COUNTY OF CONFLICT

RICHARD LOMAS

COUNTY OF CONFLICT

NORTHUMBERLAND FROM CONQUEST TO CIVIL WAR

Location photography by
MICHAEL J. STEAD

TUCKWELL PRESS

First published in Great Britain in 1996 by

Tuckwell Press
The Mill House
Phantassie
East Linton
East Lothian EH40 3DG
Scotland

ISBN 1 898410 80 1

British Library Cataloguing in Publication Data

A catalogue record for this book is available
on request from the British Library

Designed by JUSTIN HOWES
Typeset in Adobe Caslon by Combined Arts, Rushden
Printed and bound by Cromwell Press, Wiltshire

To my family and all our
Northumbrian friends

Contents

Illustrations

Tables

Maps and Plans

Prologue

This book is the product of three considerations. The first is purely personal: an abiding affection for, and attachment to, the county of Northumberland. The second is, as I argue in the first chapter, that Northumberland became a county in 1095 and that as a result 1995 was its 900th anniversary. I feel it is a cause for some regret that the public local authorities currently responsible for the historic county seemingly failed to note this fact. Finally, since any history is a revision of perceptions prompted by fresh facts and new perspectives, reinterpretation is always likely to be of some value. What follows, therefore, is a combination of my own researches and thoughts with those of other scholars who have studied aspects of the county's past into what I hope will be a coherent analysis.

The underlying theme of the book, as its title suggests, is that, as Northumberland came to be a county on the border between two states, England and Scotland, and since those states were rarely at peace, conflict and upheaval were the distinguishing features of its condition over many centuries. All this should have ended, of course, in 1603 when the two kingdoms came to have the same king, James VI and I. But it is clear that old habits died hard, and that the suppression of cross-Border violence took the best part of that king's reign. Moreover, within fifteen years of his death Northumberland was again subject to invasion from the north. Consequently, I have extended the span of the book to 1647 when the Scottish army withdrew across the Tweed.

The first two chapters are narrative in style, aimed at explaining how the emerging kingdoms of England and Scotland created and then influenced Northumberland. The first chapter ends in 1237; the second does not begin until 1296. There is a simple reason for this gap: for about sixty years the two kingdoms were at peace; consequently life in Northumberland was largely undisturbed. The very brevity of this period, however, only serves to draw greater attention to the normality of the animosity, disagreement and conflict which characterised Anglo-Scottish relations in the medieval centuries.

In the next three chapters the approach is thematic. These explain of the origins and workings of the social structures and institutions which formed, directed and controlled the lives of Northumbrians. The final chapter,

however, returns to the more narrative style with descriptions of
Northumberland's involvements in five major national upheavals.

The book will be of use to those engaged in the academic study of the
past; but I have written it with a wider public in mind, and have aimed both
to arouse their interest and to satisfy their curiosity.

I gladly and unreservedly give thanks and pay tribute to the many
scholars, past and present, whose work I have used, I hope with complete
accuracy and full consideration. Equally, I am most grateful to my wife: the
book owes a great deal to her perceptive and constructive advice. Finally, I
must thank Lisa Nelson, Wendy Shoulder and Jane Bee of the Durham
University History Department office for so quickly, quietly and efficiently
turning manuscript into typescript.

CHAPTER ONE

A Border County: England or Scotland?
924-1237

Northumberland is a border county, a fact of fundamental importance in its history. The purpose of this chapter is to explain how that border came into being, and why Northumberland came to be on one side of it rather than the other. The outcome was not inevitable, but the consequence of a complex series of events and circumstances. Moreover, it was a long process in that, although the Border appears to have become fixed shortly after the year 1000, it took almost another two and a half centuries to be fully accepted and undisputed.

THE ENGLISH CONQUEST TO 1066

Why and how the Tweed became the northern boundary of England and of Northumberland must begin with the end of the Roman period. Then, it is important to recognise, there was no England and no Scotland; nor any intimation that either kingdom would emerge in the future. Nor was there any suggestion that a two-fold division of the island of Britain was inevitable. Admittedly, the Romans had divided the island into two unequal parts, firstly along the Tyne-Solway line, then on the Forth-Clyde line, but finally reverting to the earlier boundary, and leaving the land to the north to be ruled by native chiefs or princes. But with the end of Roman rule their dividing line ceased to be of any significance.

When, in the early fifth century, the Imperial government decided that it was no longer viable or worthwhile to hang on to its British provinces, the island became divided into an uncertain number of petty states with native rulers. Of particular concern to the history of Northumberland were the peoples known as the Picts (mainly north of the Forth) and the Votadini (between the Forth and the Tees). There are also references to the kingdoms of Strathclyde (based upon Dumbarton), Rheged (around the shores of the Solway Firth) and Elmet (in West Yorkshire). Into what was probably a confused and fluctuating situation came intruders from outside the island. In the north-west the Celtic Scots from northern Ireland established themselves in Argyll. More numerous were the Germanic Angles and Saxons from the continental North Sea littoral who entered

3

Table 1: KINGS OF BERNICIA / NORTHUMBRIA

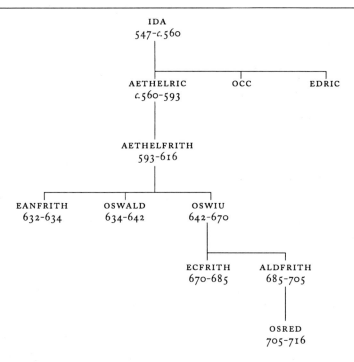

IDA
547-c.560

AETHELRIC   OCC   EDRIC
c.560-593

AETHELFRITH
593-616

EANFRITH   OSWALD   OSWIU
632-634   634-642   642-670

ECFRITH   ALDFRITH
670-685   685-705

OSRED
705-716

NOTE: Between 616 and 632, Bernicia was under the control of the king of Deira, Edwin. After 716, the kings of Northumbria were descended from two of IDA's younger sons:

OCC: COENRED 716-718   EDRIC: ALCHRED 765-774
      CEOLWULF 729-737   AEFWOLD 779-788
      EADBERHT 738-757   OSRED 788-792
      OSULF 757-759

along the east and south coasts between the Humber and Southampton Water. As Northumberland was distant from both of these invaders, it is not surprising that their arrival between Tyne and Tweed was long delayed. In fact, it was not until the middle of the sixth century (the year 547 is the traditional date) that the first Anglian settlers established themselves at Bamburgh and began to create the kingdom known as Bernicia. South of the Tees, Anglian settlement had begun earlier so that the kingdom known as Deira was well established in eastern Yorkshire by 500. Meanwhile in midland and southern districts other Anglian and Saxon kingdoms came into being through conquest, infiltration and merger. The consequence of these developments was that by about 600 much of the eastern and southern parts of the island was controlled by kings who spoke Old English, while in the northern and western areas other political divisions were dominated by Celtic-speaking rulers.

Our concern is with Bernicia. In the early years of the seventh century its king, Aethelfrith (593-616), united it with Deira to form the larger kingdom of Northumbria. Then between 633 and 685 three kings, Oswald (634-42), Oswiu (642-70) and Ecfrith (670-85), rapidly expanded westwards and northwards until they ruled an area between the Humber-Mersey line and the modern counties of Ayrshire and West Lothian. In other words, they united politically peoples of both English and Celtic traditions. This expansion came to a sudden end in 685 when Ecfrith was defeated and killed by the Pictish king, Brudei, in a battle near Forfar in modern Angus. With Ecfrith's death the era of Northumbrian dynamism ended.

In the eighth century the dominant kingdom was Mercia in the English midlands under two long-lived and powerful kings, Aethelbald (716-57) and Offa (757-96). Early in the following century, the most southerly kingdom, Wessex, under its king, Egbert (802-39) rose to challenge Mercian supremacy, while in the far north the kingdoms of the Scots and the Picts were united to form Scotia shortly after 840 as the result of the Scottish king, Kenneth I (843-57), defeating his Pictish counterpart.

It was into this situation that the Norse Vikings came. The earliest notice we have of them is the year 793 when they attacked and looted the famous monastery of Lindisfarne. While this act caused deep concern throughout Western Europe, the Norse threat did not really become acute until after 865 when a concerted effort was made to conquer parts of Britain and create Norse states. The only kingdom to withstand their onslaught was Wessex. For Northumbria, long moribund, the Norse intrusion was disastrous. The kingdom was effectively ended: Norse settlers came into Cumbria and Dumfries in considerable numbers, while east of the Pennines a Norse kingdom based upon York came into being between 867 and 876. All that remained was a rump north of the Tees, and probably extending towards the Forth, ruled by men with lower status than that of king.

The Norse tide reached its high water mark about 900, and from that time the story is one of recovery by native rulers. In the south the Norse thrust was halted by the kings of Wessex, Alfred (871-99), and his son Edward (899-924) who regained control of the midlands. His successor, Athelstan (924-39), defeated the Norse king of York, while in the north the Scottish king Constantine II (900-43) established his control over the kingdom of Strathclyde and acquired northern Bernicia as far south as the Lammermuir Hills or even the Tweed. In the 950s, in fact, the political situation in Britain at last acquired a semblance of stability. The Norse kingdom of York was finally suppressed in 954 by the West Saxon king, Eadred (946-55), who united Yorkshire with the land north of the Tees and placed the whole area under Osulf, who was styled earl of Northumbria. He and his family had controlled the land north of the Tees since at least 912, and were probably descended in some way from the

Table 2: KINGS OF WESSEX / ENGLAND, 871-1066

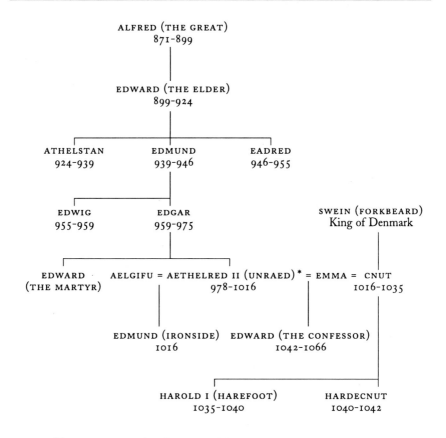

ALFRED (THE GREAT)
871-899

EDWARD (THE ELDER)
899-924

ATHELSTAN   EDMUND   EADRED
924-939   939-946   946-955

EDWIG   EDGAR   SWEIN (FORKBEARD)
955-959   959-975   King of Denmark

EDWARD   AELGIFU = AETHELRED II (UNRAED) * = EMMA = CNUT
(THE MARTYR)   978-1016   1016-1035

EDMUND (IRONSIDE)   EDWARD (THE CONFESSOR)
1016   1042-1066

HAROLD I (HAREFOOT)   HARDECNUT
1035-1040   1040-1042

UNREAD: The meaning is 'unadvised', not 'unready'

Northumbrian royal house. At the same time the English Crown acknowledged the control of the Scottish king, Indulf (954-62), over Cumbria, which had become part of the kingdom of Strathclyde, and Lothian, the land between the Forth and the Tweed, including the modern counties of Berwick, Roxburgh, Selkirk and Peebles, as well as the three Lothians.

In effect, Britain had become politically divided into two unequal kingdoms. The southern kingdom, which may now be called England, was the more powerful. This was clearly demonstrated by Athelstan who invaded Scotia in 934 and forced Constantine II to submit and give hostages, and in 937 when he defeated the combined army of Scotia, Strathclyde and the Norse kingdom of Dublin at *Brunanburgh*, the whereabouts of which is as yet unknown. It was further emphasised in 973

Table 3: KINGS OF SCOTIA / SCOTLAND, 843-1057

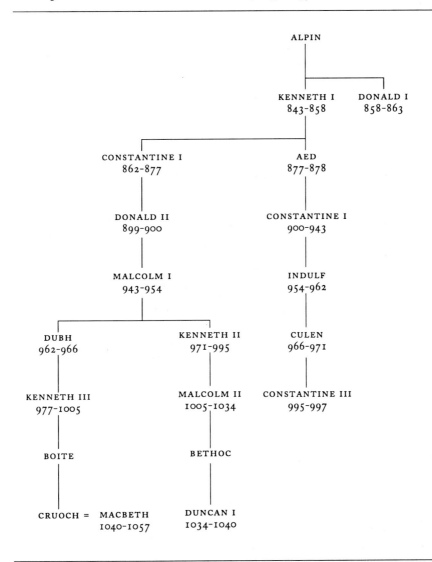

when the English king Edgar (957-75) was able to require six lesser kings, including Kenneth II (971-93) of Scotland, to wait upon him at Chester and give an undertaking as to their friendship. At the same time it is clear that there were limits to the English king's power in the north. While he might force the Scottish king from time to time to bend a submissive knee, he could not impose permanent control over him. Equally, he found it politic to concede immediate rule over Northumbria to a native earl. (Similarly the Scottish king had to tolerate a semi-independent ruler in Strathclyde.)

In the century after 960 two gradual developments of importance to the future Northumberland took place. The first was the settling of the Anglo-Scottish frontier in the east. Although the picture is very obscure, it seems likely that the Northumbrians regained control over all or part of Lothian towards the end of the tenth century. This proved to be a temporary recovery: in 1018 the Scottish king Malcolm II (1005-34) defeated a Northumbrian army at Carham on Tweed, an event which is often considered to have finally fixed the boundary of England and Scotland. This is true, but only in retrospect. As we shall see, several of Malcolm's successors seriously entertained an ambition to extend the frontier of their kingdom south to the Tyne or the Tees. Indeed, Malcolm himself made such an attempt early in his reign during the war in England between King Aethelred II and the Danish King Swein and his successor, Cnut. However, his invasion was defeated at Durham in 1006.

The second development was the gradual reduction of the independence of the native earls. The process began in 1016 when Earl Uhtred, King Aethelred's appointee, and forty of the leading men of the earldom were murdered at York at Cnut's instigation. Immediately, Uhtred was replaced by a non-native, Eric of Hlathir, who had been Swein's and Cnut's viceroy in Norway. Under this man, however, Uhtred's brother, Eadulf, surnamed Cudel, was allowed to continue as the immediate ruler north of the Tees. In 1031 Eric was replaced by Siward, who was a Dane, which may not have been a disadvantage in Yorkshire where there had been extensive Scandinavian settlement. He also took the precaution of marrying Aelfleda, Earl Uhtred's granddaughter. This might be seen as a concession to separatist feelings north of the Tees, but against this is his elimination by political murder of the subordinate earls who ruled that part of the earldom: Ealdred (his wife's father who replaced Eadulf Cudel at an unknown date) in 1038 and Eadulf (Ealdred's cousin) in 1041. Thereafter, Siward was earl over the whole of Northumbria until his death in 1055. The power of the English monarch was then again demonstrated: the ideal candidate, Waltheof, Siward's son by Aelfleda, was passed over in favour of Tostig, the brother of Earl Harold of Wessex, then the dominant force in English politics.

Neither earl was popular. Siward maintained his position by successfully defending the region from Scottish raids, and by maintaining a large force of *huscarls* (professional warriors) whom he paid out of the income from his extensive estate in Northamptonshire and Huntingdonshire. Tostig, however, was eventually driven out. In October 1065 there was a widespread revolt in the face of which Tostig fled south. The cause may have been threefold. The first was his failure to defend the region against the new Scottish king, Malcolm III (1057-93), who launched a successful raid in 1058. Perhaps more influential was his attempt to impose taxation from which the earldom had been previously exempt. Finally, there was the

Table 4: NATIVE EARLS OF NORTHUMBRIA, c.900–1074

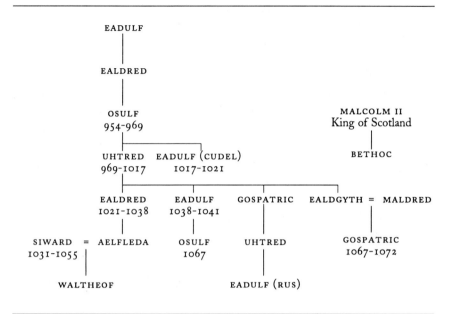

treacherous murder in 1063 or 1064 of three Northumbrian aristocrats, who may have been members of the family of the native earls.

Such was the ferocity and unanimity of the revolt that the English government was unable to restore Tostig and was forced to agree to the Northumbrian choice of Morcar, the brother of Earl Edwin of Mercia.

THE NORMAN CONQUEST: THE ADVANCE
TO THE TYNE, 1066–1080

On 28th September, 1066, William II, duke of Normandy, landed with a formidable army to pursue what he considered to be his claim to the throne of England as the rightful successor of Edward the Confessor (1042–66). On 14th October, near Hastings, his army defeated and killed Harold II, the former earl of Wessex, who had succeeded Edward earlier in the year; and on Christmas Day he was crowned king of England as William I. The Norman Conquest could therefore be seen as a brief episode. In fact, it was a much longer and more complex and arduous process, and for Northumberland the Norman conquest did not really begin until 1080, fourteen years after 1066.

As the successor of Edward the Confessor, William I inherited the problem of retaining, defending and governing the far north of England; in other words, completing the task undertaken by his English predecessors. But, such was his preoccupation with the more urgent problems of pacifying and controlling the southern and midland regions, that for the time being he was forced to resort to a series of expedient solutions which amounted to little more than a holding operation. Essentially, this consisted of continuing the practice of entrusting the rule of Northumbria to earls with vice-regal powers.

His first appointment, to whom he sold the earldom early in 1067, was a Yorkshire landowner, Copsig. This was an astonishing choice in that Copsig had been the deputy of the hated Tostig. Not surprisingly he did not last long: a few weeks after his appointment he was murdered by Osulf, Earl Morcar's deputy north of the Tees and the son of the Earl Eadulf murdered in 1041. Copsig met his death on 12th March at Newburn upon Tyne when the church in which he had taken refuge was fired. Osulf did not long enjoy the benefit of his violence since he too was murdered later in the same year.

Copsig's replacement, Gospatric, seemed more fitted to the role, being of high birth and related to the royal houses of both England and Scotland. But his appointment was also unsuccessful in that he joined the revolt of 1068 and upon its failure fled with Edgar Aetheling (great grandson of King Aethelred II) to the court of his cousin, the king of Scots. The collapse of this revolt brought William I a little closer to Northumberland. For the first time he crossed the Humber, built a castle at York and sent a force of knights under Robert de Comines to occupy Durham, ninety miles further north. This expedition met with disaster in January 1069 when it was entirely wiped out in a surprise attack. The revolt spread rapidly southwards into Yorkshire, forcing William to come north again, and this time with devastating effect. Late in 1069 he conducted what came to be known as the 'harrying of the north', the complete destruction of life and property through two swathes of land in Yorkshire and, to a lesser extent, in Durham. Violent and vicious though this was, it did not lead to a complete and satisfactory solution of the Northumbrian problem. It is true that Yorkshire now became Norman, with a royal sheriff and an inflow of settlers, but the land north of the Tees was restored to Gospatric at a meeting between him and William at Christmas 1069 held significantly on the banks of that river. The clear implication of this was that William did not yet feel strong enough to impose direct rule north of Yorkshire.

This situation continued until 1072 when at last William became free to give serious attention to his northern border. In that year he led an expedition into Scotland which ended with his meeting Malcolm III at Abernethy in Perthshire, when the Scottish king acknowledged William as his overlord, handed over hostages including his eldest son, Duncan, and agreed to expel Edgar Aetheling and other English exiles from his kingdom. On his way home William took the opportunity of improving the arrangements for Northumbria: Gospatric was dismissed as earl and replaced by Waltheof, son of Earl Siward and Earl Ealdred's daughter, Aelfleda, and also now husband of the king's niece, Judith. Waltheof would seem to have been the ideal choice: as a descendant of the ancient comital house he would attract the loyalty of native Northumbrians, while as a member of the royal family by marriage he could be expected to ensure the region's loyalty to William. If these were William's calculations, they were not fulfilled. In 1074 Waltheof joined the revolt of the Norman earl of East Anglia, although why is not clear. He did, however, use the opportunity of settling an old score by killing the sons of the man who had murdered his grandfather, Earl Ealdred, in 1038. It may be an indication of William's disappointment that after the collapse of the revolt, he had Waltheof executed in 1076.

William again resorted to selling the earldom to the local man most likely to be able to deal with the situation. This was Walcher, whom he had appointed as bishop of Durham in 1072, and to whom he had given charge of the castle he built close to the cathedral. Walcher's rule was not successful, essentially because he failed to reconcile native and Norman. In order to be on the right side of the former he appointed to his staff a man of considerable local status, Ligulf, the husband of one of Earl Ealdred's daughters, Aelgitha, and therefore uncle by marriage to Earl Waltheof. This aroused the hostility of his Norman subordinates, Leobwine his chaplain, and Gilbert, one of his relatives whom he had appointed administrator of the earldom. At Leobwine's instigation, Gilbert murdered Ligulf and his entire household. This was an outrage, and Walcher's failure to punish Gilbert, even to the extent of retaining his services, enraged Northumbrian opinion. No doubt in the hopes of negotiating a peaceful settlement, Walcher agreed to meet Ligulf's family and supporters at Gateshead on 14th May, 1080.

Walcher totally misjudged the temper of the Northumbrians, who were intent upon revenge not reconciliation. Faced by an angry crowd, Walcher and his party took refuge in the church. Gilbert was forced or persuaded to leave the building, no doubt in the hope that his death would assuage Northumbrian anger. It did not do so, and the besiegers fired the church to force out Walcher and Leobwine. Both were killed as they emerged, Walcher by a cousin of Earl Waltheof's called Eadulf Rus.

The consequence of this act, which was tantamount to rebellion, was the ravaging of Northumbria upon William's orders by his half-brother, Odo, bishop of Bayeux. This was followed almost immediately by a second expeditionary force under William's eldest son, Robert, which advanced into Scotland as far as Falkirk, probably to remind Malcolm III of the Abernethy agreement and to deter him from seeking to profit by the disturbed conditions south of the Tweed. Returning from the foray, Robert built a castle on the north bank of the Tyne at what was then Monkchester. With this the Normans were poised to take control over the future county of Northumberland.

THE NORMAN CONQUEST: THE EMERGENCE
OF NORTHUMBERLAND, 1080-1095

The events of 1080 radically altered the situation in Northumbria.
Although details are lacking, it seems likely that Odo of Bayeux' violent
sweep through the region ended or severely reduced the native will to resist,
and possibly led to the deaths of some, perhaps many, of the Northumbrian
nobility. Certainly a new and entirely Norman regime was imposed without
any sign of resistance. As earl, William appointed a certain Aubrey de
Coucy. We know virtually nothing about this man, who it was thought held
the post for a very brief time. However, William Kapelle has suggested that
his tenure of office was as long as five years and that he was not replaced
until 1085. More significant is the fact that his was a straightforward
appointment: for the first time the earldom did not change hands for
money.

Equally important was William's appointment of William of St. Calais
as the new bishop of Durham. St Calais was the abbot of the monastery of
St. Vincent at Le Mans in Maine, which Seton Offler pointed out was also
a turbulent border province. The new bishop's most significant decision,
taken in 1083, was to disperse the members of the Community of St.
Cuthbert, who had staffed the cathedral at Durham and guarded the saint's
tomb, to churches at Auckland, Darlington, Norton and Easington, and to
replace them with the Benedictine monks who had come to the region nine
years previously to restart monastic life at the famous sites at Jarrow and
Monkwearmouth. Writing a generation later, the chronicler of the new
institution, the monk Symeon, strove to convince his readers that the
reason for the old Community's destruction was its debased and scandalous
condition. David Rollason has effectively shown that Symeon's charges
were greatly exaggerated if not totally false, and that the real reason was
political, namely the strong and close association between the community
and the old Northumbrian ruling class. The destruction of the community
in fact removed one of the main pillars of the pre-Norman native
establishment.

Except for the replacement of Aubrey de Coucy by Robert de Mowbray
as earl, probably in 1085, the arrangements of 1080 remained in force until
William I's death in 1087. His successor as king was not his eldest son,
Robert, who was given the paternal duchy of Normandy, but his second son
and namesake, William, surnamed Rufus. This may have led Odo of
Bayeux, the dead king's half-brother, to rebel in 1088, a move which both
Earl Robert de Mowbray and Bishop William of St Calais chose to
support, although for reasons that are far from clear. In their treachery they
were removed from office and exiled for four years until 1092, leaving
Northumbria without its rulers.

The developments which finally brought Northumberland fully under

Table 5: KINGS OF ENGLAND AND SCOTLAND BEFORE 1066

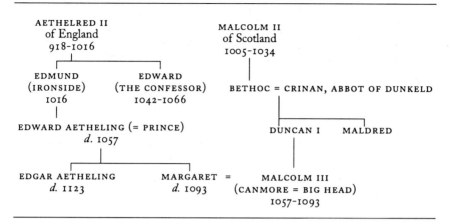

Norman control took place between 1091 and 1095, and reveal William II as a determined and vigorous ruler. The train of events began in May 1091 when Malcolm III of Scotland raided Northumbria for the fourth time in his long career. Taking the opportunity of a political vacuum to enrich himself and his followers with booty (which he and they certainly did) may have been the sole reason, although it is probably not without some significance that at that time Edgar Aetheling, his wife Margaret's brother, arrived in Scotland, having been expelled from Normandy by William II who was there pursuing a quarrel with his brother, Robert.

This incident naturally provoked a violent response. Having patched up their differences in 1092, the two brothers led an army into Scotland where Malcolm III again acknowledged the English king as his overlord, with its implied commitment to peaceful coexistence. In addition to the by now conventional response to Scottish raids, Rufus dealt with the problem of Cumbria, whose allegiance was still a matter of doubt and dispute. The situation there in 1092 is obscure: all that we know is that it was ruled by a certain Dolphin, who appears to have been largely or entirely independent of both English and Scottish control. Rufus rapidly and radically changed this. He expelled Dolphin and built a castle with an adjacent borough at Carlisle as a means of establishing the authority of the English Crown; and he also had farmers brought from the south to colonise the immediate hinterland. Later two powerful and trusted Normans were granted extensive baronies based upon Penrith and Kendal. By these actions he demonstrated his intention to have the northern boundary of his kingdom west of the Pennines resting on the Solway. For Northumberland this had a most important implication: beyond its western boundary would be English rather than Scottish territory.

The annexation of Cumbria, or perhaps, as William Kapelle has

suggested, William's refusal to honour an earlier promise to restore it to
Scottish control, provoked Malcolm III's final invasion of Northumbria.
This move was clearly expected since he was surprised by Earl Robert on
the banks of the Aln on 13th November 1093. The English victory was
complete with Malcolm and his heir, Edward, among those killed.
Malcolm's wife died four days later, whereupon the Scottish nobility chose
Malcolm's brother, Donald, surnamed Bàn (Fair), as the new king. In
doing so they passed over Malcolm's sons by his English wife. Duncan, the
eldest, who had spent many years in England as a hostage for his father's
good behaviour, was briefly successful in 1094 but was killed on 12th
November that year. His place was taken by a younger brother, Edgar, who
eventually overthrew Donald III in 1097. As both men were dependent
upon Rufus' backing, and Donald III was not a particularly effective king,
the Scottish threat, which had been serious for so long, disappeared.

It was during this phase that the final act of the conquest of Northumbria
took place. In 1095 Earl Robert revolted against William II. William
Kapelle has argued that he joined a nation-wide conspiracy that failed to
develop, prompted perhaps by a decision in 1094 to exclude the bishop of
Durham's estates from his authority. There is probably truth in this,
although it also needs to be recognised that the two men had never enjoyed
an easy relationship, and that the immediate issue between them was the
earl's refusal to obey the king's command to restore confiscated goods to
some Norwegian merchants who had put into the Tyne. Rufus' vigorous
reaction ensured an early end to the revolt, and thirty years in prison for the
defeated earl.

The true significance of 1094 and 1095 was not the defeat and
deposition of Robert de Mowbray; it was the fact that he was not replaced
as earl. Henceforth, the land north of the Tyne (or most of it) would come
directly under royal authority. In particular, the sheriff, the chief executive
officer of the shire, would be appointed by and answerable to the Crown.
But within his estate the bishop of Durham continued to enjoy full comital
powers, which were the foundation of the palatinate for which Durham
became famous. The geographical division was far from neat. North of the
Tyne, the bishop had compact blocks of land around Norham, Holy Island
and Bedlington, which were excluded from the sheriff of Northumberland's
authority and became known as North Durham. On the other hand the
sheriff was responsible for three enclaves on the north bank of the Tees,
collectively called the wapentake of Sadberge, which did not belong to the
bishop until Richard I sold them to Bishop Hugh of le Puiset in 1189. The
sheriff was also excluded from two other areas north of the Tyne:
Hexhamshire belonging to the archbishop of York, and Tynemouthshire,
the property of St. Albans abbey in Hertfordshire. Northumberland, it may
be argued, originally comprised all the land between the Tees and the
Tweed and between the mountains and the sea, but because of the peculiar

powers and the extensive lands of the bishop of Durham, it came to be confined to those parts north of the Tyne. In 1536, its situation was simplified when an act of parliament swept away liberties and franchises, leaving Northumberland as a whole and regular country or shire.

THE NORMAN SETTLEMENT, 1095-1135

Military conquest and political control were the first and necessary aspects of the Norman conquest. At the same time they were also a prelude to expropriation, the dispossession of native landowners and heads of institutions in favour of Norman incomers, a process that was primarily the work of the Crown, which needed to reward its supporters and cement their loyalty. Consequently, it was not until after 1080 that Normans could settle north of the Tyne. Between that date and 1095, when the area was under the control of the Norman earls de Coucy and de Mowbray, Norman settlement became a possibility, but since there is no clear evidence of this, it is safest to assume that during these fifteen years the Normans occupied, but did not settle in, what was to be Northumberland. The one possible exception is Hubert de La Val, who may have been granted an estate by Earl Robert.

Otherwise, it seems all but certain that the influx of Norman landowners occurred in the forty years between 1095 and 1135, that is, in the later years of William II's reign (1087-1100) and that of his younger brother, Henry I (1100-1135). Although there is little contemporary evidence, the main developments can be pieced together from later documents, particularly the enquiry into tenants-in-chief of the Crown ordered by Henry II in 1166, which was designed to reveal the situation in 1135 when his grandfather died as well as at the time of the enquiry. In responding to the king's questions several Normans claimed that they and their families had possessed their estate since the Conquest. The very vagueness of such statements makes them ambiguous, which was possibly the intention. This suspicion is given some support by the well-known claim that Redesdale was granted to Robert de Umfraville, said to be known as Robert with the beard, by William I. The document is a forgery, but its early date suggests that this family, like many since, liked to believe or have others believe that it came to England with the Conqueror.

In fact, only two Normans apart form Hubert de La Val have a serious claim to have been settled in Northumberland before 1100: William de Merlay at Morpeth and Guy de Balliol at Bywell. The others almost certainly came during Henry I's reign, although it is impossible to give or even to suggest a precise date of arrival, and in some cases even the name of the first Norman is uncertain.

Thus far the term 'Norman' has been used rather loosely. Here it needs to be recognised that the settlement of Northumberland took place between thirty and seventy years after the 1066 invasion. Consequently, the men involved were second – or even third – generation settlers for whom the description Anglo-Norman would be more appropriate. This of course does not preclude the possibility that some came direct from Normandy, but this is less likely than migration from other parts of England.

Also imprecise has been the use of terms like 'settler' and 'incomer'. Greater precision is now needed. The 1166 enquiry reveals that by 1135 the English Crown had created twenty-one baronies in Northumberland. The word 'baron' derived from the late Latin word *baro*, which meant a man in the sense of follower of a leader. In the end the use of the word came to be restricted to those men with a direct and precise relationship with the king. More specifically the Northumberland barons received from the Crown grants of land in return for which they had certain obligations, the most important of which was military service in the form of furnishing the king's army with a quota of knights, that is, fully armed and competent cavalry soldiers.

Except for their obligations it is difficult to generalise about these baronies since no two were alike, and each had its own history; and there is no evidence to suggest that they were the result of a preconceived plan or scheme. The largest, that centred upon Alnwick, included over sixty townships and had an obligation of twelve knights. In contrast, the barony of Bradford comprised a single township and carried the service of one knight. In some cases, such as Wooler, the lands of a barony were contiguous or concentrated in one area of the county; but there were also examples of very scattered estates, such as Ellingham which was made up of Ellingham and Doxford in the north and Cramlington, Jesmond, Heaton and Hartley in the south. Why this was so, and how the estate of each barony was put together, are questions that cannot at present be answered.

Given their military role, it is not surprising that the larger baronies were centred on major roads and river crossings: Bywell and Prudhoe protected the Tyne Gap; the three roads out of Scotland via Berwick, Coldstream and Yetholm passed through Wooler's territory; and the crossings of the Tweed, Aln, Coquet and Wansbeck were dominated by Wark, Alnwick, Warkworth, and Morpeth and Mitford respectively. Three, however, were created for administrative rather than strategic reasons. That at Embleton, which was comparatively small, comprising Embleton, Stamford, Craster and Dunstan in Embleton parish together with Burton and Warenton in neighbouring Bamburgh parish, was granted to Odard the sheriff. The intention may have been that either the office should be hereditary in Odard's family, or the estate should be held by the current office bearer. Neither possibility was in fact realised: the barony remained in the hands of Odard's family, who adopted the surname Viscount, the French equivalent of sheriff, but the office was held by other men appointed by the Crown on an annual basis. Dilston and Bradford were related to this development in that they were created to pension off two Englishmen, Aluric and Adred,

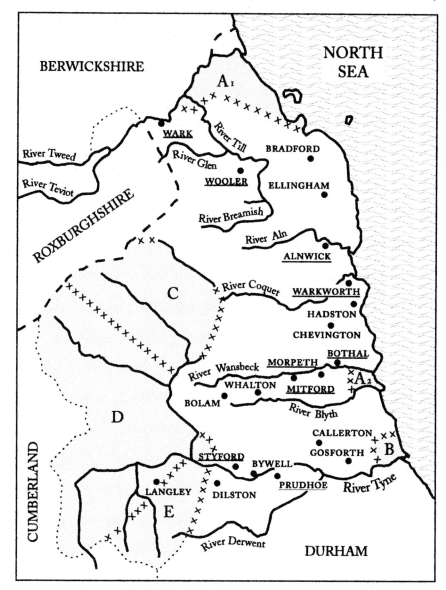

1: *Norman Franchises and Baronies*

The names underlined are those of baronies where a castle was erected shortly after the
barony was created.

A1 North Durham (Norhamshire and Islandshire)
A2 North Durham (Bedlingtonshire)
 B Tynemouthshire
 C Redesdale
 D Tynedale
 E Hexhamshire

Langley Barony was small and its lands were intermingled with those of Hexhamshire and
Tynedale liberties.

who had been the king's reeves between respectively Tyne and Coquet and Coquet and Tweed but became casualties of the reorganisation of the county's administration.

These men apart the other barons were Normans or Anglo-Norman, with one exception. The small barony of Gosforth, which comprised North Gosforth in Northumberland north of the Tyne and land in the wapentake of Sadberge, that is, Northumberland south of the Tyne, was granted to, or more likely allowed to continue in the possession of, Siward, son of Eilsi, an English landowner whose mother was of the family of the pre-Conquest earls. By the end of the twelfth century the descendants of this man had adopted the name Surtees.

Once in possession, each baron had the task of ordering his estate to meet his personal needs and wishes. How he did so, it seems, was his business, and consequently there is again no observable uniformity. One of his major problems was how to meet his military obligation. As elsewhere in the Norman world, this was largely solved by settling knights on properties within the estate, known as knight's fees, in return for military service. This process, which we call subinfeudation, was not governed by any rule or custom, with the result that there was no obvious correlation between the size of a knight's fee and the obligation it carried. In some places, for example Littlehoughton (Alnwick Barony), the knight's fee very simply comprised one township from which the service of one knight was owed. In the same barony, however, the same service was required from a much larger fee comprising Lucker (including Hoppen), South Charlton and Fallodon. A single township not infrequently carried an obligation of half a knight as at Rudchester (Prudhoe Barony), but in contrast the two townships of Brenkley and Dinnington (Mitford Barony) were charged with only a quarter of a knight. Fractions, in fact, were common; and we must assume that their service obligation was met by means of the money composition known as scutage. In all, the Northumberland barons owed a total of $67\frac{1}{3}$ knights. Precisely how many they endowed by 1135 is difficult to calculate due to discrepencies and inaccuracies in the evidence, but it is likely that the total exceeded the aggregate quota by as much as a quarter. This conclusion hides considerable variation. Some barons, such as Gosforth, could not afford or did not need to create knight's fees, while others like Wark, who seemingly could and should have done so, chose not to. On the other hand baronies like Alnwick settled more than their quota. It is likely that most of these knights were of Norman stock, but the appearance of Liulf son of Alwold among the knights of Wooler Barony warns against sweeping generalisations: the Norman barons may not always have found it easy to attract men of their own race from the south; and equally they may have found suitable natives willing to be part of the new regime.

In addition to knight's fees the barons created socage tenancies. The word derives from an Old English term implying the right of one person to demand the attendance of another at his court. Socage tenants, therefore, were saddled with the obligation of suit of the baron's court, that is, they had to attend its meetings and support its operation. The quantities of land granted to such men were small, ranging from 12 to 120 acres. The rents, which were fixed, took the form of cash, spices and such items as gilded spurs and hunting hawks. Socage tenants were clearly of lower social status than knights, but were useful or necessary members of the estate. Whatever grants were made, a portion of the estate remained under the baron's direct control, and this too had to be organised and administered.

Nine barons (Alnwick, Bolam, Bothal, Mitford, Morpeth, Prudhoe, Styford, Wark and Wooler) each built a castle. The obvious purpose was military, but as Matthew Strickland has shown, there is no evidence of a strategic defence plan for the county to which they were required to conform. Consequently, it is hard to say why these nine built, but the rest did not. Obviously some were insufficiently endowed, while others must not have felt the need of a castle, and were not encouraged by the Crown to build one. The castle was also the administrative centre of the barony, and in several instances, such as Alnwick, Wooler and Morpeth, it was part of an ambitious development which also included a borough to provide market and manufacturing facilities, and a parish church or monastery to cater for spiritual needs.

In addition to the twenty-one baronies there was the lordship of Redesdale, held not by military service but by the obligation of keeping the dale, which carried one of the main roads between England and Scotland, free of thieves. When it was created is not known, but almost certainly the original grantee was Robert de Umfraville, lord of Prudhoe Barony, the first known reference to whom occurs in 1130. It is likely, therefore, that the lordship was created by Henry I, although Percy Hedley thought it may have been the work of the Scottish earl of Northumberland between 1139 and 1153. Beanley too was not a barony held by military service but was classed as a grand sergeanty. It was almost certainly created by Henry I for Gospatric, the son of Earl Gospatric who was deposed from the earldom of Northumbria and deprived of his lands in 1072, and who fled to Scotland where his cousin, Malcolm III, gave him the lordship of Dunbar. Recently, William Scott has suggested that Henry I's grant may in fact have been a restoration, with the bonus of having a man of substance on both sides of the Border capable of dealing with cross-Border problems.

The word 'sergeant' derived from an Old French word for servant, but as with 'baron' the term had a precise meaning in the Norman world. Sergeanties were of lower status than baronies and were normally much smaller in size. Their duties were not military but services of an administrative nature. By the late twelfth century there were six sergeanties in Northumberland, in addition to Beanley. Only in the case of Brotherwick, whose holder was the king's falconer in Northumberland, can the origin be traced back to Henry I's reign. However, it seems likely that the others were also created at that time when the earliest scheme for the royal administration of Northumberland was being put into place. They seem in fact to be closely akin to the barony of Embelton, created for the sheriff, the chief royal officer in the county. Nafferton and Bamburgh were held by the coroners of the districts south and north of the Coquet; Byker and Corbridge were responsible for collecting royal debts and delivering writs; and Ditchburn was the king's forester in the county.

Creating these twenty-nine baronies, lordships and sergeanties involved a massive transfer of land in which the ownership of at least 350 townships changed hands. There were, however, parts of the county that remained outside the scope of the Crown's activity, most notably the thirty townships of the bishop of Durham's estate centred on Norham, Holy Island and Bedlington. There during the reign of Henry I, Bishop Ranulf Flambard can be seen following a similar course to that of his royal master. In 1121 he built a castle at Norham, and at various times he created knight's fees at Ross, Heaton and Tillmouth, each for the service of half a knight. Likewise at Ancroft, although by 1135 Allerdean and Felkington had been added and the obligation increased to one knight. The tenant of this fee, a man named Papedy, was the sheriff of North Durham, and the similarity between him and Odard at Embelton is obvious.

The other two areas not involved in the royal reconstruction were also church property, and both had been until recently associated with Durham. Hexhamshire was until the early 1070s controlled by men closely connected with the Community of St. Cuthbert. But, as the result of the changes and upheavals in Durham between 1071 and 1083, they transferred the overlordship to the archbishops at York. The history of Tynemouthshire is not too dissimilar. It was intended to restart monastic life in the ancient monastery there with monks from the revived house at Jarrow; but the removal of the Jarrow and Monkwearmouth monks to Durham in 1083 and a quarrel between Bishop William of St Calais and Earl Robert de Mowbray led the latter to transfer ownership of Tynemouth and its estate to the Hertfordshire abbey of St. Albans.

In addition to the three ecclesiastical estates, fifteen others in lay owner-ship appear to have remained untouched. Three were described as thanages, and were probably examples of the larger and more important type of pre-Conquest English estate. That of Halton comprised Halton, Clarewood and Great Whittington in Corbridge parish, while that of Hepple had Hepple, Bickerton and Fallowlees in Rothbury parish, but also Hurworth on Tees in the wapentake of Sadberge. In this respect it was like the barony of Gosforth, which was probably a converted thanage. In fact, Hepple too became a barony at a later date. The third thanage, comprising Kyloe, Berrington and Low Lynn, was in the episcopal estate of Holy Island.

Three townships would appear to have been the standard size of a Northumbria thanage, and therefore it is surprising to find Whittingham, which comprised Whittingham, Barton, Thrunton and half of Glanton classified as a drengage. Drengages were of inferior status, and normally had a single township or even part of a township by way of endowment. This was certainly the case with the other Crown drengages: Eslington, Callaly, Mousen, Beadnell, Yetlington, Lorbottle and Little Ryle; with those belonging to the bishop: Thornton, Goswick, Buckton and Beal; and with those belonging to Tynemouth Priory: Whitley, Seghill and Backworth.

Thanages would appear to have had a status not unlike that of the post-Conquest baronies. Drengages, however, were clearly service tenements and as such integral elements in the pre-Conquest administrative units known as 'shires', which were common throughout northern England and southern Scotland. The drengs of Mousen and Beadnell, who were members of Bamburghshire which covered over 34,000 acres and included twenty-four townships, owed money rents but less were required to perform specific ploughing, harvesting and carting duties; and they were liable to payments such as *merchet* (for permission for a woman to marry) usually associated with the base forms of tenure. Finally, it needs to be stressed that it was not only the tenements and forms of tenure that survived; the names of the tenants, where known, were English, indicating that some families, as well as institutions, managed not to be swept away by the incoming Norman tide.

As far as can be discerned from the available evidence, the transformation of Northumberland was rapid and was essentially complete when Henry I died in 1135. This is underlined by the fact that only two major transfers of land took place in the following seventy years. In 1157 Henry II granted Tynedale, comprising his valleys of the North Tyne, South Tyne and West Allen, as a lordship to the king of Scotland in compensation for his loss of the earldom of Northumberland (see below p.30). And in 1204-5, John sold the ancient royal estates of Corbridge, Newburn and Rothbury to Robert son of Roger, lord of Warkworth. In so doing, he reduced the Crown's direct interest in Northumberland to Bamburgh, the old Bernician capital, and Newcastle, its Norman successor. Also significant is that after 1135 there was little further subinfeudation, and what there was was on a small scale in terms of both quantity of land and weight of obligation. The one carucate (probably 120 acres) of land in Kirkwhelpington as $\frac{1}{20}$ of a knight's fee (Mitford Barony) and half a carucate in Wooler (Wooler Barony) as $\frac{1}{30}$ of a knight's fee are typical of the twenty-nine identifiable cases.

By way of postscript it has to be stressed that the structure created between 1095 and 1135 was not permanent. In particular, the baronies were vulnerable to failure to produce a male heir. If a baron was survived by several daughters, the estate would be divided equally between them. For example, when Roger de Merlay III died in 1265 leaving three daughters, Mary, Alice and Isobel, the barony of Morpeth was divided, although eventually only into two parts since Alice also died without heirs. Even when there was only one daughter as sole heir, major change was likely, as in the case at Embleton. When John Viscount died in 1245, the barony was inherited by his daughter, Rametta. Ten years later, she and her second husband transferred the barony of the future rebel, Simon de Montfort, in exchange for an estate in Hampshire and Dorset. In contrast, the Surtees family managed to produce a male heir for fourteen generations until the failure of Thomas Surtees VII who died in 1512. With sergeanties there was also the problem of obsolescence as county administration ceased to be based upon endowed or hereditary offices. Ralf, the sergeant of Ditchburn, solved the problem in 1200 by paying King John 50 marks (£33 6s. 8d) for the right to hold his land by the service of one knight. The role of the sergeant of Nafferton, coroner south of the Coquet, was ended in 1250, and that of his counterpart north of that river by 1292.

WOOLER: A CASE STUDY

Difficulties in making meaningful generalisations about Northumberland baronies may to some extent be compensated by looking at an example, recognising, however, that it should be seen as illustrative, not typical.

When the barony of Wooler was created is not certain, but the best evidence points to the very earliest years of Henry I's reign, possibly 1100-1102. Equally, the origins of the grantee, Robert de Muschamp, are obscure, although it seems likely that he was related in some way to one or both of the families of that name in Derbyshire and Yorkshire. The composition of the barony, however, is clear enough: it comprised a block of land running in an arc from the coast north of Bamburgh to The Cheviot. There is no evidence to show whether it was already an estate, or whether it was pieced together from the possessions of two or more landowners, although the latter seems more likely. With twenty-three townships it was one of the larger baronies, and therefore it is not surprising to find it burdened with the service of four knights. In addition, it was required to furnish part of the garrison of the royal castle at Bamburgh (castle guard), pay an ancient royal due, cornage (£1 7s. 6d), and attend the meetings of the county court.

By 1135 the lords of Wooler had enforced five knights, one more than their quota. The evidence is not conclusive, but it seems probable that they were as follows:

1	Knight's Fee		Ford, Crookham, Kimmerston, $\frac{1}{4}$ Hethpool
1	"	"	Akeld, Coupland, Yeavering
1	"	"	Humbleton, Detchant, $\frac{1}{2}$ Elwick
1	"	"	Outchester
1	"	"	Fenton

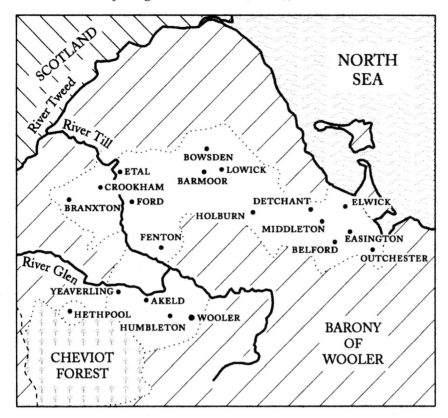

2: *Barony of Wooler*

The first three look suspiciously like pre-Conquest thanages, a notion given some support by the apparently English names of two of the tenants of 1166: Liulf son of Alwold and Elias son of Alured. Why the other fees were less ample is not clear, unless they too were pre-Conquest estates, in their cases, drengages.

Between 1135 and 1166 eight more fees were created, all of them fractional:

$\frac{1}{2}$	Knight's Fee		Etal
$\frac{1}{4}$	"	"	Heddon
$\frac{1}{4}$	"	"	Holburn
$\frac{1}{4}$	"	"	Barmoor
$\frac{1}{20}$	"	"	1 carucate in Wooler
$\frac{1}{30}$	"	"	$\frac{1}{2}$ carucate in Wooler
$\frac{1}{30}$	"	"	$\frac{1}{2}$ carucate in Wooler
$\frac{1}{30}$	"	"	$\frac{1}{2}$ carucate in Hethpool

The first four clearly equate with Fenton and Outchester, but the others are much more akin to the nine socage tenements created at unknown dates:

Wooler   32 acres   1 pair of gilded spurs

	24 acres	1 lb cumin
	20 acres	$\frac{1}{2}$ lb pepper and $\frac{1}{2}$ lb cumin
	8 acres	1d
	6 acres	6d
	4 acres	$\frac{1}{2}$ lb cumin
Hethpool	24 acres	8s od
Lowick	24 acres	1 lb pepper
Belford	24 acres	1 lb pepper

Of the townships over which the barony retained direct control, three were of prime importance, and of these Wooler stands out. It was probably decided at the outset that it would be the *caput* (capital) of the barony. A castle was built on a site just to the east of the present Church Street. In front of it was the triangular market place, the focus of the borough which eventually had over one hundred burgage tenements. Ecclesiastically, although there is as yet no proof, it seems likely that Wooler was severed from the ancient parish of Chatton and given independent parochial status; and while no monastery was founded, a hospital was built sometime before 1288. The probable reason for having Wooler as the centre of the barony was its strategic location just south of the confluence of the valleys of the Till and the Glen which carried the main roads to Coldstream and Kelso.

Situated on the Berwick road, Belford was also of strategic importance; but the presence of the royal fortress at Bamburgh six miles to the east made a castle there unnecessary. The third major township was Lowick on the higher ground to the north, equidistant from Wooler and Belford and on the line of the Roman road known as Devil's Causeway. In addition to strategic and any other consideration, these three townships were large and by the mid-thirteenth century were reckoned to be worth about £150 a year in rent.

Wooler was a compact and apparently intelligently organised barony, but like so many others it eventually broke up. Its original owner, Robert de Muschamp, failed to produce a male heir, but fortunately he had only one daughter, Cecily. She married a Stephen de Bulmer, and their descendants adopted the Muschamp name. The crisis came in 1250 with the death of Robert de Muschamp III without a male heir. As a result the estate was divided between his two surviving daughters, Marjory (wife of Malise Graham, earl of Strathearn) and Isobel (wife of Sir Walter de Huntercombe), and Isobel the child of his eldest daughter, Cecily, and her husband, Odinel de Ford, both of whom predeceased him. This girl died young in 1254, with the result that her third was partitioned between her two aunts.

The Muschamp family was not extinct, however, since a cadet branch based at Barmoor maintained itself until the late seventeenth century. Many generations later, a branch of the family which had settled at Brotherlee in Weardale produced Emerson Muschamp, the grandfather of the man who founded Bainbridge's, the famous Newcastle department store, Emerson Muschamp Bainbridge.

NORTHUMBERLAND UNDER SCOTTISH RULE, 1136-1157

When Henry I died on 1st December 1135 the question of whether Northumberland would be in England or Scotland must have seemed clearly settled: the Norman kings of England, William I and his two sons William II and Henry I, had conquered the land and settled their chosen men on most of it; and they had forced the kings of Scotland to recognise them as their overlords. Yet within three years this situation was to change fundamentally, and for a period of twenty years Northumberland was to be effectively part of the Scottish realm. This startling reversal was the consequence of a particular circumstance and the actions of the men and women involved.

The circumstance was the problem of the succession to the English throne which began on 25th November 1120 when Henry I's only legitimate son, William, was drowned when the ship bringing him from Normandy to England was wrecked off Barfleur. Henry had only one other legitimate child, a daughter Matilda, who was eighteen years of age and married to the German emperor, Henry V. Upon his death in 1125, Matilda was recalled to England as part of Henry's plans to retrieve the situation. On 1st January 1127 he required his barons to swear that they would support Matilda as his successor, assuming he had no male heir by

Table 6: KINGS OF ENGLAND, 1066-1189

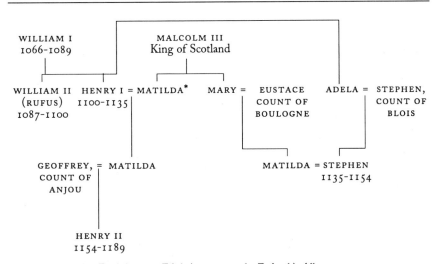

* Also known by her English name, Edith (more correctly, Eadgyth). All women named Matilda were also known by the diminutive, Maud.

his second wife, Adelaide, daughter of the duke of Lorraine; and in the following year he arranged a second marriage for Matilda, to Geoffrey, the son and heir of the count of Anjou, whose lands bordered Henry's continental territories. Adelaide appears to have been unable to have children, but Matilda and Geoffrey, in spite of strong mutual dislike, had two sons, the elder of whom, Henry, born in 1133, was to become King Henry II of England and one of the two most powerful European rulers of his day.

In the short term, however, these schemes proved to be disastrous. When Henry died the succession problem became acute. Matilda, who never forgot or let others forget she had been an empress, would not accept the role of guardian for her son but insisted on being sovereign in her own right, something the male-dominated society of the day would not allow. Nor was her husband, Geoffrey, acceptable, partly because of his unattractive personality, but also because as an Angevin he was hated on racial grounds by the Norman and Anglo-Norman baronage. They in fact turned to a third candidate, Theobald, count of Blois, the eldest grandson of William I. The situation was thrown into complete turmoil, however, by the audacity of Theobald's younger brother, Stephen, count of Mortain and Boulogne in Normandy and a leading member of the English baronage, who crossed the Channel and secured the support of London and the backing of his own brother, Henry, bishop of Winchester, who persuaded the archbishop of Canterbury to Crown him on 26th December.

Whether Stephen would get away with this daring coup d'état would depend upon his abilities. Unfortunately, while he was a very personable man with many attractive qualities, he rapidly demonstrated a lack of political skill. Within eighteen months he had effectively lost control of Normandy, and was facing a growing rebellion in England in favour of the Empress Matilda organised by her half-brother, an able but illegitimate son of Henry I, Robert, earl of Gloucester. A situation was rapidly developing in which those with ambitions could hope to advance them.

One such was David I, king of Scotland, whose aim was to detach Northumberland (and also Cumberland and Westmorland) from England. To understand why we must examine his personal history. David was born about 1080, the youngest son of the king of Scotland, Malcolm III, and his English wife, Margaret. From 1100, when his sister, Matilda (Maud), married Henry I, he lived in England as an increasingly prominent member of the baronage. Clearly able and loyal, he was handsomely rewarded by the English king in 1113 in the form of a wife, Maud. At first glance this may not seem to have been a rare gift, since the lady was approaching middle age and was the widow of Simon de Senlis, an Anglo-Norman baron, by whom she had three sons. This, however, hid her political worth: she was in fact the daughter and senior co-heiress of Earl Waltheof from whom she inherited the earldom of Huntingdon with its extensive lands in eleven

Table 7: LINKS BETWEEN THE RULING HOUSES OF ENGLAND,
SCOTLAND AND NORTHUMBRIA

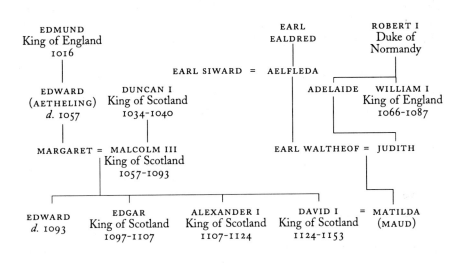

south midland counties of England. More significantly, she carried with her the claim to the ancient earldom of Northumbria, although this was a contentious matter. Like their English predecessors, the Norman kings did not accept that earldoms were anything but offices at the Crown's disposal. Moreover, hereditary right, although recognised and having some strength, was not paramount in that the rules governing inheritance had not yet hardened into law. Nevertheless, the claim David acquired by his marriage was an asset of considerable use and value.

David was essentially an Anglo-Norman baron, but when his brother, Alexander I, died in 1124, he succeeded him as king of Scotland. His new status, however, had no observable effect on his relationship with his mentor, Henry I of England, with whom he continued to be on very good terms. But, immediately upon Henry's death he made rapid and hostile moves, which suggests that his plans had long been laid and were unconnected with Stephen's usurpation. In January 1136 he occupied Cumberland and Northumberland, secured the surrender of all its castles except Bamburgh, and laid siege to Durham. Consequently, Stephen, although still insecure in the south, was forced to come north in person to deal with his problem. The two kings met in Durham in February and after prolonged negotiation came to an agreement by which David's son Henry was granted the earldom of Huntingdon, together with Carlisle and the manor of Doncaster. Stephen also conceded that, should the earldom of Northumbria be revived, David's claim would be given serious consideration. This fell short of David's ambition, but for the moment it was the most he could persuade Stephen to agree to.

There the matter rested until the summer of 1138, when Stephen's political position began to crumble in the face of Robert of Gloucester's rebellion in support of the claims of his half-sister, Matilda. David immediately recognised this as an opportune moment to renew his claim to Northumbria. Again, his demand was turned down, with the result that he launched an invasion of England with a large and polyglot force, which included badly disciplined elements from Galloway who committed many atrocities. This venture came to grief on 22nd August when an English army under the leadership of Archbishop Thurstan of York inflicted a total defeat on Cowton Moor, six miles north of Northallerton. Because of the presence of the banners of the churches of York, Beverley and Ripon, this became known as the Battle of the Standard. Among those who fought on the Scottish side was the most powerful of the Northumberland barons, Eustace son of John, lord of Alnwick, which suggests that the leading men of the county may not have been entirely averse to David's aims.

The disaster in Yorkshire was more apparent than real, since it did not hinder David's efforts to consolidate his control north of the Tyne. Moreover, Stephen was being slowly driven to recognise his inability to fight a war on two fronts, against the Empress Matilda in the south and the king of Scotland in the north. The upshot was the second Treaty of Durham, agreed on 9th April 1139, whereby Stephen confirmed to David's son Henry all that he had granted three years earlier, but added Northumberland, except for the royal castles of Bamburgh and Newcastle. Also specifically excluded were the lands of St. Cuthbert, that is, those belonging to the bishop of Durham. In return, David agreed to keep the peace, and gave hostages to this effect. The agreement was further cemented by the marriage of Henry, now earl of Northumberland, and Ada de Varenne, who was closely related to several of Stephen's supporters among the English barons. Shortly after, the barons of Northumberland did homage to Earl Henry.

David kept his promise of peace until February 1141, when the political situation in England was changed dramatically by Stephen's defeat and capture at Lincoln. David at once gave full and active support to Matilda's cause. This proved to be a costly mistake: Matilda and David were driven from London and suffered a serious military reverse at Winchester. Robert of Gloucester was captured, but David was fortunate in escaping from the débâcle and returning safely to Scotland. Stephen was released in exchange for the earl of Gloucester, and his reviving fortunes in southern England meant that David lost control of the earldom of Huntindgon. Thereafter, he confined his activity to northern England. He gave some support to the attempt of his Chancellor, William Cumin, to seize the bishopric of Durham following the death of Bishop Geoffrey Rufus in May 1140. This act led to a three-year war in Durham between Cumin and those who supported his rival, the royal candidate, William of Ste.Barbe, the dean of York. Significantly, David did not take an active role in this struggle, but doubtless would have been happy had Cumin not Ste.Barbe been the victor.

In 1148 the Empress Matilda left England, in effect resigning her claim to the throne to her elder son, Henry. The following year Henry, now sixteen, visited David at Carlisle in order to receive the honour of knighthood (his advisers argued that someone hoping to be king should not be knighted other than by a king). Before agreeing to perform this important ceremony, however, David extracted from Henry a promise that if he became king he would accept Scottish possession of all the land between Tweed and Tyne, including Newcastle. The immediate ruler of Northumberland, Earl Henry, died in 1152, and David, who was now in his seventies, installed as the new earl, William, the second of his grandsons. The following year David himself died, and was succeeded as king by his eldest grandson as Malcolm IV.

The main events of David's career may be clear enough, but not so the precise nature of his aims. Obviously his ambition was to establish Scottish political control to the Tyne, and perhaps to the Tees (and equally far south to the west of the Pennines). What is less certain is whether he hoped to absorb these lands entirely, making them integral parts of Scotland, or whether he was content for them to be in England but permanently held by the Scottish king, or more probably his heir. Such a sharp distinction may be anachronistic: twelfth-century rulers and their leading subjects thought more in terms of allegiance than of nationality, since most of them belonged to the French speaking élite that dominated much of western Europe. Whatever the truth, in Northumberland the reality was that for eighteen years after 1139 the county was governed by successive heirs to the Scottish throne, Earl Henry and Earl William, a situation the baronage appears to have accepted without undue difficulty. That their view may have differed from David's is possibly indicated by their insistence that their homage to the Scottish earl was limited by their allegiance to the English king. Equally, they may have recognised that the arrangement of 1139 was likely to be an interlude arising from the temporary incapacity of the English Crown.

If this was their perception, they were wise in it. With the death of his eldest son, Eustace, in 1153, Stephen, now old and worn out, recognised Henry, the son of his rival, the Empress Matilda, as his heir; and Henry duly became king of England when Stephen died on 25th October, 1154. For almost three years Northumberland remained unaffected by this change of ruler. In 1157, however, Henry II felt able to turn his attention to his northern frontier, and in doing so he acted from a position of strength. He summoned Malcolm IV, still only sixteen years of age, to meet him at Chester, where he dictated terms. The Scottish king had the earldom of

Huntingdon restored to him, but was forced to return Northumberland
and his other northern lands, in return for which he was given the lordship
of Tynedale by way of compensation.

THE LONG RESOLUTION, 1157-1237

Malcolm IV's surrender in July 1157 could, perhaps should, have solved the
Northumberland problem. And it may well have done so had it not been for
the tenacity, longevity, and some might argue perversity, of one man. In
surrendering to Henry, perhaps too easily and tamely even allowing for his
youth, Malcolm was not giving away his own property but that of his
younger brother, Earl William. Malcolm did not marry, and as a result
when he died in 1165 William became king of Scotland. He was then in his
early twenties, and throughout his long reign of almost forty-nine years the
recovery of Northumberland (and also Cumberland and Westmorland) was
probably his leading ambition. In this he showed himself as a typical man of
his age in his concern for what he saw as his property rights, but also to be
less than acutely perceptive of the realities of political power in Britain. The
simple fact was that a powerful monarch like his older contemporary Henry
II had no need, and could not be forced, to part with bits of his realm.
William's persistence, however, meant that the question of whether
Northumberland was to be English or Scottish remained, in theory at least,
unresolved.

Having had two peaceful requests or demands turned down in 1166 and
1170, William resorted to force in 1173 and 1174, which proved to be an
act of disastrous folly. The occasion was the rebellion against Henry II of his
heir (also Henry) known as the Young King. The matter between father and
son had nothing to do with William, but he saw their quarrel as an
opportunity to further his great ambition. His first move was to try bribery:
he offered to give King Henry his support in return for Northumberland.
When this was rejected, he threw in his lot with the rebels, who were willing
to buy his support with the gift of the entire earldom of Northumbria
(Northumberland, Cumberland and Westmoreland). This agreed, William
entered Northumberland with an army in the summer of 1173 and
conducted a seemingly aimless campaign of short and fruitless sieges of
castles, mainly in Northumberland, but without any attempt to co-ordinate
with the English rebels in the south. On the approach of an English army
he retreated to Roxburgh where he agreed to a truce to last until March the
following year. When this expired he again came into Northumberland
with no greater sense of purpose than the previous year, and this time his
invasion met with disaster. On 13th July he was camped in front of Alnwick
castle with possibly as few as sixty men (the rest of his army was away
plundering elsewhere in Northumberland) when he was surprised by a
superior English force. In the skirmish that followed he was prevented from
escaping when his horse was killed and pinned him to the ground.

He was taken as a captive, first to Northampton and then to Normandy, where Henry II imposed humiliating terms which he formally sealed on 8th December and which came to be known as the Treaty of Falaise. Not only had he lost all hope of recovering his earldom, but he was deprived of all his English lands, including Tynedale, and had to surrender the castles of Berwick, Roxburgh and Edinburgh. He and his brother David were released on 15th February and returned to England where in August they and all the Scottish baronage had to do homage and swear fealty to Henry II in York Minster. Thereafter, he was very much the subordinate king who was required to visit his master's court every year. Henry's attitude did mellow slightly in later years: in 1185 he restored the earldom of Huntingdon to William's younger brother and (at that time) heir, David, following the death of Simon de Senlis, the son of his grandfather's first wife; and in the following year he handed back Edinburgh castle. But these were relatively minor adjustments in what for William was a humiliating relationship.

With Henry's death in July 1189, William's prospects brightened considerably. He and the new king of England, Richard I, got on well; so much so that the Falaise agreement was cancelled and as a result Tynedale was returned to Scottish control, and in William's mind the question of the earldom again became live. Richard, however, promptly sold the earldom to the ambitious bishop of Durham, Hugh of le Puiset, for 2,000 marks (£1333 6s. 8d) as part of his effort to raise enough money to finance his commitment to the Third Crusade. William's disappointment did not stop him contributing the like sum towards the cost of ransoming Richard from the duke of Austria into whose hands he had fallen while returning from the Holy Land. This act of calculated generosity may have encouraged Richard, who arrived back in England in the spring of 1194, to be more sympathetic towards William in the matter of Northumbria. While in London for Richard's second coronation in April, William offered 15,000 marks (£10,000) for the earldom, which Richard accepted, subject to his retaining control of the castles. William refused to agree to this condition, and so the deal fell through. Given the depth of his commitment to recovering the three northern counties, William's action is surprising, since even without the castles he would have achieved a substantial part of his ambition and been in a strong position to gain full control sometime in the future.

These negotiations were in the realm of political reality; what followed was not. The two kings concocted a fantastic scheme for the marriage of William's daughter, Margaret, and Richard's favourite nephew, Otto, whose father was the deposed ruler of the German duchy of Saxony. The couple's dowry was to comprise Northumberland and Cumberland in England and Lothian in Scotland, but with the Scottish castles held by Richard and the English castles by William. This scheme was soon dropped in the face of opposition in both countries.

William's dealings with Richard's successor, John, were far less happy. Matters came to a head in April 1209, when following the death of the bishop of Durham, Philip of Poitou, John came to Northumberland in person. He ordered substantial repairs to the episcopal castle at Norham, and also began to build another castle on the bishop's land at Tweedmouth. This was a provocative act, to which the Berwick garrison reacted by crossing the river, killing the builders and demolishing the structure. As a result John returned to Northumberland and met William at Norham on seventh August. The Scottish king was now old and in ill-health, which may explain why he allowed himself to be bullied into giving up his claim to the earldom, agreeing to pay large sums to compensate for the destruction of Tweedmouth castle and to gain John's good will, and handing over his two daughters on the promise that the elder would eventually marry John's son, Henry. All he got in return was an understanding that Tweedmouth castle would remain unbuilt. Three years later the two kings met again at Norham when William agreed to allow John to find a suitable bride for his son, Alexander. John had now effectively reduced William to the subordinate status he had endured between 1174 and 1189.

William I died in December 1214, and was succeeded by his sixteen-year-old son, Alexander II. The arrival of a new king in Scotland occurred on the eve of the baronial rebellion in England which led to the 'signing' of Magna Carta and a subsequent civil war in which Louis, the son of the French king, Philippe II, was invited to accept the English Crown. Such turbulent times were an excellent opportunity for the young Alexander to reopen the question of Northumbria. In fact, the rebel barons were willing to concede the three northern counties in return for Scottish support, and on 22nd October 1215 the Northumberland barons again did homage to a Scottish king. This success was short-lived, and by early 1216 John had restored his authority in northern England.

The arrival of Prince Louis of France afforded a second chance, which Alexander took, promising support to the Frenchman in return for Northumbria. The likelihood of this being permanent was destroyed by John's death in October, the defeat of Prince Louis' army and the gradual acceptance of John's young son as Henry III. Towards the end of 1217 Alexander accepted the situation and did homage to the new king for the lordship of Tynedale.

The matter of his earldom remained dormant but unresolved for almost twenty years, until it was again raised in September 1236 when Alexander and Henry met at Newcastle. The outcome was another conference at York in the following year, when an international mediator, the papal legate, Otto, played the leading role in bringing about a permanent settlement. Alexander finally gave up his family's claim to the earldom of Northumbria; and in return Henry agreed to increase the size of the Tynedale lordship, which he did in April 1242 when he handed over five manors in Cumberland. With territorial issues resolved, it became possible to come to an agreement about the March Laws by which cross-Border disputes were resolved and which were already of considerable antiquity. This business was completed on 14th March 1249 on the basis of a joint enquiry held in the previous November by twelve knights from each country.

For almost a hundred years Northumberland had existed in a state of uncertainty, and indeed insecurity. To us it may be inconceivable that the Anglo-Scottish border should be other than where it is; but we must recognise that this is the result of nothing but long use. Between Northumberland on the one hand, and Berwickshire and Roxburghshire on the other, there were no significant differences of race, language and way of life at any level. And, in particular, we must recognise that the French-speaking baronage was as willing to accept a French-speaking king of Scotland as a French-speaking king of England. In the end, it was the greater ability of the latter to enforce allegiance that finally determined that Northumberland would be an English county.

CHAPTER TWO

A Border County: England and Scotland, 1296-1603

On 26th March 1296, Edward I of England led an army out of Northumberland and across the Tweed into Scotland and in so doing began what Herbert Honeyman called the Three Hundred Years' War. In fact the war lasted 307 years all but two days, that is, until 24th March 1603 when, with the death of Queen Elizabeth I of England, James VI of Scotland became sovereign of both kingdoms. As one of the two front-line English counties, it was inconceivable that the development of Northumberland and the lives of its people would not be seriously and significantly affected by this long conflict.

From the outset it must be recognised that the conflict took two forms. The more obvious was the campaigns in which one nation attacked the other by means of armies led by its king or a commander appointed by its king. These acts of state were relatively rare, but in most cases well documented. In contrast, unofficial aggression across the Border by the inhabitants of the two countries living close to it is harder to trace. Indeed, it scarcely deserves the term 'war' since it amounted to no more than brief raids in search of booty or in pursuance of feud. Both governments sought to suppress, or at least control, this activity, although they were not above giving it covert encouragement when to do so served their interests. This form of warfare was mere banditry with its participants as likely to perpetrate their crimes against their own countrymen as against the members of the other nation.

Between these two forms of warfare there were two obvious differences. One was size: cross-Border raids were on a smaller scale than state-organised invasions; they were the work of gangs rather than armies. The other difference was one of distance. Raiding parties did not normally penetrate far beyond the Border, so that the real danger zone was shallow, probably not much more than twenty or thirty miles. In contrast invading armies could and sometimes did advance considerable distances into their opponent's territory.

The length of the war was determined by the refusal of the kings of England to accept or acknowledge that Scotland was, and was entitled to be, a completely separate and fully independent kingdom. Their problem

34

began in 1072 when William I of England forced Malcolm III of Scotland to do homage at Abernethy, with the clear implication that the king of England was the overlord of the king of Scotland. Thereafter, William's successors enforced, or tried to enforce, or demanded the same submission. Inevitably, the kings of Scotland, while on occasions being forced to bend the knee, rejected the notion of subordinate status and strove to maintain full independence. As this struggle took place within and as part of the kaleidoscopic diplomatic and military activity involving all European states, any country at war with England would find a sympathetic hearing in Scotland; and since England was almost constantly in conflict with France, the 'auld alliance' between that country and Scotland was a natural consequence.

THE OUTBREAK OF WAR, 1296

Why did the war start in 1296, particularly as the two kingdoms had been at peace virtually throughout the thirteenth century and had apparently settled their differences in 1237? The answer lies in the succession crisis that blew up in Scotland. Alexander III, who became king of Scotland in 1249, had two sons and a daughter by his wife Joan, the sister of Henry III of England. Unfortunately, all three predeceased him, and neither son left an heir. His daughter, Margaret, however, who married King Eric II of Norway, did have a child, a daughter also named Margaret. Thus, when Alexander himself died in 1286, prematurely as a result of a riding accident, his only direct heir was an infant girl.

Even before his death Alexander had envisaged the marriage between this granddaughter and Edward of Caernarfon, the son of Edward I of England, and in the four years following 1286 the diplomatic moves between the English king and the six Guardians (three barons and three bishops) who ruled Scotland gradually moved in that direction, although with misgivings on their part in the light of the implications for Scottish independence. This solution, which would have anticipated the Union of 1603, was frustrated by the death of the young Margaret, known as the Maid of Norway, in Orkney in October 1290.

There now began what was called the Great Cause, the debate to determine who should be the next king of Scotland. Those with the best claim were the descendants of the daughters of David, earl of Huntingdon, the younger brother of William I of Scotland, in particular John Balliol, lord of Bywell in Northumberland (and also of Barnard Castle in County Durham), the grandson of the eldest daughter, Margaret; and Robert Bruce, the son of the second daughter, Isabel. But, there were many others who could make out a case for themselves, including Edward I, who not only could point to his descent from Malcolm III, but also could argue that, as all the claims were relatively weak or flawed, the kingdom of Scotland should revert to him as its feudal overlord. In the end, after a debate

Table 8: KINGS OF SCOTLAND, 1124-1286

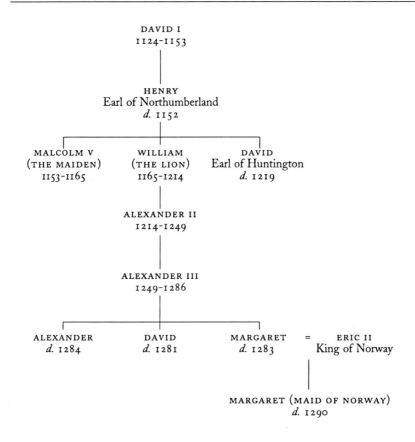

inevitably made lengthy by the lack of a clear and precise law of succession, the commission set up to decide the matter came down in favour of Balliol. On 30th November 1292, he was enthroned at Scone as King John of Scotland; and on 26th December he did homage to Edward I at Newcastle, where the English king was spending Christmas.

The reign of King John of Scotland lasted a mere four years, and ended ignominiously with his deposition by Edward I. The fact was that the two men had markedly divergent views as to John's role. He regarded himself as a legitimate King of Scotland with the same rights and powers as his predecessors had possessed. Edward, however, wanted someone who would govern Scotland according to his wishes and instructions and would be, in effect, a viceroy in all but name. The issue came to a head when in 1294 Edward went to war with France and demanded that the Scottish barons performed military service for him in Gascony. Reaction in Scotland was

Table 9: CLAIMANTS TO THE SCOTTISH THRONE, 1286-1306

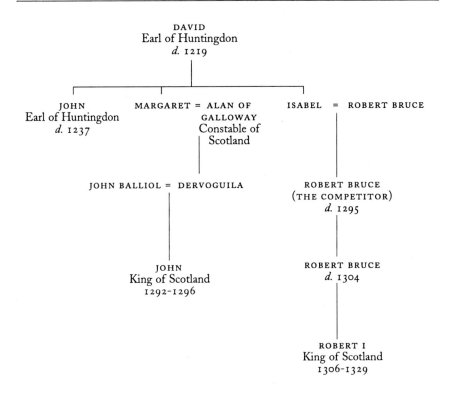

hostile, with the result that in July 1295 an alliance with France was concluded, although with misgivings on King John's part. In Edward's eyes this was a clear case of treason which fully justified extreme measures.

The 1296 campaign in Scotland was brief, brutal and one-sided. Berwick was captured and sacked; a Scottish army was crushed at Dunbar; and the English forces then swept through Scotland taking all its major castles. John was captured and in a humiliating ceremony was publicly stripped of the symbols and badges of kingship. Edward made it clear that John would not be replaced: the Stone of Destiny was removed from Scone to Westminster; and henceforth Scotland would be ruled by England as Wales and Ireland were. In brief, no longer would Scotland be a kingdom with a king, but a land with a lord.

That this did not happen was basically due to an inborn patriotism in the Scottish people, who were unable to stomach an enforced union with England. For such feelings to be effective, however, they had to be activated and harnessed. This was the work of two men, both genuine patriots but also with personal grievances against the English regime: William Wallace, the son of a Lanarkshire knight, and Andrew Moray, the heir to an important barony in the north-east. Against the odds Wallace defeated the main English army on 1st September 1297 at Stirling Bridge, and thus at a stroke Edward's work of the previous year was undone. Wallace's place centre stage lasted less than a year: on 22nd July 1298 his army was completely crushed by a new English force at Falkirk, and as a result the leadership of Scottish resistance passed back to the nobility.

And resistance there was. But the inexorable pressure Edward I exerted through annual and well-organised campaigns gradually had its effect, and one by one the leading members of Scotland's political nation made their peace with the English king. By 1305, Edward was able with some confidence to draw up the Ordinance for the Governing of Scotland. The apparent English victory was again disrupted by an individual. Also in 1305 Robert Bruce, son of the claimant of 1290, died. His heir, also Robert Bruce, unlike his father and grandfather neither of whom was strongly motivated towards the Crown, had a total commitment to what he believed to be his family's rights. In 1302, he too had made his peace with Edward I, and had the English king recognised his status as a claimant to the throne and granted him a significant role in governing Scotland, he might have remained loyal. Edward's refusal to do so, combined with his imperious attitude, drove Bruce to bid for the Crown. He probably intended to wait until Edward, who was old and in poor health, died; but by an act of extreme rashness, he was forced to show his hand early: on 10th January 1306 he murdered John Comyn, lord of Badenoch, in the church of the Franciscan friars at Dumfries, probably because Comyn refused to back his claim to the throne. Before the full effects of this could be felt or worked out, the political situation was changed by the death of Edward I and the accession of his son and unworthy successor, Edward II.

ROBERT BRUCE AND NORTHUMBERLAND, 1307-1329

Robert Bruce, as King Robert I of Scotland, was to inflict upon Northumberland the darkest and most miserable conditions it has ever had to endure. But before he was in a position to do so, he had to make himself master of his own country. This involved subduing the opposition of certain members of the Scottish nobility, particularly the Balliol and Comyn families and their followers who were strong in the south-west and north-east parts of the country, and securing the surrender of the English garrisons occupying the important castles in southern and eastern Scotland. This required a long and difficult struggle, substantially complete by 1311 but not finally over until the surrender of Berwick in March 1318.

Bruce's success was very much to do with his own abilities. In addition to his total commitment and ruthless determination, he had military ability of a high order and was able to attract the loyalty of able subordinates such as Sir James Douglas and Thomas Randolph, earl of Moray. He also had

Table 10: THE SCOTTISH ROYAL HOUSE, 1306-1625

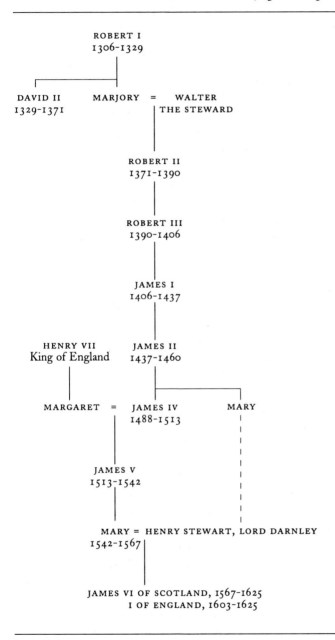

ROBERT I
1306-1329

DAVID II   MARJORY = WALTER
1329-1371   THE STEWARD

ROBERT II
1371-1390

ROBERT III
1390-1406

JAMES I
1406-1437

HENRY VII   JAMES II
King of England   1437-1460

MARGARET = JAMES IV   MARY
             1488-1513

JAMES V
1513-1542

MARY = HENRY STEWART, LORD DARNLEY
1542-1567

JAMES VI OF SCOTLAND, 1567-1625
I OF ENGLAND, 1603-1625

considerable political skill which enabled him to operate effectively in the constantly shifting world of European diplomacy. But perhaps his greatest advantage was the king of England: Edward II was completely unqualified to perform the role, so much so that rumours circulated that he was not in fact Edward I's son. He lacked interest and competence in matters martial and military; he failed to recognise the political necessity of maintaining a sufficient balance between the competing and conflicting individuals, families and groups within the baronage, a failure compounded by his homosexual addiction to favourites like Piers Gaveston and Hugh Despenser; and he proved incapable of building up a group of men on whose loyalty and devotion he could rely. Consequently, from the outset he was embroiled in domestic political problems which left him little time, even had he had the inclination, to maintain the momentum of conquest in Scotland. Apart from one campaign in 1310, which was frustrated by Bruce's adoption of the classic tactic of avoiding battle, Edward neglected his Scottish inheritance until 1314, when the imminent surrender of the strategically vital fortress of Stirling made action essential. This, almost predictably, ended catastrophically on 24th June when his army was crushingly defeated at Bannockburn by a force smaller and less well equipped but commanded by a man who knew his business.

The north of England was now completely exposed to Scottish aggression. Northumberland had already had a foretaste of what was to come. In 1296 there had been a raid into Redesdale, and in October and November the following year William Wallace as a follow -up to his victory at Stirling spent thirty days pillaging along the south bank of the Tweed and into the North Tyne valley. Fourteen years elapsed before another major incursion, but in August 1311 Bruce raided Tynedale from the west and in the following month came into north Northumberland across the Tweed, visits which gained him £2,000 by way of payment to secure a truce.

After Bannockburn, however, Scottish attention to Northumberland was almost incessant until peace was finally made by a distracted English government in 1328. This phase was studied by Jean Scammell, who demonstrated that Bruce was not so much interested in fighting battles or taking castles, as concerned to acquire plunder (essential in gaining and maintaining enthusiastic support), and cash from blackmail, even if that involved advertising a coming raid. This tactic worked admirably with victims distant from the Border: Durham in fact spared itself considerable damage by devising effective machinery for collecting and delivering money to Bruce. Northumberland, near to the Border and unable to organise itself adequately, suffered accordingly.

How bad did conditions become? A precise and completely accurate answer is not possible since the evidence is so limited, and in some cases to be suspected of exaggeration. This is particularly so of the petitions submitted to the Crown by monasteries. Admittedly as static and pacific institutions they were particularly vulnerable, but they were staffed by literate and educated men who were well versed in making a good case to their own advantage. Nevertheless, Blanchland's claim in 1327 that it had lost 40 acres of wheat and rye, 100 acres of oats, 100 of hay and 500 sheep does not seem incredible, and probably justified the 20 marks (£13 6s. 8d.) worth of food sent from the royal depot at Newcastle. The interesting aspect of this petition was that the canons attached blame not only to the Scots, but also to English government purveyors who were legally entitled to take goods on the promise of future payment.

Much more substantial and reliable are the financial records of the south Tweedside estate of the monks of Durham Cathedral. This comprised the churches of Norham and Holy Island which were entitled to tithes and a variety of other spiritual income (see Chapter 4) from thirty-one townships, twelve in Norham and nineteen in Holy Island. In addition, the monks owned the townships of Shoreswood (in Norham) and Fenham and Holy Island (in Holy Island), and drew rents from properties in Norham, Tweedmouth, and ten other places in Holy Island parish.

This estate and the income from it were divided between the cathedral priory's chief financial officer, the bursar, and its out-station or cell on Holy Island. The bursar's portion comprised the church revenues of Norham and above half of those of Holy Island together with Shoreswood and a handful of rents in Norham. The remainder of Holy Island parish, Fenham and Holy Island and rents from ten places in the parish belonged to the cell. The monks there administered their properties directly, but management of the bursar's portion was in the hands of an on-the-spot officer known as the Proctor of Norham. His job was to collect the income out of which he paid the stipends of the vicar of Norham and the chaplain at Cornhill and then send the surplus to Durham. Since all three institutions and officers kept accounts, we have good evidence from this most exposed part of the country for most years between the late thirteenth century and the Reformation.

For this period the evidence contained in the accounts of the bursar and his proctor is revealing and conclusive. Up to and including the financial year 1313/14 the proctor's income from all sources normally totalled between £400 and £420. The collapse thereafter was dramatic and is completely revealed in the following figures (to the nearest £):

1314/15	280
1315/16	243
1316/17	missing
1317/18	25
1318/19	9
1319/20	16
1320/21	23

It would seem therefore that the two-year truce agreed in December 1319 had little or no beneficial effect. The loss of the accounts for the following six years is frustrating, but the income of £22 in 1327/28 suggests that the truce agreed in June 1323 following Edward II's fruitless expedition into Lothian the previous year led to no significant improvement. We must be

cautious here, however, since Bruce broke the truce in 1327 after Edward II
had been deposed, twice coming personally into Northumberland, which
he threatened to annexe, and sending other expeditions under three of his
lieutenants into northern England.

Lest it be thought that, being on Tweedside, Norham and Holy Island
suffered exceptionally, evidence from elsewhere in the county is equally
depressing. For example, in 1325 the inquest *post mortem* into the
possessions of the earl of Pembroke, Aymer de Valence, who died in 1323,
revealed the following situation at Ponteland, a village well away from the
border.

| | *Peacetime Value* | | | *Value in 1325* | | |
	£	s	d	£	s	d
manor house		10	0			6
demesne arable	5	16	9		13	0
demesne meadow	11	8	0	1	0	0
park		6	8		0	0
bondlands	5	12	6		18	0
cottages		12	0		2	0
mill	10	0	0	1	6	8
	34	5	11	4	0	2

A similar situation existed two years later at Ingoe in Stamfordham parish.
Peacetime values were said to be:

	£	s	d
demesne arable	1	13	4
demesne meadow		10	0
bondlands	4	0	0
cottages		6	0
	6	9	4

In 1327, although most of the demesne lands were leased for £1 5s. 0d.,
none of the tenant holdings were let, because they had been destroyed by
the Scots. Likewise further north at Thirston near Felton in 1324 all twelve
bondlands were vacant for the same reason. In fact, the surviving bit of
evidence of the 1320s invariably reveals a dire and desperate situation in
which there were no tenants, or far fewer than there should have been, and
something like an eighty per cent fall in the landlord's income.

The landed nobility and gentry not only lost income and tenants, they
also suffered financially in other ways through their active engagement in
the war. By fighting they risked capture, which meant the loss of expensive

military equipment, notably war horses, and the raising of ransom money to secure their release. Like the monasteries, they could also suffer from the actions of their own side, since the Crown did not always pay promptly what it owed them in wages for themselves and their men, and in compensation for equipment they had lost. Much of their suffering is summed up in the petition of 1320 from the lord of Ellingham, Robert de Clifford, who requested an annual pension of £62 in compensation for the war losses he had sustained: £100 ransom following his capture at Bannockburn; compensation for the loss of horses and armour worth 100 marks (£66 13s. 4d); and service in the Berwick garrison at his own expense when his loss of income from his estate came to £100 over a six-year period. Clifford clearly had soldiered on; others decided to give up the fight. John of Rothbury, for example, applied to be allowed to enter a monastery on Humberside, claiming that the war had led to the deaths of his parents and to his own destitution.

Others reacted more violently, one particular incident causing considerable and prolonged upheaval. On 31st August 1317 a gang of men led by Sir Gilbert de Middleton and including Sir Walter de Selby of Seghill ambushed the newly elected bishop of Durham, Lewis de Beaumont, and his brother Henry, at Rushyford, ten miles north of Darlington, as they were on their way to Durham for the bishop's enthronement. To make matters worse, in Beaumont's party were two cardinals, Gaucelin D'Eauze and Luca Fieschi, who were travelling to Scotland as international mediators to negotiate with Robert Bruce. Although relieved of their goods, the cardinals were released, but the Beaumonts were carried into Northumberland to Mitford castle, to be held for ransom. Middleton's wild escapade was soon over: early in December he and his brother John were captured at Mitford by Sir William de Felton, who transferred them to London for trial and execution as traitors on 26th January 1318. Selby, however, escaped and continued to defy authority from the tower at Horton near Blyth which he had seized from his neighbour, Sir Bertram Monboucher. From there he fled to the Scots who installed him as their agent in Mitford castle, where he was able to maintain himself for two further years. He then surrendered to the English government on the promise of a pardon. This was not kept, however, and Selby languished in the Tower until 1327.

At first sight all this was a case of ruffians taking advantage of troubled times and weak authority to engage in lawless activity. But, the fact that no fewer than seventy-four Northumberland landowners became involved suggests that there was more to it than mere banditry. It is in fact possible to argue that the incident was born of frustration with a government which appeared to have wilfully failed in its duty to defend the country and to have abandoned the people of Northumberland to their fate. It was this same failure which drove Andrew Harclay, a man with a distinguished military career on the Border who had saved Edward II in 1322 by defeating the rebel Thomas, earl of Lancaster, at Boroughbridge, to negotiate on his own initiative a peace treaty with Bruce. He was executed for his pains. That service and loyalty did not pay is also illustrated by John de Fawdon, one of Gilbert de Middleton's captors, who was rewarded with an annual pension of 20 marks (£13 6s. 8d.). A few years later he was driven to petition for the payment of arrears, pointing out that in addition to his part in capturing Middleton, he had twice been captured by the Scots and had to be ransomed, and had his house burnt three times.

Northumberland's long years of agony were brought to an end by the events of 1327 to 1329. Early in 1327 Bruce restarted the war. In part this move was prompted by the coup d'état in England in September 1326 when Edward II's queen Isabella, and her lover Roger Mortimer, deposed her husband and had her fourteen-year-old son crowned as Edward III. It is also very likely that Bruce was equally influenced by an awareness that the disease he had contracted, possibly leprosy, would soon prove fatal. He therefore determined to use the short time left to him and the political opportunity to bring his long struggle to a successful conclusion. His own attack on Northumberland and the raids of the earls of Mar and Moray and Sir James Douglas were serious enough to bring a large English army north to Durham. Not only did they fail to bring the Scots to battle, but the cost of the expedition bankrupted the English treasury. Consequently, the English government had little option but to accept Bruce's terms for peace. By the treaty which was formally ratified at a parliament held at Northampton in May 1328, Bruce got what he had always wanted, English recognition of Scotland as a fully independent kingdom and of himself as its legitimate king. Thirteen months later, on 7th June 1329, he was dead.

The peace treaty and Bruce's death were immediately reflected in the fortunes of south Tweedside as revealed in the financial records of Durham Cathedral. The proctor's receipts, to the nearest £, were:

1327/28	22
1328/29	63
1329/30	194
1330/31	220

Northumberland, it would seem, had managed to survive and was coming back to life.

THE ENGLISH ASCENDANCY, 1329-1377

The next phase lasted almost fifty years, and covered two long reigns of Edward III of England (1327-1377) and David II of Scotland (1329-1371). Its essential characteristic was a reversal of the previous balance of power between the two countries: instead of Scotland controlling the situation, she was forced on to the defensive by English aggression. This was the consequence of major political changes. In England the eighteen-year-old Edward III overthrew the regime of his mother and her lover in 1330 and assumed personal control of the government. He was able and ambitious, and unwilling to accept the 'shameful peace' of 1328, which, he argued, while made in his name, did not have his approval. In contrast, in 1330 the Scottish king was only six years old, which meant a long period of minority government.

Edward's first move to undo the 1328 settlement was covert. He backed, but did not join, the group of English nobles known as the Disinherited who had forfeited their Scottish estates by choosing to give their allegiance to the English king. Led by Henry de Beaumont, the group included two Northumbrians, Gilbert de Umfraville and David of Strathbogie, who claimed the earldoms of Angus and Atholl respectively. Attached to this group was Edward Balliol, the son of King John, who aimed to recover his father's kingdom, for which he was willing to do homage to Edward III.

Against all the odds this enterprise had immediate success. Having landed on the Fife coast early in August 1332, they defeated a much larger Scottish army on Dupplin Moor on 11th August, and on 24th September Edward Balliol was crowned at Scone. This success was too easy. Scottish resistance recovered from the earlier defeat, and just before Christmas Balliol was surprised at Annan by a group of young patriots led by John Randolph, earl of Moray, and was forced to flee to Carlisle almost naked and on an unsaddled horse.

Edward III now had to abandon Balliol or give him greater support. He chose the latter course, and in May 1333 joined Balliol who had laid siege to Berwick in March. The Scots under Sir Archibald Douglas invaded Northumberland, but this move failed to divert the besiegers, and by July Berwick was on the verge of surrender. In fact, the Scots now faced the same dilemma as they had posed at Stirling in 1314. And the result was the same: the relieving force, this time Scottish, was completely routed at Halidon Hill, just north of Berwick, on 19th July. Berwick surrendered the following day, and again Edward Balliol appeared to be victorious, so much so that he was able to call a parliament and restore the Disinherited to their estates. On 12th June 1334 he met his master, Edward III, at Newcastle, where he paid his debt to the English king by handing over, as he had secretly promised, the counties of Berwick, Roxburgh, Selkirk, Peebles, Dumfries and the three Lothians to be permanently annexed to England.

Meanwhile in May the young David II had been taken to France for safety, and the 'auld alliance' was reactivated. The Scots, passive since their defeat at Halidon Hill, again rose against the two Edwards with widespread success. To conquer Scotland would require a long war of attrition, from which Edward III was diverted by the growing urgency of his quarrel with France over his right to Gascony, which in 1337 he chose to enlarge by laying claim to the French throne. This shift of attention gave the Scots the

46 COUNTY OF CONFLICT

Table 11: THE ENGLISH ROYAL HOUSE, 1272-1603

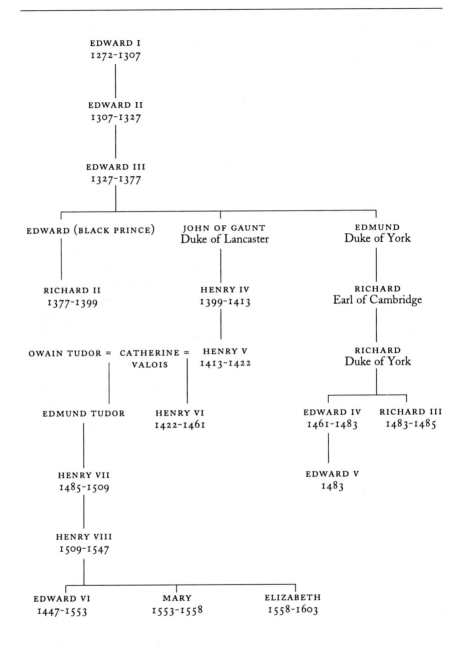

respite they needed to capture and destroy (to prevent future use) English-occupied castles. By June 1341, the process of reconquest was far enough advanced for David II to return home.

Now old enough to rule, David proved to be an aggressive king bent on ridding his kingdom of its enemies. Early in 1342 he made plain his intention by raiding Northumberland as far south as the Tyne, and then securing the surrender of Roxburgh and Stirling. This period of hostility culminated in October, 1346 when he led a large Scottish army in an invasion of England in response to French pleas for help after their crushing defeat at the hands of Edward III at Crécy on 26th August. The Scottish host mustered at Perth, and entered England on the west, having spent three days capturing the small fortress of Liddell. Tactically and strategically this was pointless, and the most likely reason for it was that its defender was Sir Walter de Selby whom the Scots regarded as a traitor for having given up Mitford castle nearly thirty years before. The memory of this betrayal still rankled, and Selby and his sons were summarily executed as soon as they surrendered.

The Scottish army was briefly in Northumberland. Coming down the Tyne valley, they devastated Hexham and its neighbourhood, and then crossed the Derwent and headed for Durham. On 17th October, on the western outskirts of the city, they were utterly defeated by an English army specially assembled for this purpose. The battle of Neville's Cross was an unmitigated disaster for the Scots. Apart from huge losses in and after the battle, David, wounded in the face by an arrow, was captured. Courtesy between kings led Edward III to send his private surgeon from York to attend to the wound; but the Scottish king was now a prisoner of his cousin by marriage, and would remain so for eleven years. The débâcle was completed by the rapid reconquest by English forces of the areas of southern Scotland that the Scots had worked so hard to recover.

From 1347 until the death of Edward III in 1377 the two countries were at peace, except very briefly in late 1355 and early 1356, when Berwick was captured in a surprise attack by the earls of Angus and March. Edward III's response was immediate and vigorous: within two months he had retaken Berwick and had devastated south-east Scotland in a savage raid known as Burnt Candlemas. It was a salutary reminder of the strength of English military power in the hands of a determined king. More significant was Edward's victory over the French in September 1356 near Poitiers in which the blind French king, John, was captured. With France neutralised, Edward could afford to release David, who returned home early in October 1357, but saddled with a 100,000 mark ($£6,666$ 13s. 4d) ransom. Such was the stability of the situation that the annual instalments continued to be paid after David's death in 1371 by his successor, Robert II (1371-90), until Edward III died six years later.

This brief outline of political and military events serves to demonstrate that, in contrast to his father's reign, that of Edward III was a period when most of the fighting was done in Scotland. Northumberland was on the front line, but was invaded on very few occasions. The most serious of these was in connection with the siege of Berwick in 1332. In the early 1330s the proctor of Norham was able to sell the tithes of corn for over £100, but in 1333/34 they fetched only £68. In the same year the rents owed by the tenant farmers of Shorewood, six miles south-west of Berwick, were abated as the result of the destruction caused by a Scottish raid in which the village smith had been killed. The record of deaths in the parish, however, suggests that this was an isolated killing, not part of a massacre. Not surprisingly, therefore, the account for the financial year 1335/36 shows that life returned to normal: the corn tithes were valued at £130, and the Shorewood tenants paid their rent in full.

A similar picture is presented by the financial records of the Holy Island cell. Rent income, normally amounting to £21, fell to little over £10 in 1333. Subsequent accounts, however, reveal no serious loss of income, except in 1340 when a Scottish raid prevented the collection of tithes at Scremerston. Other helpful evidence is the sums sent by the proctor of Norham to the cathedral bursar at Durham. After 1330 they normally amounted to between £160 and £190, but in 1341/42 and 1342/43 they fell to £71 and £117 respectively, probably the combined result of Edward III's brief campaign in November 1341 and the Scottish raid in the spring of the following year. All in all, the picture is one of a society recovering, in spite of occasional setbacks, from a period of disaster, without being able to realise earlier levels of output and income.

But was war the only, or indeed the main, problem? The fact that a very similar fall-off in output and income can be observed in Teesside communities well away from the war zone suggests that it was not. Here we must note that the onset of Bruce's onslaught coincided with a natural disaster. Throughout Britain and much of Europe harvest failure occurred in 1315, 1316 and 1317 as the result of appallingly wet summers, and this disaster was followed by widespread disease which killed many animals. The extent of this catastrophe is still being calculated, but it is now commonly thought that the population may have fallen by as much as fifteen percent between 1300 and 1330. If this is true, evidence of a reduction in economic activity is not surprising.

THE SECOND CRISIS, 1377-1406

The death of Edward III and the accession of his under-age grandson, Richard II, adjusted the political advantage in Scotland's favour. Ransom payments ceased, and during the following seven years English control in southern Scotland was gradually reduced to the three castles at Berwick, Roxburgh and Jedburgh and their immediate neighbourhoods. When the long truce agreed in 1369 ended in 1384, war between the two kingdoms again became open. Early in the year Northumberland was raided by the earl of Douglas, and in December Berwick was captured, but almost immediately regained by the earl of Northumberland. The following year fighting was on a larger scale. A Scottish force, with a substantial French contingent, crossed the Tweed and took Wark and two smaller castles. In return the English government mounted a full-scale invasion, in which the young Richard II took part, which achieved nothing because, to French disgust, the Scots declined battle.

An uneasy peace followed until 1388, when the Scots launched a major assault on northern England. They chose an opportune moment in that, like Edward II, Richard II was embroiled in a serious political crisis over his predilection for favourites and his style of government. In July a raid reached Tynemouth and returned unscathed with a large number of ransomable prisoners. This was merely the prelude to the large offensive launched the following month. The main thrust, led by the king's son, the earl of Fife, was into Cumberland and Westmorland. The attack on Northumberland, led by the earls of Douglas and March, appears to have been a subsidiary or diversionary move, and possibly the result of political differences within the Scottish high command. But it was this sideshow that gave the Scots their main success in one of the best known but least understood events in Northumberland's history.

The Scottish forces penetrated as far as Newcastle, which was well protected by its walls. Returning home via Redesdale, Douglas, the Scottish commander, decided (possibly because of a challenge) to give battle to the English force he knew would be in pursuit under the leadership of the earl of Northumberland's son, Sir Henry Percy, known for his impetuosity as Hotspur. (The rise of the Percy family to dominance in Northumberland is described in the following section.) Douglas chose his ground carefully, a ridge a few hundred yards north of Otterburn. He was, however, surprised by the speed of Hotspur's pursuit and his decision to attack after nightfall. The battle was fought by moonlight, probably on 9th August, St Oswald's Day, on the land close to where the Percy Cross now stands. The Scottish victory was complete and included the capture of Hotspur and his brother, Sir Ralph Percy, but marred by the death of Douglas. The extent of the English defeat may be indicated by the several hundred skeletons discovered in 1877 under the foundations of Elsdon church.

The battle of Otterburn has been portrayed in ballad and fable as a clash between two feuding border families of Douglas and Percy. While it is true that they were bitter rivals over the ownership of Jedburgh and Jed Forest, the events of 1388 were the consequence of national and indeed international politics. The numbers of men engaged were large, and certainly in the Scottish ranks were contingents from districts distant from the Border. For the Scottish government the underlying aim of the campaign was not personal gain or advantage but the ending of English occupation and thereby the completion of Robert Bruce's work. In this light, in spite of the great victory at Otterburn, and the successful raid as far as Tynemouth a year later, the campaign was not a real success in that the truce agreed in 1389 left English forces in occupation of the castles of Berwick, Roxburgh and Jedburgh.

The war of 1388-89 was followed by eleven years of peace. What then occasioned the renewal of hostilities was the desertion to England of George Dunbar, earl of March, as the result of a bitter quarrel between him and the third earl of Douglas, Archibald (the Grim), in which the Scottish king, Robert III (1390-1406), had favoured the latter. For the new English king, Henry IV, who had deposed and murdered Richard II in 1399, this was an excellent excuse to invade Scotland to enforce English overlordship. His expensive campaign, which left Newcastle early in August 1400 and was back there by 3rd September, achieved nothing other than the extension of the truce. War again broke out, this time more conclusively, in 1402. A raid by the self-exiled earl of March into Berwickshire was answered by a Scottish incursion into Northumberland led by Sir Patrick Hailes, which came to grief at Nesbit Muir. In revenge a larger raid was organised by the fourth earl of Douglas, Archibald (the Tyneman=loser), which initially had considerable success, reaching as far south as Newcastle without opposition. Returning home via the Till valley, however, they were caught by an English force commanded by Sir Henry Percy. On 14th September Hotspur had his revenge for his defeat at Otterburn by winning a decisive victory, which included the capture of Douglas, on the slopes of Humbleton Hill.

This victory brought the Percies to the height of their power. Within three years their fortunes were in ruins. For a variety of reasons their mistrust of Henry IV, whom they had helped to gain the throne, grew rapidly. As a result in 1403 Hotspur took part in a revolt and was killed in battle at Shrewsbury. Two years later his father, the earl of Northumberland, fled, having been implicated in a second revolt organised by the archbishop of York, Richard Scrope. After three years as a fugitive in Scotland, Wales and France, he made a desperate bid to restore his fortunes by military means, but his small force was defeated and he himself killed in a skirmish at Bramham Moor in Yorkshire on 19th February 1408. The rehabilitation of the Percy family did not begin until 1416 when the title and some of the estates were restored to Hotspur's son, the dead earl's grandson.

Equally important for Northumberland was the weakening of the Scottish government. Because of the dangerous state of Scottish politics, the ailing Robert III decided early in 1406 to send his twelve-year-old son and heir, James, to France for safe keeping. Unfortunately, the ship in which he was travelling was intercepted off Flamborough Head and the boy was made prisoner. The news of this catastrophe almost certainly hastened his father's death. James I, as he now was, was to remain in captivity in England for eighteen years, which meant weak government in Scotland and greater security for Northumberland.

Two facts stand out about this period. One is that the two sides were fairly evenly matched and each had its share of military success. The other is that fighting took place in under half of the thirty years. Nevertheless, fighting there was, and so it is not surprising that petitions were sent to Westminster appealing for help or relief from taxation, that Mindrum and Presson, which were worth over £28 in peacetime were valueless in 1380, and that five years later Halton, Clarewood and Great Whittington were wasted by the Scots. What is hard to explain, however, is the almost total collapse of economic life along the Border, which began during the 1370-1384 truce and lasted until after 1406. In 1373/74, the income of the Holy Island cell amounted to almost £201, its main components being corn tithe (£92), farm rents (£37) and rents of Tweed fish weirs (£17). By 1379/80, the total was little more than half that sum, with all elements equally affected. After 1380 conditions worsened so that corn tithes were rarely worth more than £20, and of the land rents, which should have yielded over £37, up to £28 was not paid. The same story is told by the records of the proctor of Norham. Until 1376/77 he was able to send over £100 profit every year to Durham – in that year it actually exceeded £118. By 1379/80, however, it had fallen to nothing, and thereafter until 1406, £30 was the most that was ever sent, and in nine years his income failed to cover his expenses.

There are several possible reasons for this depression which was more prolonged than that after 1314. One is that the fighting was more severe than appears; another is that evidence of a similar nature from central and southerly districts of the county would reveal a less desperate situation. Alternatively, plague, which ravaged the county in 1349 and on several occasions thereafter, may have been having a delayed effect. (The plague and its effects is discussed in Chapter 3.)

THE CONSEQUENCES OF CONFLICT

As well as the immediate devastation caused by raids and the passage of armies, the endemic enmity between the two nations had long-term effects on Northumbrian society, which were readily apparent by the early fifteenth century. One of the most obvious was the disappearance of the cross-Border estate, which both Edward I of England and Robert I of Scotland refused to allow. The lordship of Tynedale, confiscated from the Scottish kings, rapidly passed through the hands of six owners until it became Crown property in 1336 when acquired by Edward III's wife, Queen Philippa. Bywell barony, taken from John Balliol in 1296, was granted in 1331 to the widow of the earl of Pembroke, Aymer de Valence, who died without heirs in 1323. In 1336, the reversion of the estate was awarded to

John Neville, lord of Raby in Co. Durham. The Nevilles had a long wait, however, since the dowager countess lived for another forty years. Similarly, Beanley barony, surrendered by Patrick, earl of Dunbar, when he chose to be a Scot, was granted to Henry Percy, lord of Alnwick, in 1335. Lower down the social scale, Sir Henry Prendergest lost his small estate in the townships of Akeld and Yeavering in 1359 when he too finally decided to settle north of the Border.

Likewise, the reverberations of the Middleton episode continued long after the event. In 1335 the estate of John Middleton, which included Belsay manor, which was at that time in the possession of two men, one of whom was a king's clerk, was granted for life to John de Strivelyn (Stirling), a man much engaged in Border affairs, as a means of compensating him for the heavy ransom he had been required to pay to secure his release from captivity in Scotland. Another loser was Adam son of Nicholas (or Nicson) who was the tenant of Tynemouth priory for a 68-acre farm in East Lilburn. This was confiscated after the rebellion had been put down and granted by the Crown to a John of Bewick for life at only a third of its normal rent. The priory only regained control of this property when John died in 1352.

The most remarkable change in land ownership was the rise of the Percy family: in 1300 they possessed nothing in Northumberland; by 1400 they dominated the county and bore the title of earl. In part they owed their advance to the Crown, which generously rewarded their border service. But they also furthered their own interests by purchase and by marriage, and in doing so they showed a readiness to engage in sharp practice and cynical opportunism. That this was tolerated may have been the result of Edward III's adoption of a policy of devolving responsibility for Border defence on to regional forces, which made powerful local leadership essential.

The foundation of the Percy empire in Northumberland was laid by Henry I (d.1314). He and his predecessors were Yorkshire barons, and it is important to note that throughout the period the Percies remained essentially a Yorkshire family. In 1309, Henry Percy bought the barony of Alnwick for £5,000 from the bishop of Durham, Antony Bek. The transaction was rather dubious in that Bek may have been holding the estate in trust for the family of William de Vesci, the previous baron who died in 1297 without legitimate heirs.

Percy's grandson, Henry III (d.1368), added two important estates. In 1327 he contracted with the Crown to serve on the Border for an annual fee of 500 marks (£333 6s. 8d.), but he exchanged this for the barony of Warkworth (to which Rothbury, Corbridge and Newburn were attached) which reverted to the Crown in 1332 on the death without heirs of Sir John Clavering. Three years later, as we have seen, Percy also acquired Beanley barony, granted to him by Edward III after its surrender by the earl of Dunbar.

Table 12: THE PERCY FAMILY

EARLY HISTORY: Although settled in England from the reign of William I, the Percy family had no connection with Northumberland until the early fourteenth century.

WILLIAM DE PERCY, *d.* 1096
|
ALAN DE PERCY, *d.* 1120
|
WILLIAM DE PERCY, *d.* 1153
|
WILLIAM DE PERCY, *d.* 1168
|
AGNES DE PERCY, *d.* 1205 =   JOSCELINE
Count of Louvain
and Brabant
d. 1188

HENRY DE PERCY, *d.* 1196
|
WILLIAM DE PERCY, *d.* 1245
|
HENRY DE PERCY, *d.* 1272
|
HENRY DE PERCY, *d.* 1315

NORTHUMBERLAND

HENRY PERCY, 1272-1315, 1ST BARON OF ALNWICK
|
HENRY PERCY, 1299-1353, 2ND BARON
|
HENRY PERCY, 1320-1368, 3RD BARON
|
HENRY PERCY, 1342-1408, 4TH BARON AND 1ST EARL OF NORTHUMBERLAND
|
HENRY PERCY (HOTSPUR), *d.* 1403
|
HENRY PERCY, 1394-1455, 2ND EARL
|
HENRY PERCY, 1421-1461, 3RD EARL
|
HENRY PERCY, 1446-1489, 4TH EARL
|
HENRY PERCY, 1478-1527, 5TH EARL

HENRY PERCY, 1502-1537, 6TH EARL   THOMAS PERCY, *d.* 1537

THOMAS PERCY, 1528-1565   HENRY PERCY, 1532-1585, 8TH EARL
7TH EARL
                                 HENRY PERCY, 1564-1632, 9TH EARL

The fourth Henry Percy (d.1408), who was created earl of Northumberland in 1377, added to the estate by marriage. In 1373, he bought from the Crown the wardship of the two daughters of David, earl of Atholl, who had died in 1369. He immediately married them to his second and third sons, and inherited the property, which included the barony of Mitford, when they predeceased him. Seven years later he himself married Maud, the widow of the childless Gilbert de Umfraville, from whom he had earlier bought half of the barony of Prudhoe. By this marriage he not only acquired the remainder of the barony, but other properties to which Maud was heiress in her own right, notably Langley barony in Northumberland and the huge manor of Cockermouth in Cumberland. When Henry Percy IV died in 1408 he possessed five baronies and seventy manors in Northumberland, as well as substantial properties in Yorkshire, Cumberland and Sussex.

War also brought wealth to lesser men. Indeed, it is Anthony Tuck's argument that Crown service in war and Border administration with its fees and other financial rewards was the route to success in fourteenth-century Northumberland. The most notable, perhaps notorious, example, is John de Coupland, whose family had been established but without distinction at Coupland since the early thirteenth century. Coupland had served in minor offices before 1346, but his passport to success was his capture of David II as the Scottish king fled from Neville's Cross. He was immediately awarded an annual pension of £500, and subsequently appointed to important Border offices such as sheriff of Northumberland, sheriff of Roxburghshire and constable of Roxburgh castle and keeper of Berwick. He also proved adept at acquiring land, particularly from those who had fallen foul of the government. It was probably his not too delicate methods that led to his murder on Bolton Moor on 20th December 1363. The perpetrators were a gang led by John and Thomas Clifford, but there seems little doubt that behind it were the heads of some older families, such as Sir William Heton, who resented and feared the success of an upstart.

This was also the period when Northumberland moved rapidly towards being a heavily fortified county. In 1200 it probably contained eleven castles: Newcastle and Bamburgh belonging to the Crown and Norham to the bishop of Durham; together with baronial strongholds at Alnwick, Harbottle, Mitford, Morpeth, Prudhoe, Wark on Tweed, Wark on Tyne and Warkworth. Given the size of Northumberland and its Border location, this was not an excessive number, although it is as well to remember that these were the castles that had continued to exist and be developed. Others, such as Elsdon and Styford, had been abandoned because their owners had no need of them. It is likely that all castles began as wooden towers or enclosures on top of a mound (motte), which was either entirely artificial or a landscaped hillock protected by an enclosure (bailey) formed by an earth rampart topped by a wooden palisade. Over the course of the twelfth century those that survived were rebuilt in stone, some with a tower keep (Newcastle, Norham, Bamburgh, Prudhoe), others with a shell keep (Harbottle, Mitford, Alnwick, Wark on Tweed).

During the peaceful years of the thirteenth century before the 1290s there was little change in this situation: no new castle of any size or significance was started; and little development of existing structures took place, with the notable exception of the Black Gate at Newcastle. Troubled times, however, naturally led to renewed building activity. The main change to the old castles was strengthening by the addition of a double fortified gateway or barbican. In addition, twenty new castles were licensed by the Crown. Without doubt, the largest and most spectacular was Dunstanburgh, started in 1313 by Thomas, earl of Lancaster as lord of Embleton, which comprised a curtain wall to cut off a rock peninsula with a high double gatehouse which also served as a keep. Smaller but still of considerable size were courtyard castles like Chillingham, Ford and Ogle, which were rectangular walled enclosures with a tower at each corner. Most, however, like Haughton and Langley, were large rectangular towers of three or four storeys in which the hall, the main room of the castle, was on the first or second floor.

In the second half of the century the pace of construction increased, possibly because of a change in Crown policy. Hitherto, English kings had successfully controlled and restrained castle building by insisting that all fortified structures required their 'licence to crenellate'. After 1346, however, the government seems to have positively encouraged Northumbrian landowners to cater for their own defence needs without formal permission. The consequence was a rash of towers, although in the absence of licences we do not know precisely when they were built. Fortunately, a list of Northumberland castles drawn up in 1415 for Henry V as part of his defence precautions prior to his invasion of France has survived. This indicates that at least seventy-five towers had been built since the middle of the previous century. Archaeological work of recent years has revealed that, contrary to earlier belief, almost all of these towers were additions to existing halls, which were subsequently pulled down or replaced at a later date by more comfortable quarters. Some towers, however, were free standing from the start, notably the so-called vicars peles at Alnmouth, Chatton, Corbridge, Embleton, Ford, Ponteland and Whitton (Rothbury). By 1415, the main period of tower building was over, although another thirty-three were put up in the course of the following hundred years. Most of them were free standing, and significantly the majority were in townships very close to the Border.

Thus, by the early years of the sixteenth century there were well over a hundred towers in Northumberland. Although architectural and archaeological research has revealed differences in style, form and size, they were essentially variations on a basic uniform shape. Virtually all were three storeys high with a vaulted ground-floor basement, a hall on the first floor, and other rooms on the second floor; access from one storey to another was by means of a mural staircase. The roof was gabled with a crenellated parapet. In height most towers were between 40 and 50 feet, and their walls were usually 6 or 7 feet thick at the base, but slightly narrower in the upper storeys, and their external dimensions were between 25 and 50 feet. It is therefore clear that war and the threat of war had wrought significant changes in Northumbrian life, and established a number of significant differences between it and less vulnerable counties.

THE FIFTEENTH CENTURY

The years between the battles of Humbleton Hill (1402) and Flodden (1513) were relatively little disturbed by Scottish raids and invasions, a situation that arose from the political circumstances that affected each country. In Scotland the power of the Crown and the capacity of government were reduced by long periods without an effective king: James I (1406-37) was a captive in England from 1406 until 1424; and James II (1437-60) and James III (1460-88) were minors between 1437 and 1449 and 1460 and 1469 respectively. In all, Scotland had regency government for thirty-seven of the one hundred and eleven years. Moreover, the kings were not generally bent on war, and James III was a positive anglophile.

Much the same can be said of their English counterparts. Until mid-century they were preoccupied with gaining and then retaining an empire in France. Then from the 1440s until the 1480s they were embroiled in a series of conflicts that have come to be called the Wars of the Roses. In addition, the power of the great border families was sharply reduced. In England, the Percy family contrived always to be on the wrong side politically; and in Scotland the March family were for many years in England as rebellious traitors, while the Douglases were broken by James II in the 1450s.

Nevertheless, there were occasions when the Scots made damaging incursions into Northumberland. Although evidence from most parts of the county is lacking, that from the immediate Border districts suggests that there were seven occasions when life there was seriously disrupted. The pre-1450 incidents seem to have been of local origin and unrelated to state policy. The records of the proctor of Norham and of the Holy Island cell both reveal that after 1405 the district slowly began to recover from the fighting of the previous thirty years, and that recovery was uninterrupted for fifteen years. Then in 1420 and 1421 there was a brief setback as the result of warfare: no rents were paid by the farmers in Shoreswood in either year, and the monks on Holy Island lost three quarters of their rent income in 1420 and half of it in 1421. In 1436 and 1437 another raid occurred, but the effects seem not to have been as severe. This was also true in 1448 to 1450, although on that occasion the Scots are known to have got as far as

3: *Fortified Buildings*, 1415

In the 1415 survey, three different terms were used:
Castrum (castle), e.g. ETAL
Fortalicium (Fortalice), e.g. SWINBURN
Turris (Tower), e.g. Whitton

Alnwick, thirty miles south of the Border.

After mid-century, however, all the major incidents were the work of governments. In the 1450s James II, having assumed personal control of the government of Scotland and broken the power of the Douglas family, set about trying to end English occupation. In 1455 and 1457 he attacked Berwick, but without success; and in August 1456 he led a six-day raid into Northumberland in which he penetrated twenty miles south of the Tweed and devastated seventeen villages. The evidence of this is clear in Shoreswood, where only half the rents were paid, and in Holy Island, where income lost as the result of abandoned farms doubled. This apart, James's main success was the capture of Roxburgh castle, the last but one English stronghold north of the Tweed. Tragically, his victory was posthumous as he died from wounds caused by the explosion of one of his own cannon a few days before the castle surrendered.

The two states were now at peace for ten years; indeed Edward IV (1460-83) and the anglophile James III concluded a peace treaty in October 1474. The recurrence of war in the early 1480s was partly due to James's quarrel with his brother, the duke of Albany, who fled to England where he agreed to become Edward's vassal and cede to him large areas of southern Scotland in return for English help in deposing James. At the same time, Edward needed to appear active in foreign affairs, since his failure to wage war seriously in France in 1474, having been granted taxation to do so, had created ill-feeling in England. In 1482 a large English army led by the king's brother, Richard, duke of Gloucester, invaded Scotland, and found no opposition as the result of a coup d'état against James III by his leading nobles. While there is no evidence of Scottish incursions into Northumberland, there was a substantial falloff in rents paid in Shoreswood, Tweedmouth, Fenham and Holy Island. It is therefore possible that on this occasion the damage was done not by the Scots but by the English army passing through the district and forcibly commandeering much of its needs.

Again there was peace, which this time lasted for thirteen years until 1496. By then both countries had new kings. In England Henry VII (1485-1509) had acquired the throne by defeating and killing Richard III at Bosworth. Similarly, in Scotland, James IV (1488-1513) rebelled against his father who was killed in battle at Sauchieburn near Stirling. James was no anglophile; and he was also anxious to prove himself as a warrior, which his father conspicuously was not. Moreover, he had the very proper ambition to recover Berwick. The opportunity he needed came with the arrival in Scotland in 1496 of Perkin Warbeck, the impostor who at various times claimed to be the son of Edward IV and of Richard III.

The Scottish invasion of Northumberland was short and intended to force the English to grant favourable peace terms. James and his army crossed the Tweed on 20th September and were back on the north bank by

26th, having received news that an English army was mustering at Newcastle. In that week they had managed to ravage villages in the Tweed and Till valleys, destroy the towers at Twizel, Tillmouth, Duddo, Branxton, and Howtel and to besiege that at Heaton. A similar incursion was launched in the following year in which the towers at Thornton and Shoreswood were thrown down, and the surrounding area pillaged. Norham castle, however, held out. This bout of warfare ended with a counter-raid across the Tweed led by Thomas Howard, earl of Surrey. As intended, fighting was followed by talking, the outcome of which was a peace treaty in 1502, and the marriage of James IV and Henry VII's daughter, Margaret, in 1503. As on previous occasions, the effects of war were immediately manifest at Shorewood where the tenants were unable to pay rent between 1496 and 1498.

This phase culminated in one of the largest and bloodiest battles fought on British soil. It was the consequence of the ambition of the English king, Henry VIII (1509-47), to emulate his forebears, Edward III and Henry V, and win land and glory in France. To this end he joined the anti-French coalition known as the Holy League and invaded northern France in the summer of 1513. This situation posed a problem for James IV: he was committed to England by the 1502 treaty; at the same time he was attached to France by the 'auld alliance'. In the end, he opted for France, partly because Louis XII offered a substantial bribe, but also because of grievances against England, particularly the failure of the English government to punish John Heron, the bastard half-brother of the Sir William Heron of Ford, who five years earlier had treacherously murdered the Warden of the Scottish Middle March, Sir Robert Ker of Ferniehirst, at one of the truce days to settle cross-Border disputes held where the Redden Burn enters the Tweed near Carham.

The campaign began early in August with what the Scots came to call the Ill Raid. A small force under Alexander, Lord Home rode several miles into Northumberland and was returning via the Till valley when it was ambushed near Milfield by Sir William Bulmer, losing all its booty and many men. A few days later, on 22nd August, James and the Scottish army, which probably numbered well over 30,000 men and included an impressive artillery train, crossed the Tweed. Within six days, the main English fortress at Norham had fallen, and shortly after the smaller castles at Etal, Wark and Ford capitulated. Having achieved complete control of this bridgehead, James could have elected to return to Scotland, as he had in 1496, or to continue southwards deeper into England. Instead, he chose to remain encamped near Ford. In later accounts it was alleged that he did so because of his infatuation with Lady Heron, whose husband was a prisoner in Scotland. This romantic explanation must be dismissed in favour of a military one, namely, that James had decided to bring to battle the English army he knew would soon be sent north. The thinking behind this decision,

4: *Cocklaw Tower*

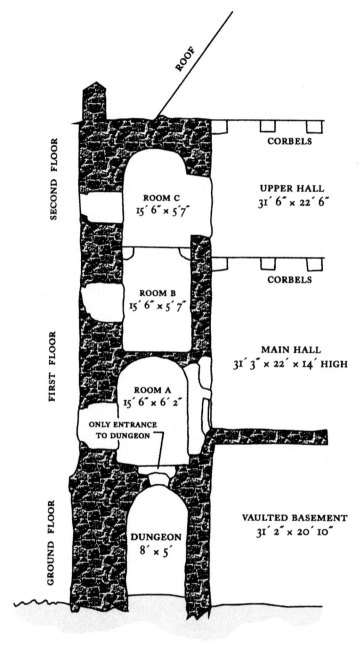

ROOF

CORBELS

SECOND FLOOR

ROOM C
15′ 6″ × 5′7″

UPPER HALL
31′ 6″ × 22′ 6″

CORBELS

ROOM B
15′ 6″ × 5′ 7″

FIRST FLOOR

MAIN HALL
31′ 3″ × 22′ × 14′ HIGH

ROOM A
15′ 6″ × 6′ 2″

ONLY ENTRANCE
TO DUNGEON

VAULTED BASEMENT
31′ 2″ × 20′ 10″

GROUND FLOOR

DUNGEON
8′ × 5′

COCKLAW TOWER - SOUTH SIDE (CROSS SECTION)

IT IS VERY LIKELY THAT THERE WERE SEVERAL OUTBUILDINGS AND THAT
THE ENTIRE COMPLEX LAY WITHIN A MOATED ENCLOSURE (BARMKIN)

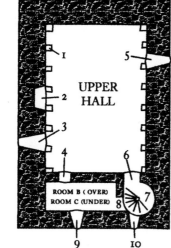

SECOND FLOOR

UPPER HALL

ROOM B (OVER)
ROOM C (UNDER)

1	CORBEL
2	FIREPLACE
3	WINDOW
4	DOOR TO ROOM C
5	WINDOW
6	DOOR TO UPPER HALL
7	STAIR
8	DOOR TO ROOM B
9	WINDOW
10	WINDOW

1	LATRINE
2	WINDOW WITH SEATS
3	FIREPLACE
4	DOOR TO ROOM A
5	WINDOW WITH SEATS
6	DOOR
7	WINDOW
8	DOOR TO MAIN HALL
9	STAIR

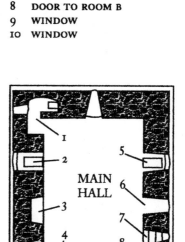

FIRST FLOOR

MAIN HALL

ROOM A

GROUND FLOOR

VAULTED BASEMENT

1	DUNGEON
2	ENTRANCE
3	STAIR

TOWER EXTERIOR DIMENSIONS :
LENGTH 50′ 6″ (NORTH - SOUTH)
WIDTH 34′ 8″ (EAST - WEST)
HEIGHT 40′ 3″
WALLS GROUND FLOOR 7′ THICK
WALLS UPPER FLOORS 6′ THICK

COCKLAW TOWER - SECTIONAL FLOOR PLANS

however, is far from clear.

In fact, the English army was already on the move. As a precautionary measure, Henry VIII had commissioned the sixty-nine-year-old Thomas Howard, earl of Surrey to be prepared to defend the Border. He stationed himself at Pontefract, far to the south, but was well prepared for an immediate response to any invasion. News of this reached him on 25th August, the day after the Scottish army had completed its crossing of the Tweed, and such was his state of readiness that by 30th, he and his troops were at Newcastle. By 3rd September he had reached Alnwick, where he was joined by his son, Thomas, the Lord Admiral, who had sailed from France with reinforcements. His force now numbered about 20,000 men, not far short of the Scottish army which had been reduced by desertions to about 26,000. On 5th September he moved to Bolton, and on the following day he arrived at Wooler. Here he was six miles south of James who had taken up a very strong defensive position on the steeply sloping Flodden Hill.

A frontal attack would have been highly risky and unlikely to succeed, the more so as the weather was wet and the ground heavy. Surrey's solution was a classic outflanking movement. On 8th September he crossed the Till and advanced eight miles eastwards to Barmoor, where he was hidden from the Scots by high ground. The following morning, Friday, he divided his army into two divisions. The larger, commanded by his son, the Lord Admiral, he sent with the artillery in a wide circling movement northwards to recross the Till by the stone bridge at Twizel. He himself led the smaller contingent across the Till by the fords between Ford and Etal. Before James fully appreciated what was happening the two parts of the English army were coming together near the village of Branxton, a mile and a half north of Flodden. Suddenly, the Scots found themselves facing the wrong way with the enemy between them and their homeland.

James now had to reverse his army and hurry to occupy Branxton Hill before the English troops could do so. It was now mid-afternoon, and by nightfall the Scots had suffered a major disaster, for which there were a number of reasons. One was accurate English artillery fire, which not only silenced the Scottish guns but also forced the Scots to advance downhill towards the English ranks. Here technology played a part. The Scots were armed with the latest weapon, imported pikes seventeen and a half feet in length which had proved highly successful in the hands of Swiss infantry. But to be successful they had to be used by tightly packed and in steadily advancing phalanxes. The Scottish battalions, however, were unable to maintain formation on the rough and marshy ground, and this gave the English troops wielding bills only eight feet in length a considerable advantage. But perhaps the crucial factor was James's own inadequacy as a commander. It is clear that he failed to heed good advice and that he fought the battle without formulating a proper plan or giving clear orders. His own

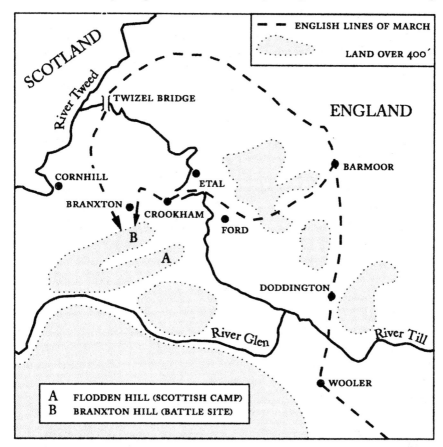

5: *The Battle of Flodden*

wild, do-or-die charge into the thick of the fray is testimony to his personal valour but also to his failure of leadership.

James died fighting and with him a very large percentage of the Scottish political nation, including his natural son, the archbishop of St Andrews, three other bishops, nine earls, nineteen lords and not far short of three hundred knights and gentry: 'the flowers of the forest were', indeed, 'a' wede awa'. For the tenant farmers of Shoreswood and their landlord in Durham things were not quite so dramatic. In 1513/14, the year of Flodden, most of the rents were paid, but the passage of armies in that year meant that payment was entirely abated in 1514/15 and 1515/16 and partly abated in 1516/17. By 1517/18, however, life was back to normal. Were many people killed? The answer would seem to be no. In 1513/14 no deaths were recorded in Norham parish, but in the following year the number was eighteen. However, this was not significantly greater than 1509/10 or 1516/17 when the corresponding figures were sixteen and fourteen.

From this brief survey of the long fifteenth century, two impressions stand out. One is that invasion was an infrequent experience. Indeed, if the district immediately adjacent to the Tweed suffered only seven incursions, most of Northumberland must have experienced fewer. The second impression is that on all occasions the damage done was relatively slight in that within three or four years it was repaired and life was in no way significantly impaired. Moreover, the rising level of profit the proctor of Norham was able to send to his master at Durham Cathedral suggests that economic growth was not unduly hindered by these rare bouts of fighting.

THE FINAL PHASES, 1513-1603

It is now fashionable to decry Flodden as a turning point in Anglo-Scottish relations, and indeed it would be foolish to argue that it alone explains why there was relatively little war between the two kingdoms in the ninety years between it and the Union of the Crowns in 1603. At the same time there is truth in the argument that such was the magnitude of the disaster which directly affected almost every noble and gentle family in Scotland that it must have impressed upon most members of the Scottish political nation that invading England was an act of folly. Not only were defeat and subsequent devastation likely, but there could be no significant benefit, even from victory: Scotland was helping France but gaining nothing for herself.

Despite this the old animosity continued throughout the first half of the century. James V (1513-42) was anglophobic, a fact he twice demonstrated by marrying French women. Tension between the two kingdoms finally led to open warfare in the 1540s. In November 1542, James decided to invade England. Significantly, many of his nobles were opposed to this venture, and their fears were fully justified when on 24th November the Scottish army was routed at Solway Moss in Cumberland. Three weeks later, James V was dead, leaving a week-old daughter, Mary, as his successor. Scotland was again faced with the problem of a long period of regency, and Henry VIII's government sought to use the situation to bring about a union of the two countries. Negotiations were successfully concluded for the eventual marriage of Mary and Henry VIII's heir Edward. The refusal of the Scottish Estates (parliament) to ratify this agreement led to what Sir Walter Scott was to call the 'rough wooing', the attempt by England to get by force what she had failed to achieve by diplomacy. The war in fact continued until the end of the decade, but it was fought north of the Border, not in Northumberland. The result was the opposite of what Henry VIII, and after his death in 1547 the governments of the young Edward VI (1547-53), intended: Mary was taken to France where in 1558 she was married to the Dauphin, Francis.

To a large extent the pattern of Anglo-Scottish relations was no different between 1513 and 1550 to what it had been since the early fifteenth century. After mid-century, however, the two countries moved closer together, a fact given formal expression in the peace treaty agreed at

Berwick in 1586. In part this accord was due to the fact that in the 1560s both governments opted for Protestantism and thus found themselves in the same ideological camp. More significant, perhaps, was that the Scottish king, James VI (1567-1625), was the heir to the English Crown, a fact made unalterable by Queen Elizabeth's refusal to marry.

In spite of this improved relationship between England and Scotland, the last third of the sixteenth century was a time of difficulty in Northumberland. One problem, which was general throughout the county, was what contemporaries termed the 'decay of the borders'. By this they meant three things: the failure of their owners to maintain towers in good repair; the growth in the number of abandoned farms; and the alarming decline in the number of men able to turn out horsed and armed with sword, spear and helmet to defend the Border. The first two problems cannot be satisfactorily quantified, but figures are available that demonstrates the truth of the last concern. The muster taken in 1538 revealed the existence of about 3250 men 'able with horse and harness'; by 1580 the number had fallen to about 1,500, and in 1595 it was under 1200. Further evidence is contained in a survey of 301 townships made in 1581, which revealed the alarming fact that no fewer than 249, that is, eighty-three per cent, were unable to furnish a fully equipped soldier.

Why this had happened was exposed in some detail by the enquiries commissioned by a worried government. Undoubtedly the government itself was partly to blame. The failed rebellion of 1569 (see Cchapter 6) resulted in the execution of the seventh earl of Northumberland in 1572 and the permanent residence of his successors at Petworth on their Sussex estates. The Percies thus became absentee landlords and ceased to be the hinge of Northumberland's defensive arrangements. More important, perhaps, were the economic changes that gathered pace in the last three or four decades of the century. Basically, rising prices combined with rising population gradually forced landlords to find ways of increasing their incomes, which in turn put a premium on good estate management. Raising rents was rarely an option since most of their tenants held their land by various forms of long-established customary tenure which included the principle of fixed rent. But they were able to raise the *gressom*, the sum of money which every tenant was required to pay upon entering his holding. As a result, tenants could no longer afford to buy and maintain the expensive equipment they needed to meet their military obligations. Also, many landlords brought back into their own hands the demesne land they had previously leased, and in some cases augmented it by enclosure, in order to create large and profitable sheep and cattle farms. By these and other means the number of tenant farmers was reduced, and many who remained were impoverished. The inclination of landowners was clearly shifting away from having a numerous, well-armed and relatively wealthy tenantry towards having a rising income. Contemporaries did not deny that 'decay' was in some cases or to some degree caused by the Scots, but they were clear that the root of the problem was in Northumberland, and that solutions were possible, given supportive legislation.

In one part of the county, however, the problems seemed intractable: Tynedale and Redesdale had become almost uncontrollable districts where lawlessness was endemic and on a grand scale. As elsewhere there was an upper level of gentry families, but beneath this layer the tenantry had formed tightly knit family groups known as 'surnames' with subdivisions called 'graynes'. This society was very similar in nature and operation to the clans and septs of the Highlands, and, as in that region, was the consequence of the failure of government to impose its authority. In Tynedale the main 'surnames' were Charlton, Dodd, Milburn and Robson, while in Redesdale the leading groups were Dunn, Hall, Hedley, Potts and Reed. Across the border in Teviotdale and Liddesdale an identical and parallel development had taken place which had given rise to 'surnames' such as Armstrong, Elliot, Graham and Nixon.

Being an upland region, the economic base was animal husbandry, with crops being of marginal importance. The habitation centres were not large villages but dispersed farms, and also small hamlets occupied by members of several 'surnames'. The quantities of arable and meadow land were small, each farmer having no more than 5 or 6 acres of each. The main asset was the thousands of acres of common grazing, particularly the high moorland where shielings, the temporary settlements occupied between April and August, were located. In contrast to the hamlets, each shieling was exclusive to a single 'surname'. The amounts of land involved are well illustrated by the situation in Elsdon parish in 1541 where 168 tenant farmers had only 790 arable and 577 meadow acres, but 4,960 acres of good pasture, 13,550 acres of grazing and over 21,000 acres of moorland for shielings.

Socially the unit above the family was the 'grayne', each with its own chosen headman, who represented his group in its dealings with the landlord and, when required, with the law courts; and was their leader in illegal activities. These were of three main sorts: blackmail (extorting protection money), reiving (stealing animals) and kidnapping (for ransom). Homicide would almost certainly provoke a 'deadly feed', that is, a feud which resulted in a series of reciprocal murders. The principal opponents or victims were of course the inhabitants of the Scottish dales, but the Tynedale and Redesdale men were not averse to raiding their own countrymen elsewhere in Northumberland. Consequently, watch had to be kept on all the exit points from the dales, especially in the October to March period, the main raiding season, when nights were long and animals well fed and strong from summer grazing. Moreover, English and Scottish borderers were willing to unite in defence of their way of life. When in January 1567, Sir John Forster, who was Warden of the Middle March from 1560 until 1595, hanged one of the Redesdale Halls along with other thieves, the dead man's brother organised a gang including Armstrongs and Nixons from across the Border and together they burned the house of one of Forster's servants and stole nearly 500 of his sheep.

The Warden was in fact the government official responsible for controlling the region, assisted by the Keepers of Tynedale and Redesdale. Theirs was a thankless and all but impossible task. The government frequently failed to pay their salaries and they had to expend a great deal of their own money on 'entertainment' in order to gather intelligence. From time to time the headmen were required to swear oaths and give recognisances to keep the peace. At other times the dales were raided and suspects arrested and held for trial in Newcastle. This was almost pointless as escapes were engineered, and when trials did take place convictions were all but impossible to obtain because witnesses were intimidated. In 1596, for example, only three convictions were obtained from fifty-nine trials in the Warden's court. Justice was also hindered by the willingness of the local gentry to collude with the 'surnames', usually to their mutual profit.

Both dales suffered from the 'decay' that affected the rest of the county, and in Redesdale the problem was made worse by the local custom of partible inheritance which virtually guaranteed smaller and smaller holdings and increasing poverty. In 1538 Tynedale could raise 391 men 'able with horse and harness', and Redesdale could muster 185. The total force was 576; but by 1580 it had fallen to 225 and by 1595 to 55. This meant that the dales ceased to be able to defend themselves. The predicament is well illustrated by an incident on 27th November, 1587. To raise a force of 800 men for a punitive raid into Teviotdale, the Keeper of Redesdale, Sir Cuthbert Collingwood of Eslington, needed the services of a large company of Yorkshire men supplied by the President of the Council of the North. In contrast, three days later the retaliatory raid led by Robert Ker of Cesford and Walter Scott of Buccleuch was supported by over 2,000 Scotsmen. This growing insecurity may explain why the bastle became the characteristic dwelling of these dales in the later sixteenth century. Whereas the normal farmhouse of the period had the accommodation for humans and castle end to end, the bastle had animals on the ground floor and humans above. Bastles were very uniform, being 35 feet long and 25 feet wide with stone walls 4 feet thick. The ground floor had a door in one of the end walls, but entrance to the upper floor was through a door in a side wall reached by means of a retractable ladder, although this arrangement was replaced by a permanent stone stair.

Arguably by 1603 the Scots were winning this local war and union of the crowns came just in time to save Tynedale and Redesdale from complete devastation. This statement is probably too extreme because there is evidence enough that cross-Border lawlessness was ended only with much effort on the part of the government. That this happened was principally the result of James VI and I's determination to be rid of the Borders and to turn Northumberland and other counties involved into what he imaginatively called the Middle Shires of Britain. Very soon after becoming king of England he abolished the special March Laws that had governed cross-Border affairs since the twelfth century, and set up a Border Commission composed of equal numbers of Scotsmen and Englishmen to suppress lawlessness. That the men of the Borders were unwilling to give up their traditional lifestyle is demonstrated by the continuing need for this and similar commissions until late in the reign.

Peace then came slowly, but come it did; and with it normality. Hints of this can be seen in the decision in 1614 of the Middleton family to rebuild the hall next to their tower at Belsay, and even more so in that of Anthony Errington in 1622 to construct a completely new house at Denton with the then fashionable E plan and without any defensive features. At the same time, however, the dwellers in Tynedale and Redesdale still felt it prudent to build castles.

CHAPTER THREE

Medieval Life: Economy and Society

POPULATION

How many Northumbrians were there at any one time, and how did conditions in Northumberland compare with those in other counties? These are important questions, but the answers can be fully appreciated only within a consideration of the broader framework of English demographic development.

The starting point for this must be the Domesday Book, the attempt by William I to discover and record who possessed what and on what terms in the kingdom he had conquered. The survey, produced in 1086, recorded the existence of some 275,000 tenants, a figure several scholars have used as the basis of their calculation of the total population of England. Their results have varied from a low of 1.1 million to a high of 2.25 million. The safest figure is probably 1.75 million. There is, however, no disagreement about the fact that at that time the population of England, and indeed of all other European countries, was rising, and that it continued to rise until the end of the thirteenth century. By that time, it is thought, the English population was at least three times higher than in 1086 and that it stood at between 5 and 6 million. Indeed, some scholars are even prepared to argue for 7 million.

Whatever the figure, this was the high point. The severe famine consequent upon disastrous rain-ruined harvests in 1315, 1316 and 1317 produced a significant mortality, which may have lowered the population by as much as fifteen per cent. This disaster, however, was nothing like as damaging as the catastrophe of 1348-49 when plague swept through the country. This disease, which arrived in Europe from Asia in 1346, and which was to be a dreaded scourge until the late seventeenth century, had three forms. In the commonest, the bubonic, the bacilli were transmitted to humans by fleas from infected rats and attacked the lymphatic glands, causing swellings in the groin and armpits and a high fever. Death was normal, though not invariable, within two to five days. Bubonic plague tended to be seasonal since the fleas were active in temperatures normally experienced in England only in the summer. Moreover, it could not be transmitted directly from person to person. In contrast the pneumonic plague, which was concentrated in the lungs and caused certain death, was contagious and not seasonal. The third form, septicaemic plague, was rarest but most severe: infection was so massive that certain death occurred within hours.

The number of plague deaths has been calculated with some confidence as to accuracy for a good many places throughout England, and these studies show a wide variation from as low as twenty to as high as eighty per cent. Overall, the national mortality was probably between forty and fifty per cent, and if so by 1350 the population was probably less than 3 million. This conclusion is given some support by the evidence from the 1377 poll tax returns. This impost, which supposedly affected all subjects, male and female, over the age of fourteen, proved highly contentious and unpopular, and an attempted repeat in 1381 helped to spark the uprising in the Home Counties known as the Peasants' Revolt. The returns record not far short of 1.4 million taxpayers, and as there was probably a large under-fourteen population and widespread evasion, a total population of around 3 million is likely.

Had the Black Death, as it was known, been an isolated event, the population could well have recovered within a couple of generations. What prevented this were the recurrent outbreaks, of which there were about a dozen on a national scale between 1350 and 1500, and which to a considerable extent wiped out any gains made since the preceding episode. Consequently, the demographic low did not occur until the middle decades of the fifteenth century when England's population probably did not exceed 2.5 million. By the end of the century, however, there were signs of growth, and by 1541 the total had reached nearly 2.8 million. This figure is the result of detailed analysis of the baptisms, weddings and burials in the 404 parish registers which are complete and unbroken from their inception in 1538. The same analysis also indicates that from 1541 there was a continuous increase in the size of the population, which totalled about 5.1 million in 1650.

To what extent did Northumberland conform to this uneven development? At once it must be said that there is very little evidence on which reliable calculations can be based. And it is especially unfortunate that there are no Domesday figures. In the 1080s the land between Tyne and Tweed, like the future counties of Durham, Cumberland and Westmorland, was only nominally under the control of the English king, and consequently it was not included in the survey. As a result there is no way of calculating how many people in 1086 were living in what was to be Northumberland.

In 1377, however, there were just over 16,800 taxpayers, which may imply a population of up to 35,000. How many people had died in the Black Death is completely unknown, but figures available from certain Durham townships indicate a fifty per cent mortality between Tyne and

Tees. If this was also the case in Northumberland, its immediate pre-plague population could have been as high as 70,000, with an even higher figure for 1300 before not only the great famine of 1315-17 but also the disruptions of the Scottish wars.

What happened after 1377 is almost totally obscure. By 1541 there may have been about 50,000 people, a figure based upon the assumption that the county's 1801 population of 157,000 was the product of a rate of increase in line with that of the country as a whole. This figure, however, seems rather high if, as seems likely, the mid-fifteenth century population was not much above 30,000.

How did Northumberland compare with other counties and other parts of England? Here it is necessary to rely on the calculations published in 1948 by the American historian, Josiah Russell. Although these are now considered to be underestimates, this does not invalidate their comparative value. Russell's work in fact shows that by all yardsticks, Northumberland was very close to the bottom of the league. The 1377 poll tax data suggest that only Cumberland and Westmorland and the two very small counties of Rutland and Huntingdon had smaller populations. By comparison, Yorkshire, although somewhat larger in area, had five times the number of people. Inevitably, Northumberland had a very low density, just over seventeen people per square mile compared with thirty-seven in Yorkshire; only in Durham, Cumberland and Cheshire was the figure lower. Likewise, in Northumberland there were 37 acres per person compared with 17 in Yorkshire. And it follows almost automatically that settlements were generally smaller. Russell reckoned that twenty per cent of settlements in Northumberland had fewer than twenty-five inhabitants and only eight per cent more than 100. This compares badly with Yorkshire where a quarter of settlements had over a hundred people, or even worse with, for example, Northamptonshire and Kent, where the respective percentages were thirty-five and thirty-eight.

In Northumberland, therefore, we are concerned with a county which, although probably following the national trends, was one of the most under-populated in England. Overall, it can be said that although it was the fifth largest physically, it was the third smallest demographically.

TOWNSHIPS, HAMLETS AND FARMS

The central and eastern parts of Northumberland, that is, the lowland districts, were a region of townships, each with a population that lived on and worked the land as a community. It would be risky to suggest an exact number, but the total was not far short of 450. They ranged in size from 500 to 4,000 acres, although the overwhelming majority, probably eighty-five per cent, were under 2,500 acres. No two were identical, but they all had common features so that they can be regarded as individual variants of a common form; and all of them changed in the course of time. To appreciate their form and history it will be best to begin with an assessment of what they were like in the late thirteenth century, and then to consider their origins and subsequent evolution.

The core of every township, although not necessarily at its geographical centre, was a village. Any attempt to describe these villages must rely heavily on the work of Michael Jarrett and his teams who in a fifteen-year period from 1966 extensively excavated the site of West Whelpington, a village abandoned about 1720 as the result of a fundamental reorganisation carried out by the lord of the manor, Mark Milbank, and his principal tenant, John Stott.

Their work confirmed West Whelpington as a typical Northumbrian village in that its farmsteads faced inwards on to a central green. Evidence from other townships reveals greens of various shapes, including circular and triangular; but the most common, as at West Whelpington, was an elongated rectangle. West Whelpington was also typical in having an east-west axis, so that the two long rows of houses were along the north and south sides of the green.

Each farmstead comprised a long rectangular enclosure, end-on to the green and divided into two unequal parts. The smaller, abutting the green, was the toft in which the house was built. All the houses appear to have been what are called long houses, single buildings divided into two parts, one for humans, the other for cattle. Entrance to both parts was by a common door towards the centre of the long side facing the green, adjacent to which was a wooden screen across the width of the house to separate the two rooms. The total floor area varied between 300 and 500 square feet. As regards their construction, they consisted of a timber frame with a wattle and daub infill resting on a low foundation wall of stone. Almost certainly the roof was supported on 'crucks' and thatched with ling (heather). In the living room there was an open hearth made of flat stones, but no chimney, the smoke escaping through a hole in the roof. The byre was paved and had a drainage channel sloping away from the living room.

Behind the toft was a larger enclosure, the croft, bounded by either a ditch and bank topped with a quickset hedge, or a wall of upright slabs round a rubble core. The croft had a variety of uses: growing vegetables and fruit, and also flax and hemp; keeping pigs, hens, ducks, geese and bees; and grazing horses.

Immediately beyond, and in most places surrounding, the village was the township's arable land. This was in the form of several hundred (or in large townships thousands) of long narrow strips known as rigs. In plan they had a flattened and inverted S shape, the result of having to turn a cumbersome six- or eight-ox plough team at the end of the furrow. Whenever possible, rigs were 220 yards or a furlong (=furrow long) in length and 11 yards in width so that they were half an acre in area. As ploughing was always in the same directions, the soil was turned inwards to create a continuous ridge between two gullies. Consequently, in profile a line of rigs formed a continuous corrugation. The rigs normally followed the slope of the ground to facilitate drainage.

Rigs were grouped in units known as flatts, each with its own name which in most cases has been lost. The size and shape of each flatt was dictated by the number of farmers in the township and also, of course, by the natural conformation of the land. Between the flatts were irregularly shaped pieces of ground, the balks, which were not cultivated, either because they were too steep, or because they were bisected by burns or narrow water courses called sikes. Flatts too narrow for full-length rigs were known as butts.

In turn the flatts were grouped into large units, usually three in number, called fields and normally distinguished by the terms north, south, east or west. These fields were invariably unequal in size. At Longhoughton, for example, they contained 544, 375 and 182 acres, while at Bilton, a smaller township, they were 217, 176 and 138 acres. The total acreage, 1101 at Longhoughton and 531 at Bilton, give a good indication of the amount of land township communities cultivated.

The sole purpose of this complex arrangement was the production of cereals, wheat, barley and oats principally, but also peas and occasionally rye. Wheat and rye, the hard corns, were sown in autumn, but oats, barley and peas were spring-sown. Roughly one third of the arable would be sown with winter corn, another third with spring crops, while the remaining third lay fallow to regain its fertility, a process assisted by the application of such manure as the animals of the community could produce. Ploughing was done with a heavy wooden plough with iron-shod cutting and turning edges drawn by a team of six or eight oxen. Seed was broadcast by hand, and harrows were drawn by horses rather than oxen.

A much smaller area, often low-lying along the banks of a burn, was the meadows, whose function was to produce one, and hopefully two, crops of hay for winter fodder. The meadows were enclosed in the spring as soon as the grass began to grow, but thrown open for grazing after the hay had been won, usually around Lammastide (1st August).

The third category of land was pasture, the primary purpose of which was to support the oxen of the community during the grass-growing months in spring, summer and autumn. The size of these reserved areas – at Longhoughton and Bilton they extended to 165 and 166 acres respectively – indicates their importance. Oxen, in fact, were at the heart of the farming process, and without them no community could have functioned. Consequently, it was necessary to ensure that every member of a community could feed his oxen. This was done by allotting to every farmer a specific number of 'gaits'. These were expressed as a number of acres, but this is misleading in that no farmer had a separate part of the pasture for his exclusive use. But the term did indicate how much grazing

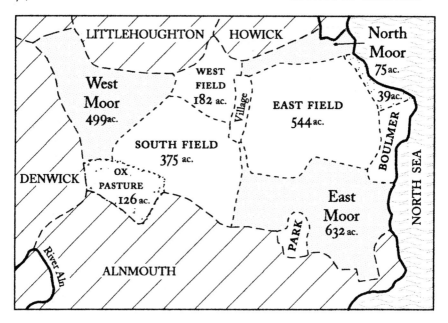

6: *Longhoughton*

each was entitled to, and the extent of his access to the common resource.

Finally, a considerable portion of every township consisted of
uncultivated and undivided moorland. At Longhoughton there were
three moors with a combined area of 1206 acres, which was forty-five per
cent of the township. A similar situation obtained at Bilton where a single
moor of 532 acres accounted for forty per cent of the township's land.
These percentages were in no way exceptional, and since in most places
much if not all the moorland was capable of cultivation, they clearly support
the view that Northumberland was far from being over-populated.
Although it could be the source of stone, coal and wood, the primary
role of the moorland was rough grazing for the cattle, sheep and other
animals owned by members of the community. The number each was
allowed to put on to the common, his 'stint', was governed by the number of
arable acres he possessed.

Who were these farmers? Immediately, it must be noted that they were
tenants, and therefore before they can be discussed, something must be said
about their landlords. The fact was that the lordship of every township
belonged to somebody, individual or corporate. The simplest, neatest and
most convenient situation was that where the entire township had a single
lord. Such was the case at Bilton which was owned entirely by the barony of
Alnwick, except for a period from the late twelfth century until 1368 when
it was in the hands of a single feudal tenant of the barony.

In most places, however, the situation was more complex and changed
over time. Eachwick, a member of the barony of Styford, was granted

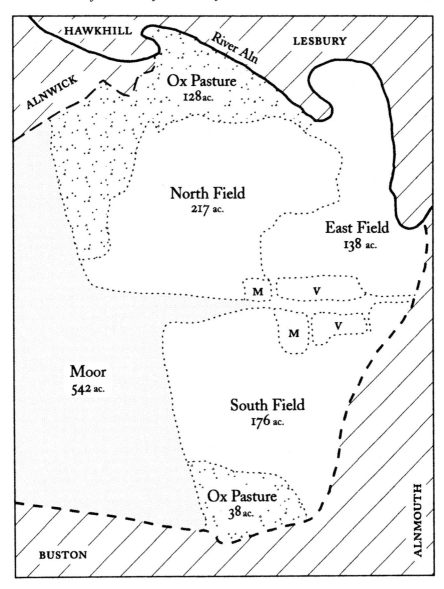

7: *Bilton*   M = Manor House   V = Village

sometime before 1138 to the Delaval family, which also possessed the
nearby townships of North Dissington, South Dissington and Black
Callerton. Later in the twelfth century, Robert Delaval and his mother,
Richelda, granted half the township to the canons of Hexham Priory. Later
still, the remaining half was divided, and the owner of one of the quarters,
Robert of Fawdon, gave the canons the reversion of the land of one of his
tenants, William of Houghton, who died without heirs in 1342. Prior to
that, Hexham had acquired two other small properties amounting to 28

acres. The other quarter, having passed through the hands of several lay owners, was acquired by Newminster Abbey in 1489. Thus, Eachwick changed from being a township in the exclusive ownership of a single lay family to a fragmented condition in which the bulk of the land was owned by two ecclesiastical corporations.

More common, perhaps, was fractured ownership arising from the failure to produce a male heir. Black Heddon, for example, was a member of the barony of Bywell granted to a family as feudal tenants. By 1322, it belonged to a Robert of Redesware, but he died leaving three daughters, among whom his estate had to be divided. Two of the three parts were soon reunited and thereafter Black Heddon comprised two estates, the smaller in the hands of a family called Paston, the larger passing through two families until finally becoming the property of the Swinburns.

Beneath these many changes of ownership a township had to function as a community. Again, it must be stressed that, in human terms as in physical, no two townships were exactly alike, although probably most of them had three categories of tenant. The largest and most important, in fact the core of the community, was the bondmen. Their number was broadly determined by the size of the township, but it was rarely less than ten or more than thirty. They each held the same quantity of land for which they owed an identical rent. The number of arable acres per bondland, however, differed from township to township, but by far the most common was 24, distributed in single rigs throughout the flatts of the three fields. In return for these acres a complex rent was due, which could include cash, cash in lieu of service, labour and farm produce. For instance, the ten bondmen of Longframlington each paid 6s. 8d. rent, four hens at Christmas and twenty eggs at Easter; in addition they had to thresh, harrow, cart corn and cart hay for one day, and to reap for two days a week throughout the harvest period, when, however, they were fed. All in all, their rent, particularly its labour element, was not excessively heavy.

However, there were some townships, although probably relatively few in number, where the bondlands were larger (30 acres or more) and carried a heavier rent. At Acklington, for example, the twenty-one bondmen each had 30 acres for which they paid 3s. 6d. in cash, 3d. in lieu of an ancient carting service, thirty-two bushels of malted barley, and a hen at Christmas. Their labour service was equally onerous: each man had to work three days a week, except on feast days; and in addition he had to reap for five days at harvest time with two men, and to cart a load of firewood from Acklington Park to Warkworth Castle. Clearly, there was a considerable difference between the two townships: when valued the rents and services of the Acklington bondmen were two and a half times greater than those of their Longframlington counterparts, although they had only twenty-five per cent more land.

The explanation of these differences is far from certain, but it must have involved the differing approach of landlords to the running of their demesne farms. Before looking at this aspect of township life, two other types of tenant must be mentioned. Virtually all townships had cottagers, tenants with little or no land who paid money rent and performed a few services. At Ovington there were only three cottagers compared with sixteen bondmen, but at Longhoughton the numbers were equal. The Ovington tenants each had 3 acres, while at Shilbottle they had 6, the maximum on record. As with the bondmen, holdings and rents were generally equal, although this was not so at Framlington, where the size of the cottage holdings ranged from a half an acre to 2 acres and the rents from 1*s.* and eight day-works to 2*s.* and ten day-works. These tenants would not have been able to earn a full living from their holdings, and they therefore must be seen as men and women who formed a pool of labour available for work at day wages.

Many, but not all, townships also had free tenants. Their number was usually small and their holdings were not particularly large. At Ovington, for example, there were eight free tenants, an above average number, but they held between them only 126 acres, on average only two-thirds the size of a bondland. The great advantage enjoyed by the free tenant was that his relationship with the lord of the township was governed by common law, not the custom of the manor. This meant that his rent was fixed in perpetuity, that he could sell his land, that his widow was guaranteed a third of it for life, and that, if necessary, he could prosecute his lord in the royal courts.

Also in a high percentage of townships the land occupancy scheme included a demesne, that is, land which the lord had chosen to retain in his own hands rather than let to tenants. At Bingfield, for example, Hexham Priory's 234 acres of arable demesne land were unevenly distributed through twenty different flatts ranging from 3 acres in a flatt called Warinlawside to 30 acres in one called Crow Law, said to be next to Erring Bridge. The canons also had 16 acres of demesne meadow in five different sites and 16 acres of pasture. In all they had retained 256 acres and let 342 acres to their bondmen and cottagers. The farm was run from what was called the manor, a complex of buildings, including a chapel and with three gardens, almost certainly surrounded by a wall or fence. Where there was no demesne land, it must be assumed that tenants would have performed their labour services at a demesne located in a nearby township.

Unlike most counties, very little evidence of demesne farming operations in Northumberland has survived. It is fortunate, therefore, that the records of Durham Cathedral Priory's Holy Island cell contain enough evidence to give some idea of how a demesne farm was run. In 1340, the monks had 117 acres under crops at their farm at Fenham on the mainland opposite the island: 48 acres of wheat, 19 acres of barley and 50 acres of oats and peas. Assuming a three-course crop rotation, a further 50 to 60 acres could have been lying fallow. The total arable acreage would thus have been about 175, probably slightly below average for the county as a whole. The work of hauling ploughs was done by twenty-five oxen, which, the presence of a bull would seem to indicate, were bred on the farm. There were also two horses and five colts, probably used to pull carts and drag harrows. Some idea of what this agrarian activity produced is indicated by the contents of the barn: 140 bushels of wheat, 136 of oats, 52 of barley and 136 of malt. The farm was not exclusively concerned with cereals, however. There was a small herd of nine cows with three heifers and two calves, and a flock of eighty-one breeding ewes and a hundred and ten wethers and young sheep. At this date, much, perhaps all, the work of the farm was performed by full-time hinds with occasional seasonal help rather than by tenant labour services. Unfortunately there are insufficient data to assess the farm's financial performance.

It is all but certain that every township would have a smithy where the basic iron work of the community was forged and fitted, an oven where members of the community baked their bread and a brewhouse for the making of ale (beer, which requires the addition of hops, may have been introduced into the county before the mid-seventeenth century, but there is no evidence to prove that it was). All these necessary services were more easily and sensibly provided by communal rather than individual facilities. Not so the grinding of corn, which could have been done in the home by means of hand querns. This did not happen, or at least should not have happened. Instead, all tenants were required to have their corn ground at power-driven mills built and owned by their lord. To add insult to irritation, they were charged a multure, a fraction of the ground flour (in most places a thirteenth) for the privilege. By no means all townships had their own mill since many were not large enough to generate sufficient business. Rather, tenants in several communities would be required to take their corn to a central mill, a further inconvenience. Thus, the mill at Lesbury also served Bilton, Wooden and Hawkhill, while the tenantry at Amble and Hauxley had to travel to the mill at Warkworth. Moreover, in addition to grinding their corn at the mill, tenants were required as part of their rent to help with its upkeep by performing such non-specialised tasks as scouring the pond and lade and carting materials needed for repairs (setting the grindstones and making and repairing the gearing called for the services of a millwright). Most mills were water-driven; only occasionally are windmills (a late invention not known in England before the thirteenth century) mentioned. At Darras Hall, however, there was one of each variety, presumably to complement each other. Almost without exception landlords did not run their own mills but leased them to millers who were thus the targets for the ill-will of those forced to use their services. The size of the rent was dictated by the number of customers, but there is no doubt that a well-patronised mill could yield a good profit.

Although the evidence is limited and fragmentary, it is sufficient to permit some assessment of the form and quality of life in these townships. The most obvious fact is that all the members of these communities were either farmers or were engaged in ancillary occupations. Consequently, the patterns of daily and annual life were dictated by the demands of soil, crops and animals. These patterns, however, were modified and at times seriously disrupted by the caprice of weather and, from the fourteenth century, by the occasional appearance of plague or Scottish raiders. But, if these were absent and the weather was not too unkind, a very reasonable standard of life was possible; particularly for the bondmen. With yields up to eight times the quantities sown they could grow enough wheat for their bread and barley for their ale, with oats and peas being fed to their animals. This was the ideal; in practice it must often have been necessary to make bread with whatever grain was available. In addition, small herds of perhaps two to six cattle would have provided milk and the wherewithal to make cheese. Sheep, however, would have been kept principally for wool, a useful cash crop. The produce of the croft was also important. A pig provided meat; poultry did likewise, as well as eggs. Flax and hemp were grown for sale, but vegetables, such as onions and leeks, and fruit would be for consumption, as was the honey from the beehives. These food-stuffs could be obtained licitly, but it is safe to assume that others would be gathered by poaching. Unfortunately, virtually nothing is known of the recipe aspect, although with only an open hearth there was scope for little but stews and broths supported by bread, cheese and fruit, with water, milk and ale to drink. Nevertheless, although not very varied by today's standards, the diet would seem to have been nutritionally sound.

We also have very little information about other facets of domestic life, partly because excavated house sites have been virtually devoid of refuse. Furniture, which must have included a table, stools, a bed or beds (with mattresses and pillows stuffed with straw or feathers) and probably a chest would be made locally, either by the householder himself or a local wright. Utensils such as bowls and cups would be of wood, containers of local pottery and at least one pot of iron; and it is possible that late in the period the better-off farmer could have afforded pewter vessels. We are equally ignorant about clothing. Locally grown wool and flax may have been turned into cloth by spinning and weaving processes in the villages, but there is no evidence of this. If not, hodden would be obtained, as were salt and other items, at local markets to which farmers would take their surpluses to sell.

The very regularity of the physical and social structures displayed by thirteenth-century townships argues that they did not develop organically or haphazardly, but were planned and imposed by men or organisations with the necessary power and authority. Unfortunately, there is an almost total absence of firm evidence as to when this occurred, although there is a suspicion that it may have been part of a systematic reorganisation conducted by, or inspired by, incoming Anglo-Norman lords. What does seem certain is that the growth of population led to the creation of new townships. One indication of this is the nearly fifty places where two (in a few instances three) adjacent townships with the same name were distinguished by adjectives such as east and west, north and south, high and low, great and little. Occasionally, the chronology is revealed as in Felton parish where West and East Thirston were also known respectively as Old and New Thirston. West Whelpington is another obvious example, having been carved out of the territory of Kirk Whelpington, probably early in the twelfth century. Another township of early twelfth-century origin is Dilston, which was created in the moor of Corbridge south of the Tyne for the benefit of the royal reeve who was being made redundant. Even more obvious are places with the element *new* in their names. Two conclusive examples are Newlands in Whittonstall and Newtown on the south bank of the Coquet opposite Rothbury, both brought into being by deliberate landlord action in the second quarter of the thirteenth century.

These townships were in the normal 500- to 2,500-acre range; but there were also smaller settlements, either farms or hamlets, mostly with only 150 to 250 acres created at the edges of existing townships. Boulmer in Longhoughton, for example, was a fishing village, but others were farming enterprises such as Bassington (237 acres) in Shipley, Bullock Hall (210 acres) in West Chevington, Gatherick (404 acres) in Bowsden, Wallridge (153 acres) in Ingoe, Crookhouse in Howtell and Wooden (276 acres) in Lesbury. Also in this category were separate demesne farms created out of wasteland by monasteries: Cheeseburn and Stelling created by Hexham and Ulgham, Heighley and Nunnykirk by Newminster are good examples.

Much more evidence has survived about post-1300 developments, most of which had contracting population as an underlying cause. The evidence from West Whelpington is of a fundamental remodelling at some time during the fourteenth century. The reason for this may have been reduced population and a reorganisation of tenancies, but it may also have been prompted by extensive damage caused by Scottish raiders. One outstanding feature of the redevelopment was the enlargement of the longhouses so that the largest had 750 square feet, with 550 square feet as the average. Perhaps more noticeable would have been that the walls were now made of stone, in most cases boulders bonded with clay. It is tempting to see this as a response to the threat of Scottish raids, but in fact change from wood to stone was widespread in England at this time. Every house had a cross-passage from a central doorway to the opposite wall, and a screen separating living room and byre. Like their predecessors, the new houses had roofs supported on 'crucks' and open hearths. Byres were generally larger than living rooms, suggesting an expansion in the size of the herd.

Also from this period there is good evidence of outbuildings. Some were small and lack any indication of function, although a reasonable guess is

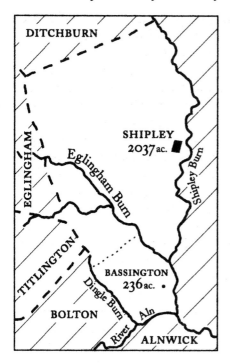

8a: *Shipley and Bassington*

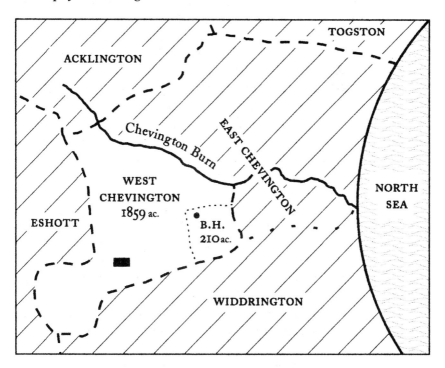

8b: *West Chevington and Bullock's Hall*

that they were stables or sheds for carts and other equipment. What are clearly identifiable are the barns. These were rectangular in shape with opposed doorways in their long walls with a threshing floor between them across which a strong draught could blow to disperse the chaff.

Although population changes led to minor modifications, the village as rebuilt endured without fundamental change for the rest of the period. How typical this was is difficult to say, but given that similar redevelopment can be observed in other parts of England, it is hard to think of West Whelpington as being unique in Northumberland.

Important social changes also occurred. To a large extent these are summed up in the replacement of the terms 'bondman' and 'bondland' by 'husbandman' and 'husbandland'. The change we know least about is the disappearance of the condition of personal unfreedom known in Northumbria as neifty. Indeed, the exact meaning of the term is unclear, although being restricted to the township of birth was certainly one aspect. In 1300 some men and women were neifs, but how many and what percentage of the population they formed cannot be calculated. By 1400, however, it is likely that their number was much reduced, absolutely and relatively. For example, of Hexham Priory's fifteen husbandmen and cottagers living in Bingfield in 1379, only one, Walter of Sandhoe (a township also owned by the canons), was a declared neif, and in their other Northumberland properties only ten other instances of neifty are recorded. At Shoreswood, a township belonging to Durham Cathedral Priory, neifs were more numerous, but still a small minority in the early 1360s: six families out of nineteen or twenty were so classified. The Shoreswood records also reveal how neifs freed themselves by simply removing to townships belonging to other lords who did not ask questions: in 1348, three Shoreswood neifs were recorded as living in Swinton, Upsettlington and Chirnside, all townships across the Tweed in Scotland and therefore beyond the prior of Durham's jurisdiction. As the population contracted and labour and tenants came to be in short supply, so the opportunities for neifs to escape their condition increased. Consequently, it is unlikely that neifty still existed in 1500. At Shoreswood it probably disappeared early in the fifteenth century when the entire township was leased to one man, who presumably had no interest in enforcing an antique condition.

There is more certainty about the substitution of money compositions for labour services. This was a simple matter since all services had for a long time been assigned cash values. What rendered them redundant was the decision of landlords to opt out of demesne farming and to lease the land for rent in cash. They did so because the economic circumstances turned against them: as population declined, wages tended to rise and prices to fall. Moreover, the almost constant threat of Scottish incursions made it attractive to shift risk-taking on to a tenant's shoulders. Although information is patchy, it is sufficient to indicate that very few landlords were engaged in farming by 1400. Certainly the Percy family had leased their demesnes, as had Hexham Priory, by 1379, the arrangement in force on their Bingfield estate being absolutely typical: the manor and all its lands were leased to three men, two of them Bingfield tenants, the other from Errington, for a term of twelve years at an annual rent of £7 for the first quarter, £7 6s. 8d. for the second quarter, and £8 for the second half of the term. There was, however, at least one exception. Durham Cathedral Priory through its Holy Island cell continued farming at Fenham, which significantly was only ten miles south of the Border, until 1426.

With tenants in increasingly short supply landlords had no scope for raising rents; indeed until the later fifteenth century they often had to accept reduced rents. Consequently the terms on which tenants held their farms (which were recorded on the rolls of the manorial courts) continued unchanged for generations. The result was copyhold tenure, which came to be regarded as unalterable. Changes also affected some of the small freehold tenants. Inflation made their rents less and less related to the true value of their land. Consequently, it made sense for their landlords to buy them out so as to be able to lease the land at an economic rent. Tynemouth Priory certainly pursued such a policy, gradually recovering nearly 2000 acres of freehold land. Hexham Priory, too, seems to have taken such opportunities as presented themselves. In Dalton, for example, the canons originally had five small freeholds ranging from one to 19 acres. By 1379 they had recovered 11¼ acres of a holding of 19 acres, and had secured the reversion of another of 18 acres upon the death of its current tenant who meanwhile occupied the farm rent-free. When she died, the priory would have liquidated 30 of the 49 acres of freehold land in the township.

In the sixteenth century the effects of gradually rising population and changes in farming practice began to be felt throughout England. In Northumberland, the vulnerable and disturbed conditions tended to inhibit any urge to modernise. Nevertheless, changes did take place. At the very end of the century the sort of depopulating enclosure which destroyed so many villages further south in the late fifteenth and early sixteenth centuries was perpetrated in a few places such as Hartley, Seaton Delaval, Tughall, Seghill and Littlehoughton. Radical upheaval of this nature was dangerous, however, since it reduced the reserve of manpower needed for Border defence. More common, therefore, was a simplification of the open-field arrangements by the division of townships into halves, thirds or quarters with each farmer having all his rigs in one section only.

With the Union of the Crowns of 1603, the Border defence problem disappeared, and landlords began to consider ways of increasing the returns from their estates. The Crown led the way by abolishing Border Tenure, and other landlords moved to break the dead hand of copyhold tenure by recourse to the courts and to replace it by the short lease at economic rent, a policy adopted with some success by the earl of Northumberland after

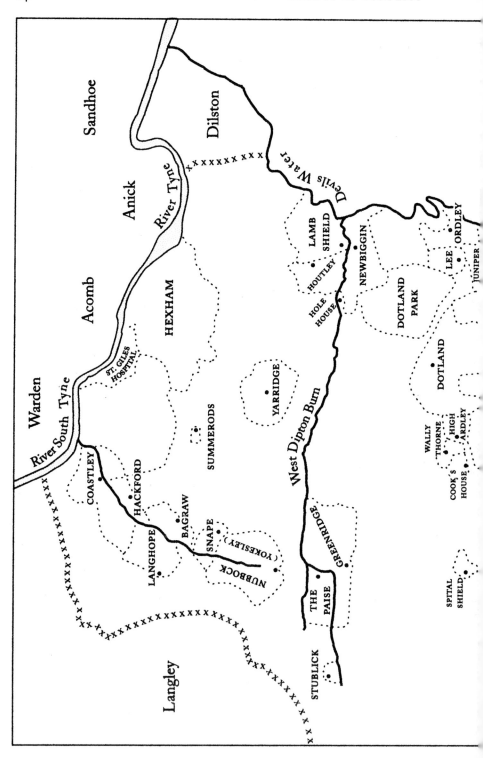

9: *Hexham*

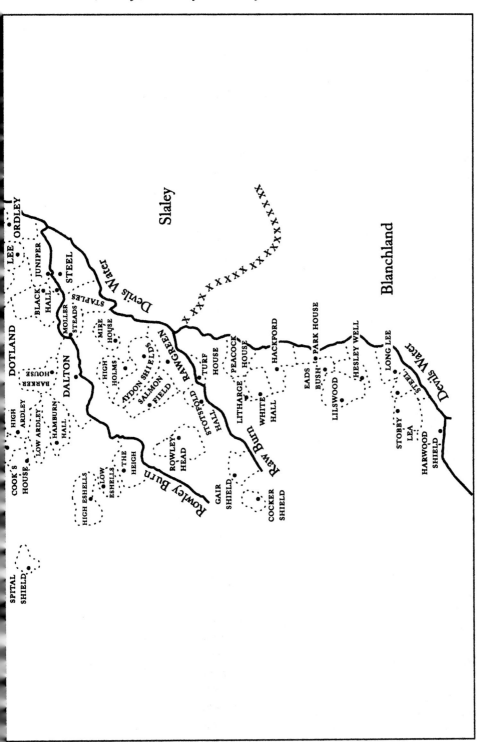

1613. Such developments, however, were interrupted by the upheavals of the 1640s and 1650s. As a result, it was not until after 1660 that the radical changes in land organisation were finally implemented which reduced so many Northumbrian villages to farms.

If lowland Northumberland was a land of settlements with commons, the upland districts in the west may justifiably be described as commons with settlements. The parts of the county to which this statement could be applied were roughly the valleys of the rivers North Tyne, Rede, South Tyne, East Allen and West Allen. There the landscape consisted of huge tracts of moorland in which lay small clusters of settlements. Moreover, the settlements themselves were small, rarely exceeding 250 acres, and in some cases being under 50 acres in size. A few large settlements of up to 500 acres existed here and there, occupied by communities of up to ten farmers, which can be classified as hamlets. The smaller settlements, however, may have been single farms occupied by individual families, although it is risky to draw too firm a distinction between hamlet and farm since over time a settlement may have changed from one condition to the other as population increased or declined.

The enclosed land of these settlements included some arable to provide essential supplies of cereals, but otherwise it was meadow for growing hay, and pasture. For example, in 1608 the farm in Slaley known as Steel Hall had only 10 acres of arable but 24 acres of meadow and 30 acres of pasture. But the greatest asset enjoyed by such farmers was the vast expanse of moorland beyond their enclosed fields on which they could graze large numbers of cattle and sheep. Nature had made this pastoral, not agrarian, country.

Unfortunately very little evidence has survived to show when these hamlets and farms came into existence, although the few fragments available hint that the larger hamlets were of twelfth-century (or earlier) origin, while many of the smaller settlements were created in the thirteenth century.

The various characteristics of this region are well illustrated by Hexham, which covered an area of almost 25,000 acres. From its northern boundary on the River Tyne it extended southwards for up to twelve miles as far as the County Durham boundary at Nookton Edge. Its eastern boundary was also clear-cut, being Devil's Water which divided it from Dilston, Slaley and Blanchland. In contrast its western limits were an ill-defined watershed across the moor which Hexham shared with Langley and Allendale. By the mid sixteenth century there were thirty-nine settlements within these boundaries, or forty-five if subdivided tenements are counted twice. As the map shows, Hexham with the hospital of St Giles bordered the Tyne, but otherwise all the other settlements with the exception of Yarridge, Summerods and Riddehamhope were located on the Darden Burn in the west and Devil's Water and its western tributaries in the east. Of these settlements, three were large enough to be classified as townships and were clearly occupied by communities rather than single families. Moreover, there is clear evidence of early foundation. Dotland (463 acres) and Yarridge (364 acres) were given by Archbishop Thurstan of York to the newly founded house of Augustinian canons at Hexham in 1113. What is not certain is whether they already existed or whether they were new settlements for a new monastery. That they were hamlets, not farms, is clearly shown in the descriptions of them in 1379 which show Dotland with ten husbandlands and Yarridge with six. The third hamlet was Coastley (304 acres) with which the hamlets or farms at Langhope (175 acres), Bagraw (79 acres), Hackford (124 acres) and Snape (94 acres) were associated. Its origins are obscure, but it was certainly in existence by c. 1200 when it was given to an Adam Bertram by the archbishop of York, Geoffrey Plantagenet, the illegitimate son of King Henry II.

About the origin of two smaller settlements we have some information. That known as Hamburn Hall began as three parcels of land amounting to 40 acres on the Ham Burn granted by Archbishop Walter Gray to a man called Richard son of Alexander in February 1229, although there may have been some previous settlement there since one of the parcels was said to have been surrendered to the archbishop by a man with the unusual name of Uduman. Archbishop Gray later added to his grant so that by 1235 Richard had 64 acres. Later information suggests that the farm grew to 109 acres, although whether by formal grant or quiet illicit expansion is not clear. The other small settlement about which we have some evidence, Park House (75 acres), was also the consequence of archiepiscopal initiative: in January 1304 Archbishop Thomas Corbridge granted 60 acres of land in Lilswood on Devil's Water to a William son of Katherine. In this instance there is no doubt that the land was still moorland since William was required to 'reduce it to cultivation'. In addition to these farming settlements Hexham Priory created Dotland Park (250 acres) in 1355 from lands acquired piecemeal from the archbishops of York.

When the acreages of the farms and hamlets and Dotland Park are added up they come to about 7,000 acres, less than thirty per cent of the total area of Hexham. And it is clear enough that the same would be the case in the other parts of western Northumberland.

BOROUGHS, TRADE AND INDUSTRY

Although most people lived in villages and hamlets or on farms, and made their living by farming or closely allied activities, there were other sorts of work and another type of settlement, all of which were important in the life of the county.

BOROUGHS

At the beginning of the fourteenth century, when the size of the population and economic activity were at their greatest, there were probably eighteen settlements in Northumberland with borough status: Alnmouth, Alnwick, Bamburgh, Corbridge, Felton, Haltwhistle, Haydon Bridge, Hexham, Mitford, Morpeth, Newbiggin, Newbrough, Newcastle, Norham, Rothbury, Warkworth, Warenmouth and Wooler. Not included was Berwick, then still in Scotland. Essentially, a borough was a precisely delimited area of land within which all, or the great majority, of properties were burgages. The holders of these properties, the burgesses, owed low, fixed rents, in most cases less than 1s., and could sell or devise their burgages as they wished. A borough was also distinguished by having its own court where transfers of title to burgages took place and were registered, and where disputes between burgesses and petty criminal cases were settled. Everywhere burgesses were ambitious to escape the control of the owner of their borough and to govern themselves through institutions they controlled. While most achieved some measure of self-regulation, only Newcastle became fully independent (see below).

Boroughs were strategically located. Some – such as Bamburgh, Alnmouth, Newbiggin, Warenmouth – were on the coast and engaged in fishing as well as being ports. Others were some way inland where main roads crossed major rivers. Ultimately, those like Newcastle, Morpeth and Alnwick, not far upriver, were more important than Hexham, Corbridge, Rothbury and Wooler, which were well to the west. Although differing in size, importance and development, all had a number of common physical features. At their centre was a market place. Shapes and sizes varied, but in all boroughs it was from the market place that the main roads diverged. Bordering the market place and the streets radiating from it were the burgages which in shape were long and thin: those at Alnwick, a borough that has been closely studied, were between 14 and 64 feet wide and 475 and 580 feet long. To maximise the number the narrow ends were to the street, and normally the house too would be end-on to the street, with a narrow passage to one side to allow access to the rear of the burgage plot. At Alnwick, one of the largest boroughs, there were not far short of 400 burgages, while at Wooler the number was 114 and at Warkworth only 76. Much more work needs to be done on this subject, especially in Newcastle.

Throughout Europe many boroughs were surrounded by walls, obviously for defence, but also to facilitate the taxation of traders visiting the borough. Only three Northumberland boroughs, however, became walled, which is very surprising given their frontier situation, although less so when the expense of building and maintaining a wall is considered. The defences at Newcastle were formidable and occupied ground almost 100 feet wide. The walls themselves were between 7 and 10 feet thick and reached a height of between 20 and 30 feet; and they were reinforced by eighteen towers and six towered gateways. To make them more effective they were fronted by a 15 foot ditch, 60 feet wide at the top. Construction began in the 1260s,

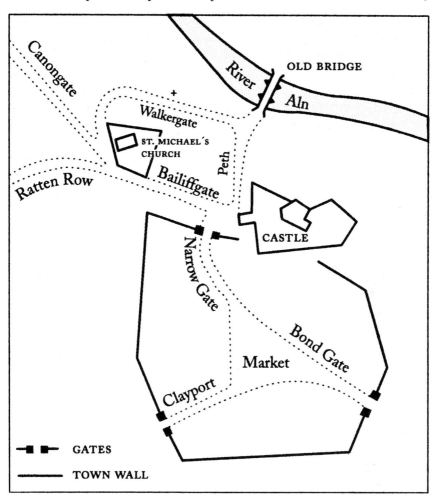

10: *Alnwick Borough*

significantly a time when there was no military threat; but they were not finally completed until the middle of the next century. Alnwick's walls were not quite so substantial as those of Newcastle, being 20 feet high and 6 feet thick. But they were not begun until after the issue of a royal licence in 1434. They took fifty years to complete and were clearly defensive in purpose. In total length, the walls of Alnwick were about 1,600 yards compared with over 3,700 yards at Newcastle.

Berwick too became a walled town. Initially defended by a ditch built on the orders of Edward I, a wall was begun by Edward II of England and completed by Robert I of Scotland. Berwick's medieval walls were somewhat longer than those of Newcastle, indicating how large and important the borough was in the early fourteenth century. When the walls were rebuilt in accordance with the most up-to-date military theory during Elizabeth's reign, the area they enclosed was much smaller, a testimony to the impact of Border warfare and transfer to English sovereignty.

Where a borough commanded a river crossing, sooner or later it constructed a bridge. Almost certainly the earliest was that over the Tyne at Newcastle which had twelve arches and was located very close to the present swing bridge. Built in the late twelfth century, it was to last until the great flood of 1771, and it replaced the Roman bridge, *Pons Aelius*, which may still have been in use. The late twelfth and thirteenth centuries were a time of bridge-building, and consequently, it is not surprising to discover that, for example, bridges were built at Corbridge in the 1230s and at Morpeth about fifty years later. Walls and bridges cost money, and to finance their construction and maintenance boroughs obtained royal licences to levy special tolls known as *murage* and *pontage*.

Boroughs were founded by persons or institutions with sufficient land, wealth and power. Most obvious was the English Crown, which was responsible for Newcastle, also for Bamburgh, Rothbury and Corbridge, although there the boroughs were not so much formally founded as allowed to develop in what had been pre-Conquest administrative centres. In addition, of course, Berwick owed its existence to the Scottish Crown in the person of David I (1124-1153). Two boroughs had ecclesiastical founders: Norham was created in the later twelfth century by Bishop Hugh of le Puiset of Durham, while Hexham owed its development to the archbishops of York. The remaining boroughs were founded by barons, the more important of whom saw a borough, together with a castle and a monastery or parish church, as an essential element in the structure of their barony.

Why did kings, bishops and barons go to the trouble of creating boroughs and attracting settlers to them? The answer is basically economic: a borough was a piece of infrastructure which, if successful, would yield considerable income. Although individually small, the burgage rents were cumulatively significant. More important, however, was the income received from rents and tolls paid by those attending and trading at

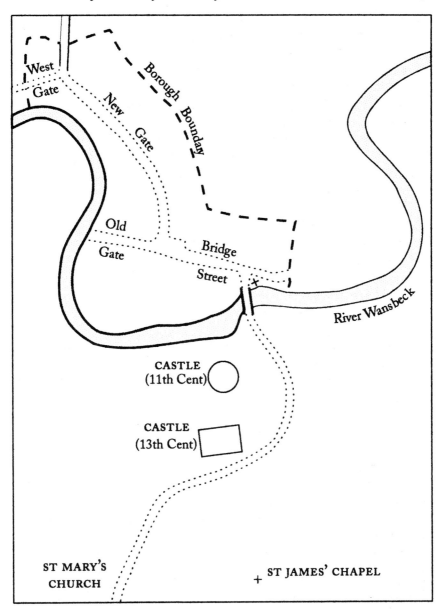

11: *Morpeth Borough*

weekly markets, and, in many cases, the annual fair. What was traded would depend upon the size and drawing power of the borough, but mostly it would be surplus agricultural produce of, and the essentials and luxuries required but not produced in, the surrounding countryside. Consequently, in addition to bakers and brewers producing for the borough itself, there would be exponents of the cloth trade (weavers, fullers, dyers) and the skin trade (tanners, shoemakers, glovers), and also workers in base metals,

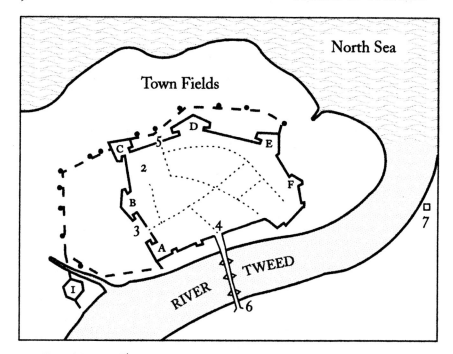

12: *Berwick upon Tweed*

- – – – – – – – 14th century walls
——————— 16th century walls
. . . . Main streets
1 Castle
2 Holy Trinity Church
3 Scot's Gate
4 Water Gate
5 Cow Port
6 Bridge
7 Spital
A Meg's Mount
B Duke's Mount
C Brass Mount
D Windmill Mount
E King's Bastion
F Fisher's Port

particularly iron, serving a wider market.

Markets were held weekly, and in the thirteenth century the demand for this sort of trading venue was such that the right to hold a market was granted to at least eleven villages which never became boroughs: Bellingham, Bewick, Bolam, Chatton, Elsdon, Embleton, Kirk Whelpington, Newburn, Tynemouth, Wark on Tweed and Whalton.

In addition, some but not all market centres also had the right to hold an annual fair, the principal purpose of which was the wholesale trade in animals. Such was the importance of markets and fairs that the Crown jealously guarded its right to license them. So, although a bishop or a baron might found a borough on his own initiative, he had to obtain a licence from the Crown before either a market or a fair could be held in his creation. As well as trade, some boroughs had an administration function: at Alnwick, for example, Bailiffgate was essentially a street created for and inhabited by men engaged in administering the castle and the estate rather than engaging in trade, and there were probably similar sorts of people living in Newcastle.

Behind the proliferation of boroughs and markets was an expanding population which increased both scope and need for trading outlets. But, with the decline of population after 1315, and particularly after 1349, most village markets disappeared and many boroughs became moribund. This was especially so in the western areas of the county where, for example, Corbridge, which had been the county's second largest borough at the end of the thirteenth century, was virtually a village by the late sixteenth century. In addition, warfare took its toll: Berwick notably, but also Norham, Bamburgh, and its outport Warenmouth and probably Wooler all appear to have suffered through being so close to the Border. In contrast, although they contracted in line with virtually every other settlement, Newcastle, Morpeth and Alnwick, on what became the Great North Road, managed to sustain a high level of vitality and importance.

NEWCASTLE: A SPECIAL CASE

Although all boroughs are interesting and deserving of consideration, because of its size and its local and national importance, Newcastle is entitled to special attention. As we have noted, its origin is obscure, although evidently in the twelfth century rather than before or at the time the castle was built. In some respects Newcastle usurped the place that anciently belonged to Newburn, four miles further up the Tyne, which, with Bamburgh, Rothbury and Corbridge, was one of the royal administrative centres of pre-Conquest Northumbria. This, and its command over a ford across the river, made it a candidate for borough status. This was not to be. Like Mitford, which was only two miles from Morpeth, it was outshone by a too-near neighbour.

Once founded, Newcastle's expansion was rapid. In the 1150s it paid a tallage (a tax levied by the Crown on its own property) only half the size of that paid by Corbridge. Forty years later the positions had been more than reversed, Newcastle's payment being six times larger than that by Corbridge. And the pace of growth was maintained. When the county was assessed for the subsidy of 1296, the number of taxpayers in Newcastle was 297, or forty-five per cent of all the borough taxpayers in Northumberland. Its nearest rival, Corbridge, had only 77 taxpayers. Another indicator of the town's thirteenth-century expansion is the creation of the Quayside between the bridge and Sandgate which involved the reclamation of something like 70,000 square metres of ground. What all this meant in terms of population is difficult to say, but at the beginning of the fourteenth century the town may have had around 10,000 inhabitants. If so, it would have been the third largest provincial borough after Bristol and York. But this was the high water mark; and the famines and plagues of the fourteenth century probably reduced it to under 5,000, a low level from which there was no significant recovery until well into the sixteenth century. By 1600, however, the population probably again stood at about 10,000, and on the eve of the Civil War it had almost certainly topped 12,000.

To what did Newcastle owe its size and importance? In brief, the answer is long-distance, seaborne trade. The most obvious direction of this trade was along the eastern and southern coasts of England, and included dealings with all ports between Scarborough and Southampton, including such major towns as Hull, Boston, Lynn, Yarmouth, Dunwich and London. In addition, there was some northward trade into Scotland, although the long periods of active hostility between the two states tended to restrict trading opportunities. Also of major importance was trade with numerous ports along the continental North Sea coasts from Hamburg to Harfleur at the mouth of the Seine, and also extending further south to Gascony in south-west France and Galicia in northern Spain. Finally, there was substantial trade between Newcastle and ports along the southern shores of the Baltic from Lübeck through Rostock, Stralsund, Szczecin (Stettin), Kaliningrad (Königsburg) and Elblag (Elbing) as far as Riga in Latvia. In the main goods were carried in foreign rather than English ships, with Newcastle vessels forming only a small minority of the latter. Almost certainly they would have been cogs, single-masted, clinker-built ships designed for North Sea and Baltic conditions and for the transport of bulky cargoes. The one excavated at Bremen in Germany and dated about 1380 was 80 feet long, 25 feet in the beam and 13 feet high. Newcastle's fleet did increase, however, and by the mid-sixteenth century some fifty ships belonged to the port, about half of which were good enough to be used as warships.

What the ships carried away from Newcastle was large quantities of a limited number of goods produced in northern England, for which there was considerable demand in many parts of the Continent. Before examining them it is important to recognise that Newcastle's role as the port from which they left owed much to government policy. From the late thirteenth century English governments devised and imposed taxes on trade, which made a major contribution to the Crown's revenue. In order to minimise tax avoidance, trade needed to be funnelled through a limited number of outlets where the king's officers could check and charge the goods being traded. Newcastle was chosen as a major trade outlet, and

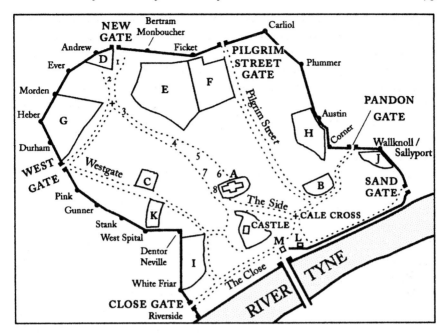

13: *Newcastle upon Tyne*

A St. Nicholas's Parish Church
B All Saints' Chapel
c St. John's Chapel
D St. Andrew's Chapel
E St. Bartholomew's Benedictine Nunnery
F Franciscan Friary
G Dominican Friary
H Augustinian (Austin) Friary
I Carmelite Friary
J Trinitarian Friary
K St. Mary's Hospital
L Maison Dieu
M St. Thomas's Chantry
1 Horse Market
2 Neat Market
3 Nolt Market
4 Bigg Market
5 Cloth Market
6 Flesh Market
7 Meal Market
8 Iron Market

consequently the Crown had a vital and vested interest in promoting and supporting the borough, particularly in its conflicts with its rivals.

The commodity that was, or rather came to be, *the* export from Newcastle was coal. How far back this trade goes is difficult to say, but there is a very strong clue that it developed rapidly in the thirteenth century: in 1281 it was confidently asserted that the value of the borough had doubled as the result of the coal trade. The quantities exported, however, remain obscure until after 1350 when customs evidence becomes available to us. By that time, however, there are clear indications of rising demand: industrial processes such as lime burning, salt boiling and iron working were all using coal; and it was gaining ground as a domestic fuel, especially in stone buildings such as castles, manor houses and monasteries where proper draught-inducing chimneys could be installed. The amount of coal being exported by the late fourteenth century is indicated by the record of 1377/8 when 158 ships cleared the port carrying 7,320 chaldrons at an average of 46 chaldrons per ship. A chaldron being 53 hundredweight, the total export was about 20,000 tons and an average shipload 120 tons. The ships were almost entirely from the foreign ports which ranged from Kaliningrad (Königsburg) in Prussia to Harfleur in France as well as many in eastern and southern England.

Between then and the early sixteenth century the size of the trade appears not to have grown to any great extent, and although it then began to increase, exports probably did not exceed 50,000 tons a year by the early 1570s. During the next seventy years, however, the coal trade expanded at a phenomenal rate, exports from the Tyne exceeding 200,000 tons by 1600 and being not far short of half a million tons on the eve of the Civil War. This staggeringly rapid growth can only have stemmed from a surge in demand combined with an ability of producers to respond to it. The expansion of the market was mainly due to the generally gathering pace of population growth, and especially to its spectacular increase in London where the number of inhabitants shot up from about 85,000 in 1550 to about 400,000 by 1640. More people meant more houses and more hearths, which led to a rising demand for fuel which the depleted woods and forests of southern England could not meet. On top of this, many of these additional people were engaged in a variety of industrial processes, many of which also demanded fuel in growing quantities.

Coal was the answer, and Tyneside could supply it, since it could be easily mined close to the river down which it could be taken to colliers below the bridge. Although considerable quantities of coal were extracted on the north side of the Tyne in places like Elswick, Benwell, Newburn and Prudhoe, the most important source was the Durham parish of Whickham and also to a lesser extent its immediate neighbours, Gateshead (east) and Ryton (west). The huge reserves of good-quality coal close to the surface had always been available, but until the 1580s exploitation was controlled by the bishops of Durham who had always followed a policy of granting leases of short duration and with limits on production, which inhibited expansion.

The solution of this problem was initiated by Queen Elizabeth, although primarily for her own profit. In February 1578, she forced the recently appointed bishop, Thomas Barnes, to lease to her, without any restriction and for seventy-nine years, the mines of Whickham and Gateshead in return for a derisory annual rent of £118. Almost immediately she transferred the lease to Thomas Sutton, a well-known merchant who aspired to join the Hostmen, the group within the Newcastle Merchant Venturers Company who dealt in coal. Admission to this body was essential because, by an act of parliament of 1529, Newcastle had the monopoly of the Tyne coal trade. The Hostmen, so called because foreign merchants coming to the Tyne for coal were assigned to them, were the middlemen who bought coal from the producers and sold it to the buyers, from whom they also collected on behalf of the Chamberlains the dues imposed by the borough. And they were tightening their grip on the coal trade by means of partnerships with the coal producers or leasing mines on their own account.

The Hostmen were not prepared to admit this 'foreigner' to their ranks, and in the end Sutton acknowledged defeat and offered to sell his lease (which had been renewed for ninety-nine years in 1582) to the mayor and burgesses of Newcastle. At this point it was discovered, to considerable embarrassment, that Newcastle was not a legal corporation and so could not buy the lease. In the emergency, the mayor, Henry Anderson, and an alderman, William Selby, personally bought the lease for £12,000, £5,500 of which came from the borough treasury and much of the remainder from a number of wealthy burgesses, on the understanding that they would transfer it to the borough as soon as its legal condition allowed. With the issue by the Crown of the charter of 1589 this became possible, but then Anderson and Selby reneged, and with their financial backers effectively hi-jacked the coal trade of the Tyne.

They could not be allowed to get away with such a blatant piece of double-dealing, and in 1598 the Privy Council, on a petition of Newcastle corporation and with the support of the corporation of London (which was concerned at the rising price of coal), forced Anderson and his associates to transfer the lease to the mayor and burgesses, but with the condition that the Hostmen became a separate company with a monopoly of the coal trade. The closed nature of this clique was apparently undermined in 1604 by a regulation allowing any burgess to join the company on payment of the prescribed fee; but in practice this did little to reduce its highly exclusive nature.

Also important, although much more poorly documented, was the export of lead, which was mined and smelted in the upper reaches of the

Tees, Wear, Tyne and Allen valleys. The most important producer was the bishop of Durham, and between 1426 and Elizabeth's reign successive bishops directly exploited this asset. During that period production increased steadily until it reached about a hundred tons annually. About sixty per cent was exported, mostly through Newcastle and often as ballast in otherwise empty ships. As with coal, the Elizabethan period saw a rapid expansion of lead mining, partly in response to demand, but also as the result of the bishop leasing his rights to an entrepreneur. By the mid-seventeenth century, over one hundred mines were in operation producing some five hundred tons a year.

Although coal and lead were important, until the second half of the sixteenth century, they were behind wool and wool cloth in value: in 1508/9, for example, the value of wool exported was only slightly less than the combined value of coal and lead. Newcastle's importance as a wool-exporting port owed much to government policy. As duties and subsidies were imposed, so the Crown sought to channel trade through nominated ports in order that its customs officers could weigh the wool (for which *tronage* at 1½d a sack was charged) and collect the imposts which came to 40s. a sack from English merchants and 53s 4d. from foreigners. From 1377 the staple, as it was known, was located at Calais. Newcastle, however, had a special and separate place in the scheme: it was designated as the port through which wool from Northumberland, Durham, Cumberland and Westmorland and from the districts known as Richmondshire and Allertonshire in Yorkshire was to pass. The reason for this, apart from geography, was that northern wool was coarse in quality and classified as being inferior to, and of lower value than, midland and west country wool. In fact, some weaving towns in Flanders banned its use, although there was ready sale for it in others producing cloth for the lower end of the market.

The wool trade was at its height in the period between 1275 and 1350, although with a prolonged depression between 1315 and 1325 as the result of war and disease. The number of sacks (at 26 stones per sack) was usually at least 600 and in 1328/9 exceeded 2,000. In addition, wool fells (sheepskins with the wool still attached) were also traded. For example, in 1305/6, one of the best years on record, some 1,910 sacks of wool and nearly 35,000 wool fells left the Tyne. In this period the trade was substantially in the hands of foreigners. An analysis of seven years in Edward II's reign for which there is detailed evidence reveals that 145 of the 216 merchants involved were foreign, principally from such towns as Amiens, Calais, Abbeville, St Valery, Brugge, Middleburg and Hamburg, but including seven Italians from several of the famous trading companies such as the Frescobaldi of Florence and the Riccardi of Lucca. However, of the seventy-one native merchants, no fewer than fifty were Newcastle based. The home contribution to transport was less impressive. Of the 205 sailings to some thirty-six continental ports, only thirty-five (in twenty-six ships) were English, and of these only seven ships were from Newcastle and they made only eleven sailings.

In national terms Newcastle was a second-rate wool port, pride of place going to Boston, London and Southampton. In 1279, for example, Boston exported 7,654 sacks of wool and 10,794 wool fells compared with Newcastle's 875 sacks and 2,260 fells. Moreover, after 1350 exports from the Tyne fell significantly, and after 1400 seldom rose above 500 sacks. One reason for this was the growth of a national wool cloth industry which led to an export of broadcloths (24 yards by 2 yards), which, although erratic, frequently exceeded 50 and occasionally 100 cloths a year.

Newcastle also exported hides. Indeed, in 1279/80 over 9,000 hides left the Tyne, putting Newcastle in first place nationally, well ahead of Southampton with 8,000. As with wool, exports of hides expanded rapidly over the next twenty-five years so that in 1305 the number had risen to over 14,000. What happened thereafter must await further research. The same may be said of grindstones, a product for which Newcastle became famous, prompting the not too flattering saying that 'throughout the world one could always find three things: a rat, a Scot and a Newcastle grindstone'. Grindstones were produced in local quarries: there were several in Heworth on the south side of the Tyne, for example. What we do not yet know is the origin, extent and development of this trade.

Far more can be said about exports than about imports, although it is clear enough that imports were substantial and varied, probably more so than exports. Perhaps the most distant commodity was iron which was brought from northern Spain. When sold it fetched up to twice the price of locally produced iron, known as Weardale iron. Whether this was because of the transport costs or because it was of superior quality is not clear. Also from the south, from Gascony, came wine. The records show that from the late fourteenth century anything up to 400 tons was imported annually, although in many years the total was under 100 tons. The rather wild fluctuations are hard to explain, given that it is unlikely that demand would have varied much from year to year. Newcastle was well down the list of wine-importing ports, and brought in far less than Hull, from where wine was sometimes forwarded to the Tyne. Also from France came what was known as Bay salt, that is, from the Bay of Bourgneuf. Another major import, in this case from the Baltic, was sawn timber, known as 'estlandbords' which was needed by the building trades. The Baltic also supplied quantities of corn, wax, oil and fish as well as luxury items such as furs. In addition a whole range of exotic products collectively known as 'spices' were brought in although in small quantities since they were expensive luxuries.

What cannot be calculated for the period as a whole is the balance of trade. In 1508, for example, the figures show a distinct deficit, imports

worth £1,292 exceeding exports by £258, but whether this was typical or
not is impossible to say. What does seem clear, however, is that trade, both
overall and in individual items, fluctuated frequently and to a considerable
degree due to a wide and varied range of factors and situations, continental
as well as domestic, and political as well as economic.

Although possessed of many advantages, including Crown support and
favour, Newcastle constantly and anxiously sought to confirm and extend
its privileges, and was prepared to react violently and unscrupulously to any
threat. The central concern of its leading citizens was to preserve the town's
monopoly of trade on the Tyne which, it was claimed, it had had since its
foundation. Specifically, it was claimed that Henry II had granted to
Newcastle jurisdiction over the river from 'the Sparhawk to Hedwin
Streams', that is, from the river mouth to the area of Newburn. Until the
sixteenth century there were two constant local threats, both from
ecclesiastical bodies. On the south bank of the river Gateshead was a
potentially serious rival, particularly as its owner was the extremely powerful
bishop of Durham. That the threat rarely became actual was largely due to
the long absences of bishops on state business and to their essentially non-
commercial outlook. Perhaps more threatening was North Shields, created
by Tynemouth Priory, which had the advantage of being located at the river
mouth. As we shall see, this threat was almost completely beaten off in the
late thirteenth century, although renewed efforts to develop North Shields
were made in the fifteenth and sixteenth centuries. The Reformation,
however, largely eliminated the problem: Tynemouth Priory was closed
and the powers of the bishops of Durham were significantly reduced. These
changes must be seen as assisting the expansion of Newcastle's size and
activity in the reign of Elizabeth.

Newcastle also benefited from war. Not only was it the base of operations
against Scotland, which brought men, money and goods to the town, but
war also reduced the competition from Berwick. The principal port of
Scotland, Berwick was significantly larger than Newcastle at the beginning
of the fourteenth century, and there is clear evidence that it handled more
trade. It was not only a magnet for north and central Northumberland
because of its proximity, it was also very attractive because of the lower level
of Scottish customs duties, especially those on wool. It was Berwick's
misfortune, however, to be on the front line, and also in the long run from a
commercial standpoint to become an English town. The reduced
circumference of its Elizabethan walls is testimony to its failure to realise
its economic promise.

In one respect, however, Newcastle burgesses often served their own
short-term advantage rather than the good of the town by engaging in
smuggling. Apart from avoidance of customs officers in Newcastle itself,
the nearness of Scotland and its financial attractions were hard to resist.
Not infrequently leading members of the town's commercial elite,

including those who held office in the customs service, were exposed as tax evaders. The numerous commissions set up by the government to investigate smuggling and trade with the Scottish enemy bear witness to the endemic nature of the problem and to the Crown's inability to eradicate it.

COAL, SALT, FISH

Non-agricultural occupations were not found only in boroughs. From Tweedmouth to Tynemouth there were coastal communities where at least some of the inhabitants were engaged in activities other than farming, notably mining coal, making salt and sea fishing. Moreover, these activities were to a great extent linked: coal was mined in order to boil sea water to produce the salt required to cure the fish caught at sea. Unfortunately, our information is so scanty that we can get only fleeting glimpses of what was happening.

Mining appears to have taken place from at least the thirteenth century virtually everywhere where coal was close to the surface. The common practice was for the owner of the mineral rights, the lord of the manor, to lease them to miners for a specified number of years, and also to stipulate the quantities of coal to be mined. Thus in 1533 the earl of Northumberland leased the mining rights at Bilton near Alnwick for sixty years with the condition that only two pits were to be in operation at any one time and that neither pit should produce more than 16 chaldrons of coal per day. These pits could have been up to 120 feet in depth and cost up to £12 to sink; and they would have been extracting coal from the High Main seam which was up to three feet thick. Most of the pits would have been 'land sale' mines, that is, relatively small enterprises catering for local markets which would have included salt boiling, lime burning and domestic heating. Although mining appears to have taken place on a modest scale in Bamburgh and Embleton parishes, and more vigorously at Bilton, the area of greatest activity was between the Blyth and the Tyne in such places as Horton, Hartley, Earsdon, Preston, Cullercoats and Tynemouth.

As we have seen, mining also took place in the townships along the north bank of the Tyne. Before the Reformation there was considerable activity in Elswick, Benwell, Wylam and Denton, directed or encouraged by the monks of Tynemouth Priory, while the burgesses of Newcastle were mining in the land adjacent to the borough, and the earls of Northumberland were doing likewise at Newburn, Prudhoe and Horsley. The levels of activity were such that the characteristic Tyneside coal transport system involving the movement of coal by chaldron from pit head to riverside staith, and then by keel down-river to below the bridge at Newcastle for loading on to colliers was fully developed well before the sixteenth century.

Coastal salt making was closely allied with coal mining. From the mid-twelfth century salt was made, probably without interruption, at such places as Blyth, Horton, Cowpen, Bebside, Hartley, North Shields and Tynemouth, but also to the north around Warkworth and Bamburgh. The most obvious fact is that most of the pans were operated by monasteries – Tynemouth, Brinkburn, Newminster, Alnwick and Durham Cathedral. It must be presumed that these houses were providing for their own needs, although there is evidence of surplus production being available for export to east-coast ports such as Hull and Yarmouth. The import of Bay salt, however, clearly points to the inadequacy of the coastal pans in relation to the county's needs. Currently available evidence suggests that salt making began earlier than mining, and therefore it is possible that mining began to improve the efficiency of the salt pans.

Because of the many occasions when the church banned the eating of meat, fish formed an important ingredient in the medieval diet. Consequently, it is not surprising that sea fishing along the Northumberland coast appears to have been a very longstanding activity: the references to *canefish*, a word of Celtic origin, at Amble and Beadnell certainly suggests great antiquity. *Canefish* was a rent comprising a quarter of the catch, and it demonstrates that sea fishing was controlled and regulated by lords of the manor to their own benefit but at little cost. Later records reveal fishing from about a dozen townships along the coast for a wide variety of fish, but especially for herring and cod and for other members of the gadoid family such as ling, saithe, whiting and pollock.

Inshore fishing was conducted from cobles, the design of which remained largely unchanged for centuries. They were about 20 feet long and 5 feet wide, with two oars and a mast and a crew of between three and five men; and from them fish were taken by means of both line and net. There is also some evidence of larger vessels operating from the Tyne, probably doggers, which were between 30 and 50 tons displacement with a crew of between twenty and thirty men, and were clearly designed for deep-sea work. Although there is little evidence, it is likely that the sea-fishing industry was stimulated in the fifteenth century by two factors: one was the mysterious migration of the herring from the Baltic to the North Sea; the other was the opening up of the deep-sea grounds beyond Shetland and around Iceland.

River fishing, for salmon and trout, was equally important. Fish were caught by means of yares, wicker weirs set into the river bed which trapped the fish as they came upstream. These contraptions can be identified in eleven townships on the north bank of the Tyne as far upstream as Hexham. There were also two lucrative yares on the Coquet, at Warkworth and Brotherwick; and the Tweed had at least a dozen between Tweedmouth and Cornhill. Some idea of what a yare could yield is indicated by the 528 salmon (including 48 grils) and 240 trout taken at Ovingham in 1506/7. Like all yares, it was owned by the lord of the manor, in this case the earl of Northumberland. Here the earl had the operation in his own hands, presumably because his large household were able to consume the catch. This was certainly true in 1471/2 when part of the catch at his other important yare at Warkworth was transported over one hundred miles to his manor house at Leconfield near Beverley. At other times, however, he and other landlords with riparian rights leased their yares to fishermen who hoped to work them at a profit.

CHAPTER FOUR

Medieval Life: Church and Religion

No account of medieval life anywhere in Europe can ignore the church, a
powerful and internationally directed body operating at all levels in society.
Not all of these, however, directly affected ordinary people, although
decisions and ideas at the upper levels could in the end influence their lives
and beliefs. This chapter, therefore, seeks to explain how the church as an
organisation operated in Northumberland. This is not too difficult a task.
Much harder is to arrive at any appreciation of men's and women's true
thoughts and feelings on spiritual matters.

THE DIOCESE

Northumberland was part of the diocese of Durham from 995, when Earl
Uhtred settled the Community of St Cuthbert, which through insecurity
had deserted Lindisfarne two hundred years earlier, on the peninsula
formed by the loop of the River Wear, until 1882 when the diocese of
Newcastle was created. However, the situation was not quite so neat and
straightforward as this statement implies. Between 1071 and 1113 control,
in both secular and ecclesiastical senses, of Hexhamshire passed to the
archbishops of York. Henceforth, it was in ecclesiastical terms a
jurisdictional peculiar, that is, a part of one diocese within the bounds of
another. Also, the parishes of Alston and Denton, although in all other
respects in Cumberland, were members of the diocese of Durham.

The spiritual head of the diocese was, of course, the bishop of Durham.
Almost all the forty men who held the office in this period were Crown
appointees who had been active, prominent and successful servants of the
state, who expected, and were expected, to continue so to be. With few
exceptions they were strangers to the region; and only one, Robert of Holy
Island (1274-84), was a native of the county. Nor did the people of
Northumberland see much of their bishops. When in their diocese, the
bishops usually resided at their manor houses at Auckland, Darlington and
Stockton in Durham, and crossed the Tyne only when state business, in
most instances to do with Anglo-Scottish relations, made a northward
journey necessary. Because bishops were frequently absent and heavily
engaged in other business, it was essential to have a bureaucratic
organisation capable of governing the diocese without their presence or

104

active participation. This came into being in Durham, as in all other dioceses, during the thirteenth century, and reached full maturity by the early fifteenth century. It was with members of this organisation that Northumbrians were most likely to come into contact.

It is unlikely that they would have seen anything of the Vicar-General, the general administrator of the diocese, or of the officers of the bishop's household, the Chancellor the Registrar and his legal counsellors. Many, however, would have met, albeit briefly, the suffragan bishop who was employed to perform those duties which required episcopal status. These men were usually friars with titles to totally inaccessible dioceses in places like western Ireland or Asia Minor. One of their functions, which would have brought them into contact with the wider population, was to conduct the ceremony of confirmation. They also had authority to admit men to holy orders. For example, in Durham cathedral on 21st September 1342, Richard, bishop of Bizaccia, the suffragan of Bishop Richard de Bury (1333-45), ordained thirty acolytes, twenty-six sub-deacons, thirteen deacons and twenty-five priests. Ten were Northumbrians, including monks from the abbeys of Alnwick, Hexham and Blanchland, the rectors of Eglingham and Morpeth, and a Corbridge man, Alan Corwell, who was the rector of a Yorkshire parish.

Another episcopal officer with a public function was the official principal who presided over the consistory court of the diocese held in the Galilee chapel of the cathedral to deal with matters subject to canon law. These included any cause involving a cleric, but also many matters of concern to the laity.

Perhaps the most important of these was wills. Written wills were made by the better off, and by a wide range of Novocastrians. Of the dozens that have survived from the years after the Reformation (there are very few from earlier times), two may serve as representative samples. On 12th October 1581, John Barnes of Newcastle, who described himself as a wait (municipal musician) and a minstrel, made a will in which he asked to be buried in St Nicholas' church-yard. He bequeathed his instruments to his apprentice, Nicholas Fletcher, unless his partner, William Bennett, should want them; in which case Bennett was to pay Fletcher 13s. 4d. To his maid he left 3s. 4d., and the residue of what was surely a small estate to a friend, Agnes Twigbird. The witnesses were William Bennett and a local doctor, Mr Walters.

Much higher up the social scale was John Heron of Chipchase, whose will was dated 5th December 1590. In it he made seventeen bequests totalling £702 to five sons and three daughters, a grandson and four friends and sons-in-law and three servants. He also provided annuities for life for a grandson and one of his servants, who also bore the name Heron. The rest he left to his wife, Margery, who was his executor. As supervisors he appointed two other Northumberland gentlemen, Ralph Grey of Chillingham and William Ridley of Willimoteswick.

Such wills presented the court with no problems. Occasionally, however, difficulties arose when testators did not follow the rules, as happened in April 1542 when it was discovered that the recently deceased Edmund Horsley had made two wills, one in 1538 in favour of his wife, Agnes, the other shortly before his death (and seemingly unknown to Agnes) in favour of his eldest son, John. William French, the chaplain of Milbourne Grange, was called in by John to testify that this will represented his father's true wishes.

In country districts where lawyers were not readily to hand, poorer people frequently made verbal wills, which required two witnesses to be valid. This was so in the case of Robert Logan, a tenant farmer of Kirkley who had died in 1563, and whose verbal will was proved in February 1564. The principal witness was a man of standing, John Ogle of Twizell, but the second witness was a local husbandman, Roger Hopper, who it is clear had been brought in from the street as he was on his way 'to see the youth of Kirkley play football'. Together these men could verify that Logan wished to bequeath his goods to his sister, Isabel, and to the children of Edward Temple, who had been the husband of another sister, Janet, who presumably was dead. Temple was also to have Logan's clothes, and to hold the farm for five years to pay for the children's upbringing. At the end of that time, the farm was to revert to Isabel.

The inheritance of property, as well as personal stigma, was also behind the occasional enquiries to determine whether or not a person had been born out of wedlock. All matrimonial matters were very much the court's concern, including petitions for the restoration of conjugal rights, and most frequently, breach of promise, which reveal the frailties and follies of our forebears. In one such case, a Ponteland woman, Janet Wood, brought an action in October 1565 against William Rand which was supported by the deposition of two men. One was her uncle, a seventy-three-year-old clerk, Edward Allenson, who testified that two years previously there had been talk of a marriage between Janet and William, but nothing had come of it after he had refused to allow the couple to live with him. The other deponent, William Loy, a Newcastle mariner, described how when Janet came to town she stabled her horse with him and then went off with Rand. Loy knew, or thought he knew, what was going on since, as he put it, he reckoned that 'those two would one day make three'. He taxed Rand with this, who clearly did not deny it, but claimed that, given the chance, he would 'make her as good as himself'.

More numerous were cases of defamation, such as that of Agnes Parker, a Newcastle woman who alleged that a neighbour, Dorothy Robinson, probably came to steal a pig not to see her and her husband; or that of Margaret Potts, also of Newcastle, who accused Bertram Smith of calling her a 'drab (whore and slut), a rotten drab and a bitchfox'. In this case, she was able to produce a witness, a twenty-two-year-old weaver, John Dag, who overheard the quarrel while in the house of Ralph Caisley with whom he was living; Dag also claimed that there were many others in the house at that time who could support his testimony.

Another important episcopal officer whose activities could have touched the lives of ordinary Northumbrians was the sequestrator-general. The bishop normally employed two such men, one for each county, and used them to take charge of vacant churches and to collect their revenues and the fines levied by the consistory court. They were also used to investigate the dilapidation of church fabric, and to examine claims to the right of advowson (see below p. 121).

Dioceses were divided into archdeaconries, and Durham was no exception; and here as elsewhere they conformed to county boundaries. The Durham arrangements evolved gradually during the twelfth century, but by the 1170s the territorial archdeaconries of Durham and Northumberland were permanently established. The archdeacon of Northumberland, who usually held the rectory of Howick, was excluded from Hexhamshire, which was part of the diocese of York, and also from the late fourteenth century from the appropriated churches (see below p. 122) belonging to Durham Cathedral, in respect of which the prior was archdeacon. As far as their appropriated churches in County Durham were concerned, the priors had enjoyed this right since the early thirteenth century; but they had failed to prevent the archdeacons of Northumberland establishing control over their churches north of the Tyne. A campaign to wrest these powers from the archdeacon began in 1331, but it took several decades of effort to achieve complete success.

In origin the archdeacon's role was disciplinary, exercised through an annual visitation of the churches within his jurisdiction, except every third year when an episcopal visitation was supposed to take place. Over time, however, this system fell into abeyance and the inspections came to be performed by other men and other means. At the same time archdeacons managed to hold on to this right to collect procurations, payments by their clergy in lieu of hospitality. The office thus became to a degree superfluous while continuing to be valuable. Consequently, it was normally in the hands of well-qualified university graduates who were absentees working elsewhere and performing such duties as inducting newly appointed clergy into their parishes by means of a paid deputy known as the archdeacon's official. In this respect the archdeacons of Northumberland conformed to the national pattern.

Also like other British archdeaconries, Northumberland was divided into rural deaneries: Newcastle and Corbridge south of the Coquet; Alnwick and Bamburgh north of it. It is not known for certain when these were created, but they were in existence by 1220. Rural deans were senior and responsible members of the resident parish clergy. They were not the archdeacon's deputies, and were appointed and dismissed at will by the bishop. Because they were under full and direct episcopal control, they were used along with the sequestrator-general in a variety of matters, particularly as members of the penitentiary commissions set up by the bishops to deal with disciplinary problems. Unlike archdeacons, they did not acquire a separate endowment or an independent status.

Although the Reformation wrought many fundamental changes in religious life, the diocesan organisation was not deeply affected. Suffragan bishops disappeared after the friars were dissolved, and English began to replace Latin as the language of record; otherwise the system continued to discharge the pre-Reformation duties of its predecessor.

PARISHES, CHAPELS AND CHANTRIES

For almost all Northumbrians the centre of their religious life, first and last, was their parish church; and therefore it is most important that the parish and the parochial system are fully explained. A cursory glance at the situation in 1295 reveals a startling fact: there were only sixty-three parishes in the county (excluding Berwick which was still part of Scotland). Given the size of the county and the fact that it contained getting on for 450 townships and at least 300 discrete farms, this would seem to be under-provision on a massive scale. Moreover, closer examination also reveals that the system was very uneven and unbalanced. At one extreme were very large parishes such as Bamburgh, covering almost 35,000 acres and containing twenty-four townships: or Simonburn, considerably larger at over 130,000 acres, but including much high moorland incapable of cultivation. There were in fact no fewer than twenty-eight other parishes with ten or more townships: Norham, Holy Island, Chatton, Kirknewton, Embleton, Eglingham, Whittingham, Warkworth, Felton, Rothbury, Woodhorn, Bothal, Mitford, Hartburn, Kirkwhelpington, Alwinton, Ponteland, Stamfordham, Chollerton, Tynemouth, Newburn, Ovingham, Bywell St Peter, Bywell St Andrew, Hexham, Haltwhistle, Warden and Newcastle.

In complete contrast, Branxton parish comprised no more than the township of Branxton which covered 1,430 acres. Fenton, Howick, Meldon (which included the hamlet of Rivergreen), Lambley, Wooler and Kirkharle were very similar. In between were parishes with between three and nine townships. Ellingham, for example, included Ellingham, North Charlton, South Charlton, Preston and Doxford, and extended over nearly 9,000 acres. In this group were twenty other parishes: Carham, Ford, Chillingham, Ilderton, Ingram, Lesbury, Edlingham, Alnham, Shilbottle, Morpeth, Longhorsley, Thockrington, Bedlington, Stannington, Whalton, Bolam, Longbenton, Heddon, Slaley and Corbridge. Finally, five parishes in the extreme west of the county were extensive in area, but sparsely settled because of their geography: Knaresdale, Kirkhaugh, Whitfield, Elsdon and Corsenside.

It is obvious, therefore, that the great majority of parishes were large in

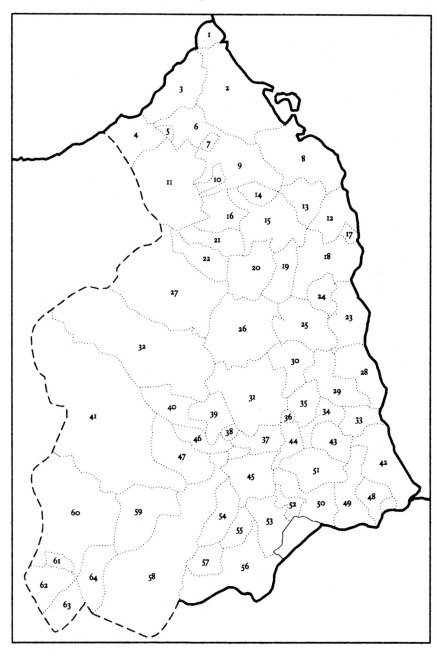

14: *Parishes in* 1300

1 Berwick	12 Embleton	23 Warkworth	34 Morpeth	45 Stamfordham	55 Bywell St. Andrew
2 Holy Island	13 Ellingham	24 Shilbottle	35 Mitford	46 Thockrington	56 Bywell St. Peter
3 Norham	14 Chillingham	25 Felton	36 Meldon	47 Chollerton	57 Slaley
4 Carham	15 Eglingham	26 Rothbury	37 Bolam	48 Longbenton	58 Hexham
5 Branxton	16 Ilderton	27 Alwinton	38 Kirkharle	49 Newcastle	59 Warden
6 Ford	17 Howick	28 Woodhorn	39 Kirkwhelpington	50 Newburn	60 Haltwhistle
7 Fenton	18 Lesbury	29 Bothal	40 Corsenside	51 Ponteland	61 Lambley
8 Bamburgh	19 Edlingham	30 Longhorsley	41 Simonburn	52 Heddon on the	62 Knaresdale
9 Chatton	20 Whittingham	31 Hartburn	42 Tynemouth	Wall	63 Kirkhaugh
10 Wooler	21 Ingram	32 Elsdon	43 Stannington	53 Ovingham	64 Whitfield
11 Kirknewton	22 Alnham	33 Bedlington	44 Whalton	54 Corbridge	

both physical size and in the number of settlements they catered for. Northumberland was very far from being a land where every village had its church or where township and parish coincided, as was so often the case in southern England. Why was this? The answer involves a consideration of the origins of parishes, and immediately it has to be said that this is a problem which is still far from having a clear and comprehensive solution. In time, no doubt, we shall have a more accurate picture, but to achieve this will require a great deal more work, particularly by archaeologists. What can be said here is that there are indications, admittedly very slight in some cases, that at least twenty-nine parish churches existed before the Conquest. In some instances – Corbridge, Bywell St Peter, Heddon, and Rothbury – the evidence points to great antiquity. In other cases the fabric seems to date from the hundred years immediately before the Conquest, and may represent not so much new building as renovation and remodelling made necessary by the damage sustained during the Viking period of the ninth century. Other churches, of course, may have existed, but built in wood, all trace of which could have been obliterated by post-Conquest replacements in stone. One obvious candidate is Warkworth where the present building is essentially post-Conquest Romanesque architecture with no evidence of pre-Conquest work, but where a church is known to have existed in 738.

One possible explanation for these very large parishes is that they were related to the 'shires', the administrative districts *cum* estates so widespread in northern England and southern Scotland. In other words, when creating a system of territorial parishes, the church simply adopted already existing secular administrative units, rather as on the Continent dioceses conformed to the basic divisions of the Roman Empire, the *civitates*. If this were the case, the search for early parishes should be assisted by evidence relating to 'shires', and vice versa. Although this method of enquiry has obvious dangers, it may be a way forward. Thus, at Corbridge, where the church is of proven antiquity, its parish may have been a 'shire'. Equally, although there is no pre-Conquest fabric at Bamburgh, the continued existence of Bamburghshire may be a pointer to its being a pre-Conquest parish. Without pre-judging the outcome, a close look at forty at least of Northumberland's larger parishes might yield interesting results.

However, it is also evident that some, but I think relatively few, parishes came into existence after, and as a result of, the Norman Conquest. The most obvious must be Newcastle, which did not exist as a settlement until the castle was built in 1080, but which developed rapidly in the following fifty years. It seems likely that what became Newcastle parish was previously part of Longbenton parish, since Cramlington, which was a member of Newcastle parish, was separated from the rest of the parish by the Longbenton townships of North and South Weetslade. An equally clear example is Lambley, which comprised the land given to the small nunnery founded there at an uncertain date in the twelfth century. At Branxton, the church built by the lord of the manor was given by him to Durham Cathedral Priory. The monks began to treat it as a parish, and in so doing aroused the fierce opposition of the Yorkshire monastery of Kirkham, which claimed Branxton as a member of their parish of Kirknewton. Being the more powerful institution, Durham won the case, although there seems little doubt that Kirkham's claim was valid. Similarly, Slaley church was built by a certain Gilbert who had been invested with the territory sometime before 1135 by the lord of Styford in return for the service of one knight. Either Gilbert or one of his descendants gave the church to Hexham Priory, which was able to separate it from the Bywell St Andrew parish. A like origin may be postulated for Wooler, where the powerful Muschamp family elected to build a castle and establish a borough as the centre of their extensive estate. One or two larger parishes may also have had post-Conquest origins. Shilbottle, for example, was substantially the estate granted before 1135 by the lord of Alnwick to Richard Tilson and was probably severed by him from Lesbury parish. Other possible post-Conquest parishes are Chollerton, Corsenside, Thockrington, Kirkharle and Fenton.

It is likely that these severances happened before 1150. After that date creating a new parish became increasingly difficult. For this there were a number of reasons, all bound up with the church reform programme developed in the third quarter of the eleventh century by a series of popes, most notably Gregory VII (1073-85), the underlying theme of which was that the church at all levels should be free of lay control. For parishes this meant that ownership by hereditary priests and lords of the manor, which earlier had been the accepted norm, was heavily criticised. This criticism had an increasing effect in the twelfth century, with the result that more and more laymen handed over their churches to the growing number of monasteries. These new monastic owners, for reasons which will become apparent in the next section, were very concerned to keep their parishes whole. Also as part of the reform movement was the growth and elaboration of canon law, one aspect of which was the increasingly precise definition of such terms as 'parish', 'church' and 'chapel'.

However, as the parochial system was becoming fixed and rigid, the population was expanding, thus creating the need for greater flexibility and fluidity. The solution was the chapel, designed to provide the growing number of people with greater convenience without diminishing the rights of the parish church and its owner. In Northumberland, a little over one hundred chapels can be identified with greater or lesser certainty. They fall into two groups. The more important were those catering for between two and six townships, which, had they been independent, would have been medium-sized parishes.

Exactly when, why and by whom these chapelries were formed cannot be known with great precision. One parish where there is some evidence is Holy Island, which belonged to Durham Cathedral Priory. Sometime before 1145 the monks divided most of the parish between four chapels at Ancroft, Kyloe, Lowick and Tweedmouth with four, eight, five and four townships respectively. The Romanesque architecture at Ancroft suggests that the division was recent in 1145, although the pre-Conquest stone cross at Kyloe raises the possibility that the priory's action may have reinforced or modified an earlier arrangement. The cathedral priory also, and probably about the same time, built a chapel at Cornhill in the neighbouring parish of Norham to cater for the three townships west of the River Till. Other monastic houses did likewise: Tynemouth divided Tynemouth parish into two parts, centring the larger northern division on the chapel at Earsdon; and at Hexham, the nine townships north of the River Tyne were formed into the chapelry of St John Lee, while south of that river chapelries were created at Allendale and Whitley to cater for the expanding moorland settlements. Other chapelries may have owed their existence to lay power. Belford, for example, was probably formed by the Muschamp lords of Wooler since its four townships comprised their property in Bamburgh parish.

These examples suggest that the larger chapelries were the work of very powerful authorities, lay and ecclesiastical. This was not true of the smaller chapels, of which there is evidence of eighty, built to serve only the townships in which they were located. Here our knowledge is very sketchy, since although eighteen are still in existence and in use, and a further six are identifiable ruins, no fewer than fifty-six have disappeared so that at present we know of their existence only through documentary evidence, and in some cases this is very slight indeed. Stamfordham parish provides two good illustrative examples. At Ingoe, the existence of a chapel is well attested by references to it in late sixteenth-century surveys, by another reference in 1293 to a man seeking sanctuary there (presumably he was a fugitive criminal), and by the presence in the 1296 tax assessment of a chaplain, Roger, whose moveable goods were reckoned to be worth £3 0s. 6d. At Bitchfield the evidence is much flimsier: references to Easter Chapel Close and Wester Chapel Close. Such evidence should not be lightly dismissed, however, since it was sufficient to pinpoint the site of the church at Kimblesworth near Durham, for the existence of which there is ample documentary support.

It is all but certain that these chapels came into existence during the twelfth and thirteenth centuries when the population was on the increase. In a few cases, such as Brandon and Seaton Delaval, a possible pre-Conquest origin has been suggested. This may be so, but it is also possible that they were built shortly after the Conquest but using pre-Conquest styles and techniques.

Why were they built? Rising population may have been an encouraging factor, but in the end it was he or she who owned the land who decided. While it would be unfair and over-cynical to deny their concern for the spiritual wellbeing or convenience of their tenants, it is more likely that landlords looked first to their own welfare, and that they found the prospect of having their 'own' church gratifying. In searching for reasons for a particular chapel, therefore, it is sensible to discover where the founders lived.

As well as building chapels, landlords had to ensure that they had enough income to support at least one priest. The minimum is perhaps represented by the provision made by Peter de Roos for the chapel he had built at Wark on Tweed in the third quarter of the twelfth century. He assigned two bovates (24 acres) of land, which was probably the standard size of a tenant farm, and required his tenants to raise 6s. 8d. annually as a supplementary salary. In contrast, a hundred years later Sir John de Plessis was very generous in providing for the chaplain who was to serve the two associated chapels he built at Plessey and Shotton in Stannington parish. In addition to a manse next to the chapel at Shotton, he assigned 159 acres, pasture for thirteen oxen and four horses (which would be needed to work the land) and 2s. out of the rent of one of his tenants in Shotton, and a further thirteen acres in Blagdon. This man could have lived like a gentleman farmer, but his counterpart at Wark would have had to labour with the men with whom he lived.

That chaplains and their flocks were subordinate to the parish church there is no doubt. Precisely how is revealed in a judgement given in October 1343 in the consistory court which ended an attempt to obtain independent parochial status for the chapels at North and South Charlton in Ellingham parish. Although the inhabitants would normally attend their chapel, they were required to visit the mother church on the four major feast days of Christmas, Easter, Whitsun and Candlemas (the Purification of the Virgin Mary on 2nd February); and for such ceremonies as christenings, churchings, weddings and burials. Thus, the parish church was assured of the fees and offerings made on these occasions. More important was the injunction that all tithe payments were to be made to the parish church. The inhabitants of each township had to bear the running costs of their chapel, and to send two of their number to Ellingham every Sunday to hear any announcements and injunctions given out in church.

Because they were the product of local and individual initiative, not of a public policy, the incidence of these chapels was uneven. The best-endowed parish was undoubtedly Chollerton, which had chapels at Birtley, Great Swinburn, Little Swinburn, Chipchase, Colwell, Gunnerton and Kirkheaton. Only Barrasford, and the later moorland settlements of Broomhope, Buteland, Tone and Cowden did not have their own place of worship. Chollerton was almost a model: a church at the central place of the parish with a chapel in each of the constituent townships. No other

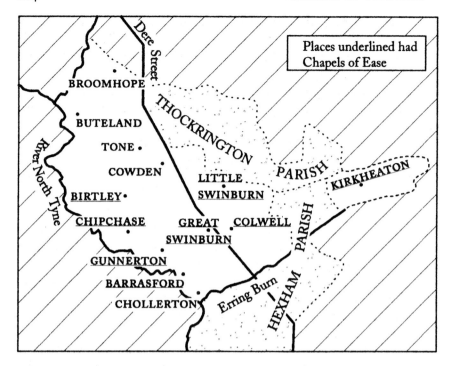

15: *Chollerton Parish*   Places underlined had chapels of ease.

parish came near to this, and some like Ovingham, with twelve townships, had no chapels.

As buildings, serving as they did relatively small communities, chapels were small in size, their naves seldom exceeding 40 feet in length and their chancels 20 feet. Perhaps the clearest idea of what one looked like originally can be seen at Old Bewick, which became a ruin but was faithfully restored, with the addition of a porch and a vestry, in the middle of the nineteenth century. Its nave measures 40 by $17\frac{1}{2}$ feet and its choir is 13 feet square. Beyond the choir is a semi-circular apse which clearly betrays its early twelfth-century origins.

Within their parish church some but not all Northumbrians would be familiar with a chantry. This consisted of an endowment to pay a priest to say masses for the souls of the founder and any one he named in the foundation deed. The institution was based upon the belief that masses would ease the soul's passage through purgatory. Chantries could be of a temporary nature, but the ones we are aware of were perpetual chantries with sufficient endowment to support a priest in perpetuity. The details recorded in the survey drawn up at the time of their closure in the late 1540s show there to have been forty-two such chantries in parish churches and chapels, and a further seven in the priories of Hexham and Tynemouth and the castles at Alnwick, Norham and Prudhoe. Of the forty-two, no fewer than twenty-three were in the Newcastle churches: eleven in the parish church of St Nicholas; the others in the chapels of All Saints (seven), St Andrew (two) and St John (three). In addition there were four in Morpeth and one each in Alnwick and Berwick.

Clearly the chantry movement was very much an urban phenomenon, and the available evidence suggests that wealthy merchants such as Richard of Embleton, who founded a chantry in Newcastle parish church in 1333, and the famous Roger Thornton, whose chantry dedicated to St Peter was founded about 1412 in All Saints chapel, were typical examples of urban piety. But the landed classes too could equally afford this sort of spiritual luxury, as the Percy chantry in Tynemouth Priory and those founded by Sir Aymer de Athol (c.1380) in St Andrew's Chapel in Newcastle and by Sir Robert Ogle (c.1410) in Hexham Priory amply demonstrate. Also, and not surprisingly, the clergy were founders of chantries, that by Prior Rowland Leschman of Hexham (died 1490) being a notable example. Elsewhere, little physical evidence has survived, largely because most chantries comprised no more than an altar set up in an existing church, sometimes in a section screened off to create a private chapel. Some idea of the appearance of such an arrangement can be seen in the south nave aisle of Newcastle cathedral (then parish church) where the chantry of St Margaret was set up. Northumberland, alas, has nothing remotely able to rival the splendour of the duke of York's chantry at Fotheringay in Suffolk.

Northumberland in fact is poorly endowed with medieval churches. In part this was because relatively few were built in the first instance, and many of them have subsequently disappeared. In addition, seventeen of the old parish churches and twelve of the chapels were entirely rebuilt in recent times. Consequently, the limited physical evidence makes it difficult to chart the development of church building with any real precision.

It is clear enough, however, that the last century before 1066 saw a wave of building or rebuilding, especially in the Tyne valley. With the Norman settlement came the Romanesque style of architecture, which is evident in many churches, most obviously those of post-Conquest foundation. According to Sir Nikolaus Pevsner and the revisers of his monumental study of the buildings of Northumberland, the thirteenth century was the great age of church building in the county. This is not surprising since it was a time of peace, prosperity and rising population. The special hallmarks of this period were the lengthening of chancels and in so doing replacing the apse by a squared end; the addition of aisles, transepts and towers; and the introduction of the pointed arch, most characteristically in the form of narrow lancet windows.

After 1300, however, there was a considerable fall off in building activity. War, poverty and a declining population all combined to leave Northumberland almost void of the splendid churches that were the products of late-medieval wealth and piety in so many southern and midland counties. The two notable exceptions were St Michael's, Alnwick and St Nicholas', Newcastle, both rebuilt in the fifteenth-century Perpendicular style. Elsewhere, renewals and additions were the limit of activity, although in some places – Bolam, Bywell St Peter, Embleton, Morpeth, Kirkharle and Widdrington – these were substantial.

RECTORS AND VICARS

How did this parochial system function? Although the evidence is sparse, it seems certain that in the late eleventh century most parishes were controlled either by laymen who appointed priests at will, or by hereditary priests who owned the churches they occupied. It was this situation that the church reformers found intolerable, hence their campaigns to create a celibate priesthood and to establish clerical control over parish churches. Almost inevitably this conflict ended in a compromise which left neither clergy nor laity in full control. By this compromise the clerical incumbent of a parish became the rector with full responsibility for the spiritual welfare of his parishioners, what was called cure of souls. His appointment was a two-stage process. The first move was made by the patron, the person or institution that possessed what was called the advowson, the right to nominate the new incumbent. But before that man could take up the office he had to submit to an examination of his qualification and fitness to hold it. This was conducted by the bishop of the diocese in which the parish lay, who thus had a right of veto. Once inducted into his parish, however, a rector could be removed only by the church, and only for a serious offence in canon law; and he was entitled for life or until he chose to resign to the emoluments of his office.

These comprised three elements. The first was the endowment in land – known as the glebe - given to the church by its founder or a subsequent benefactor. Since these endowments were in no way regulated, glebes varied considerably in size and therefore in value. More certain and more calculable was the tithe, the tenth part of every man's income, which in an essentially rural society meant the produce of farming or allied activities. Thirdly, the rector was entitled to fees for weddings, churchings, christenings and burials, traditional offerings on major feast days such as Christmas, Easter and Whitsun, and the mortuary, a death duty usually in the form of an animal. Self-evidently, the larger and more populous a parish was, the greater would be the rector's income or living.

The consequence of this compromise was that churches were severely reduced in use and value to their lay founders or owners. No longer could they make free with their wealth or appoint and remove their incumbents. As a result, in the course of the twelfth century there was a growing trend for laymen to hand over advowsons to monasteries. It was in this century that monasticism was at the height of its popularity and monastic houses were founded in considerable numbers. All required endowment, and by

I. BYWELL (ST. ANDREW).

The tower is pre-Conquest with typical tiny round-headed windows and side-alternate quoins. There are very similar towers at Warden, Ovingham, Corbridge and Bolam. The narrow, pointed 'lancet' windows in the church walls are typical of the thirteenth-century Early English style.

2. (*above*) NEWCASTLE.

The entrance to the stone keep built between 1168 and 1176 to replace the wooden structure of 1080. It is slightly smaller than similar keeps at Bamburgh and Norham built a few years earlier. The entrance at first-floor level is reached by a double flight of stairs separated by a gate, a feature found at only one other castle, Dover, and probably designed by the same man.

3. (*opposite, above*) WARKWORTH. The south wall of the outer bailey. The moat is probably twelfth-century, but the wall, gatehouse and the Carrickfergus Tower (foreground) were built by Robert son of Richard, lord of Warkworth, in the early thirteenth century.

(*opposite, foot*) 4. DUNSTANBURGH.

A completely new castle built by Thomas, earl of Lancaster after 1313 and developed in the 1380s by John of Gaunt, duke of Lancaster. Unlike twelfth-century castles, it has no keep but consists of a massive gatehouse and walls enclosing a peninsula. A very similar castle was built at Bywell in the early fifteenth century by Ralph Neville, earl of Westmorland.

5. EDWARD I and (on horseback) ROBERT I (THE BRUCE).

Edward I began his attempt to conquer Scotland in 1296, but had still not succeeded in doing so when he died in 1307. Scotland's independence was assured by the military efforts of Robert Bruce, King Robert I from 1306. In the years between 1314 and 1328 Northumberland suffered grievously at the hands of Bruce and his lieutenants. (*Illustration of Edward I reproduced by permission of The British Library (Roy 2A XXII 219v) and that of the Bruce statue at Bannockburn by permission of the National Trust for Scotland.*)

6. EDWARD III and DAVID II.

This picture is a piece of political hypocrisy. As the result of his capture after the battle of Neville's Cross near Durham on 17th October, 1346, David was a prisoner of his brother-in-law, Edward, for eleven years, and was released only on condition of a promise to pay a huge ransom. (*Reproduced by permission of the British Library (Cotton Nero D VI, f. 6rv).*)

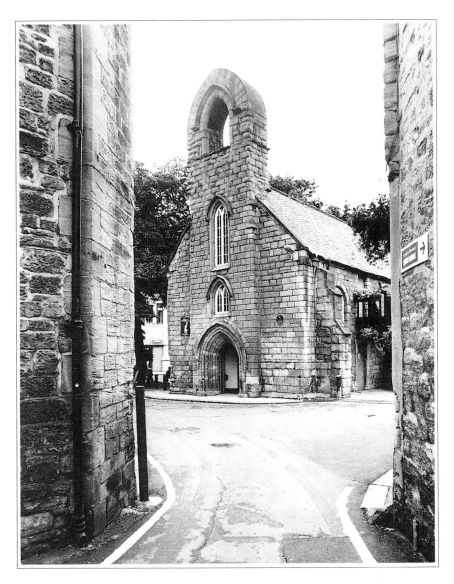

7. (*opposite, top*) WARKWORTH (ST. LAWRENCE).

Probably the most complete of the county's many Norman churches. The north wall shows the carefully dressed stone, semi-circular arches and larger windows typical of the Romanesque style of the late eleventh and twelfth centuries.

8. (*opposite, foot*) WARKWORTH.

The medieval bridge over the River Coquet, 11 feet wide and of two 60-foot spans. It was built after 1379 with a bequest from a Newcastle man, John Cook. Similar bridges spanned the county's main rivers, that at Felton being substantially intact. The protective tower at the south (town) end is a rare British example.

9. (*above*) MORPETH.

All Saints chantry built in the 1290s at the north end of the medieval bridge. It also functioned as a grammar school, which was refounded after the Reformation.

10. (*top*) HEXHAM.

The market place formed by the junction of several roads. On the far side is the Moot Hall at the entrance to the archbishop of York's manor from which he administered his liberty of Hexhamshire.

11. (*foot*) HEXHAM.

St Mary's Chare, running south from the market place, is a typically narrow medieval town street. Similar examples still exist in Newcastle.

12. (*top*) NEWCASTLE.

The Dominican Friary (Black Friars) built in the 1240s. Beyond the foundations of the church in the foreground is the cloister garth with its surrounding buildings which were used by nine of Newcastle's trade companies after the Reformation. The Carmelite Friary in Hulne Park near Alnwick is also to a large extent intact.

13. (*foot*) NEWCASTLE.

The Heber Tower (one of eighteen) and a section of the town alongside Bath Lane, built in the thirteenth century.

14. (*opposite, top*) ALNWICK.

Unlike Newcastle, where all six gates were destroyed, one of Alnwick's gates has survived. Popularly known as the Hotspur Gate, it was built in the mid-fifteenth century about fifty years after Hotspur's death.

15. (*opposite, foot*) BERWICK.

The early Elizabethan ramparts between the Cumberland and Brass Bastions. The stone wall is only about 14 feet high, but it is backed by a huge earthwork capable of resisting artillery fire.

16. (*above*) ALNWICK (ST. MICHAEL).

A rare example in the county of a pre-Reformation church built after 1300. The result of a complete reconstruction carried out after 1464, it displays the very large windows with fine tracery of the Perpendicular style.

17. BELSAY.

Built *c.*1370 by the Middleton family, it is typical of the more substantial tower built by wealthier landowners. Next to it is the manor house built *c.*1614 after the accession of James I when purely domestic accommodation became safe. A very similar development occurred at Chipchase.

18. CORBRIDGE.

The so-called Vicar's Pele. In fact, a more modest tower than Belsay, but serving the same purpose, it was built of stones from the Roman fort.

IACOBVS · 4 · D GRATIA
REX · SCOTORVM

19. JAMES IV.

An authentic portrait of one of the two Scottish kings killed in battle in Northumberland.
James met his death at Flodden on 9th September, 1513. The other king, Malcolm III, was
killed at Alnwick on 11th November, 1093. (*Reproduced by courtesy of the Scottish National
Portrait Gallery*).

20. THOMAS PERCY, 7TH EARL OF NORTHUMBERLAND.

The earl's failure in the rebellion of 1569 and his execution at York on 22nd August, 1572 marked the end of the political dominance of the Percy family in Northumberland. They continued as wealthy aristocrats, but for the rest of the period they were exiled to their estate at Petworth in Sussex. (*The painting, at Petworth House, is reproduced by courtesy of the National Trust Photo Library.*)

21. JAMES VI AND I.

The accession of James, king of Scotland since July 1567, to the throne of England in March 1603 meant the end of over three hundred years of conflict which had seriously affected life in Northumberland. (*The painting, by Adam de Colone, is reproduced by courtesy of the Scottish National Portrait Gallery.*)

giving an advowson, a layman would earn the gratitude, and more importantly the prayers, of the recipient monks; and would be seen to be generous without significantly diminishing or damaging his family's estate.

Monasteries, however, needed to find ways of benefiting financially from these acquisitions. They did so initially by imposing an annual pension on the rectors they appointed, what would today be called top-slicing the profits. Much greater income, however, could be gained by appropriating their churches. In doing so they made themselves the permanent corporate rectors of their parishes. But, as cloistered monks, they were not permitted to serve as parish priests. Consequently, they had to appoint a qualified deputy to do the work. Initially such men were stipendiary priests, but their vulnerability to the whims of parsimonious or inefficient abbots led the papacy to legislate in favour of a more secure arrangement. The Fourth Lateran Council held in Rome in 1215 laid down that henceforth the resident deputy should be assigned a specific share of the endowment which would give him control over his own income. Although no prescription was issued, the classic division awarded the glebe and the tithe of grain (usually far more valuable than the tithes of all other produce) to the rector, and the small tithes and the dues and offerings, known as altarage, to the resident priest. Under such an arrangement the priest was known as the vicar (the word derives from the Latin *vicarius* = deputy) and his share of the endowment as the vicarage. In England until 1279 the appropriation and the setting up of vicarages was a matter for canon law and the church authorities, in particular the bishops. In that year, however, the Statute of Mortmain brought the matter into the field of English law as well by making any transfer of property to the church subject to royal licence.

How did all this affect Northumberland? The problem is that we do not know for certain who owned such parishes as there were at the end of the eleventh century, and consequently we have no certain start line. The best guess is that four – Norham, Holy Island, Hexham and Tynemouth – were owned by the church. Another eight belonged to the Crown: Bamburgh, Rothbury, Warkworth, Whittingham, Corbridge, Newburn and Simonburn were on estates which had belonged to the kings of Northumbria, while Newcastle was of very recent creation. The remainder we must assume belonged to laymen. By the end of the fourteenth century this situation was almost totally transformed: in only seven parishes – Ford, Ingram, Bothal, Morpeth, Elsdon, Knaresdale and Kirkhaugh – was the advowson owned by a lay person.

Three parishes had been acquired by Oxford colleges: Embleton and Ponteland by Merton and Longbenton by Balliol; and one, Thockrington, had been handed over to the archbishopric of York early in the thirteenth century by Richard de Umfraville to expiate offences against Hexham Priory and the archbishop. The others were in the possession of monasteries. All six Northumberland houses had benefited. The most fortunate were Alnwick, Hexham and Tynemouth. Alnwick acquired seven: Alnham, Chatton, Chillingham, Fenton, Lesbury, Shilbottle and Wooler, although the number was reduced to six when Fenton was absorbed into Wooler in 1313. Hexham also had six, having added Chollerton, Ovingham, Slaley, Stamfordham and Warden to its home parish. Likewise Tynemouth acquired Haltwhistle, Hartburn, Eglingham, Whalton and Woodhorn to add to Tynemouth. Blanchland secured Bolam, Bywell St Andrew, Heddon and Kirkharle; Newminster was given Kirkwhelpington and Stannington; and Brinkburn acquired Felton. Two of the three nunneries also profited, Holystone acquiring Holystone, Corsenside and Alwinton, and Lambley the parish formed by its estate.

Fifteen parishes, however, fell into the hands of monastic houses in neighbouring counties. In Cumberland, Lanercost secured Longhorsley, while Carlisle Cathedral acquired the important parishes of Newcastle, Warkworth, Rothbury, Newburn and Corbridge. Durham Cathedral Priory also benefited considerably, adding Bedlington, Ellingham, Howick, Meldon and Branxton to its origin possessions of Norham and Holy Island. Finally, two Yorkshire monasteries were beneficiaries of lay generosity: Nostell acquired the valuable parish of Bamburgh, while Kirkham obtained Kirknewton, Carham and Ilderton.

The twelfth century was the main period for the transfer of advowsons from lay to monastic hands, and in Northumberland some thirty such transactions took place. A further five occurred in the thirteenth, notably those to the Oxford colleges. The last ten changes of ownership were effected in the fourteenth, the final instance being the grant of Haltwhistle to Tynemouth Priory in 1379 by Richard II, the advowson having been in the gift of the Crown since the forfeiture of the king of Scotland. Space will allow for only a few further examples. Most notable was Henry I's decision to divest the Crown of all its Northumberland advowsons. He gave Bamburgh to the Yorkshire house of Augustinian canons at Nostell near Wakefield and the others to found another Augustinian house at Carlisle, which became the cathedral chapter when the diocese was created in 1133. His example was followed by one of his leading baronial associates, Walter l'Espec, who was originally settled in Yorkshire and founded an Augustinian Canonry at Kirkham in the Vale of Pickering. Subsequently, he was given the barony of Wark on Tweed, which included the churches at Carham, Kirknewton and Ilderton, the advowsons of which he bestowed upon his Yorkshire foundation.

It is obvious that to contemporaries parish churches were valuable assets capable of yielding considerable income. How valuable were Northumberland's churches? One very useful guide is the valuation for the purposes of papal taxation made in the 1290s, when population was at its highest and churches at their richest. Although it may not be fully accurate or reliable, this document reveals three major features. The first is the very wide discrepancy in wealth. At the top end of the scale the annual income of Bamburgh parish was reckoned to be a little over £264 and that of Holy Island almost £231; and there were twelve other parishes worth over £100 a year. In contrast, Kirkhaugh and Slaley were both valued at under £10 and Knaresdale and Thockrington at £10 and £10 4s. 2d. respectively. The average value was £56, but this disguised a clear difference between the northern and southern deaneries, parishes in Bamburgh (£88) and Alnwick (£65) being worth considerably more than Newcastle (£54) and Corbridge (£39). Northumberland north of the Coquet was, it seems, wealthier than the districts south of that river.

This income, as we have noted, was derived from three sources. Of these the glebe is most difficult to pin down, partly because there was no rule to offer guidance, but mainly because the subject has not yet been properly investigated. In some large ancient parishes the glebe may have comprised entire townships: thus it is suggested that Shoreswood and Fenham were respectively the glebes of Norham and Holy Island parishes. Probably more typical, however, were the $87\frac{1}{2}$ acres at Kirkwhelpington or the $37\frac{1}{2}$ acres at Chillingham.

About tithes and altarage payments there is enough information to give a very fair idea of what accrued. The data from a single year will serve to show what various sources yielded. In 1487/88, the grain tithes of the whole of Norham parish and half of Holy Island parish produced an income for Durham Cathedral Priory of £49 19s. 0d. This was not the result of collection and then sale, but of leasing the right to the tithes to local men, who we must assume expected to make a profit. The lesser tithes produced in total £25 17s. 0d. made up principally of the tithe of the fish weirs on the Tweed, and lambs, which numbered 460. Other tithed products were hay, hemp, wool (34 stones), cheese (56 stones), calves, pigs, hens and geese. A further £11 11s. $11\frac{1}{2}d$ was produced by the sale of blessed bread, fees for weddings, christenings and burials, Easter offerings and the mortuaries of seven recently deceased parishioners. The relatives of the richer ones rendered an animal and an article of clothing (or the value thereof) while poorer parishioners were required to give only a garment. Thus, John Brown's family gave a horse worth 10s. and a cloak worth 10d., while the relatives of William Chapell's widow handed over a dress worth 1s. This example is from a time when population had contracted, and with it cereal production. In the late thirteenth and early fourteenth centuries tithe income was much higher, the grain tithes alone of these same townships being normally worth over £300 a year.

Given the size and wealth of so many parishes, it is not surprising that in the end all but ten were appropriated. Dating this process is not a simple task since evidence is missing in many cases, and in others the process proved to be extraordinarily long and fraught with obstacles. As a result many moves to appropriate begun in the twelfth century were not complete until well into the thirteenth. A prime example is Bamburgh, given by Henry I to Nostell Priory in 1121, with permission to appropriate upon the death of its incumbent priest. This man, however, lived on until 1171, and with both Henry II and John choosing to ignore Henry I's wishes, Nostell did not gain full control of the church until 1228, and then only after papal intervention. Durham Cathedral Priory had to wait almost as long between c.1140 and 1239 to secure Ellingham, while fifty-eight years of complaint and litigation between 1274 and 1332 were needed to put Merton College into full possession of Embleton.

Appropriations after the Statute of Mortmain, of which there were twelve, were accomplished over much shorter periods and with far less bother, in part because the statute itself imposed a degree of order on the whole process. Also the documents relating to these annexations record the official reasons for them. For example, in 1340 Roger de Somerville granted the advowson of Longbenton to Balliol College, which secured immediate permission to appropriate since the intention was that the income should support six scholars and a chaplain. In the case of Kirkwhelpington, where the advowson was given by Gilbert de Umfraville to Newminster Abbey in 1334, appropriation was delayed until 1349 when the monks could with justification claim that their house was burnt, their lands devastated by the Scots and their tenantry reduced by plague so that their income had fallen to the point where they could not afford repairs, customary charity, or (a telling point) to entertain the nobility.

With appropriation came profit, but net profit, for the monastic or collegiate rector had to endow a vicarage or pay the vicar a stipend. In the case of Norham, where there was no endowed vicarage, stipends throughout the fifteenth century totalled £25 6s. 8d., £20 for the vicar and £5 6s. 8d. for the chaplain of Cornhill. Total income from all sources was about £70, which meant that thirty six per cent had to be paid to the parish clergy. This was a far cry from the opulent days of the early fourteenth century when stipends were lower (£13 6s. 8d. and £3 13s. 4d. respectively) but income massively higher. In 1309/10, for example, the grain tithe was sold for £174 and the remaining income came to £75, giving a total of £249. In that year, therefore, remuneration of the clergy consumed less than seven per cent of income. These figures amply illustrate how justified monasteries were, at least from their financial point of view, in striving to secure full appropriation of their larger parishes (small parishes were generally too poor to be worth appropriating). They also reinforce the belief that there was more than enough financial capacity to support a much greater number of parish churches.

Unlike Norham, however, most appropriated parishes had endowed vicars. How did their rewards compare? Their level of annual income was basically determined by what had been assigned to the vicarage, but it was also affected by seasonal factors and fluctuations. Perhaps the best overall guide is again the 1291 taxation figures. These show a scale ranging from an average of £9 in Corbridge deanery via £11 in Alnwick and £14 in Newcastle to £18 in Bamburgh. The overall average was £13, which interestingly is almost exactly what the vicar of Norham received.

Appropriation obviously entailed a certain amount of administration, which became more of a headache the greater the distance between monastery or college and its churches. The Durham monks found it expedient to retain an agent, the proctor of Norham, to oversee their properties on south Tweedside some sixty-five miles from the priory. Even so, fully effective supervision involved much journeying back and forth by both proctor and several senior monks. The problem was more acute for Merton, whose church at Embleton was 256 miles from the college. A document of 1464 shows that it took the college bursar a fortnight's journey there and back covering up to thirty-five miles a day, and a month's stay at Embleton, to ensure that the college secured what was due to it. Happily, the exercise would seem to have been uneventful and not without its pleasures and diversions: but it lasted from 13 August until 15 October and cost the college £6 7s. 3d. in expenses.

Finally, something must be said about the men who staffed these parishes. Those fortunate enough to hold a rectory would in most cases be wealthy as a result. Consequently, most of the time such churches would be in the hands of men of political or administrative importance. Increasingly they were university graduates employed in matters non-parochial and perhaps non-ecclesiastical, and would therefore need to employ a vicar to reside and perform the duties of parish priest. Although they were supposed to be in priests' orders, it is clear that many were not, at least at the time of their appointment. Not a few would hold rectories in the early stages of what turned out to be glittering careers, and would relinquish them as they ascended the ecclesiastical ladder. About the holders of vicarages and the stipendiary priests we know relatively little, and even less about the men in orders below that of priest who assisted in many ways with the mundane work of the parish. To the system of a resident rector or vicar there were two exceptions: Ovingham and Bamburgh were staffed by members of the monastic houses to which they were appointed. This was possible because both Hexham and Nostell were houses of regular canons not monks whose rule allowed them to work outside the cloister. These two parishes may in fact have been served by what we would now call a team ministry.

MONASTERIES, FRIARIES AND HOSPITALS

Even though they have little appreciation of monasticism, most people are aware that monasteries played an important part in European life throughout the middle ages. It is perhaps surprising therefore to discover that at the time of the Norman invasion there were no monasteries in Northumberland, or indeed in the whole of northern England. This had not always been so, however. In Northumberland monasteries had been founded at Lindisfarne, Tynemouth and Hexham, and perhaps Norham, in the early days of English Christianity in the seventh and eighth centuries. All, however, had been destroyed and abandoned during the turbulent and violent Viking period in the ninth and early tenth centuries. A monastic revival in the middle period of the tenth century, owing much to continental example, had resulted in the foundation or refoundation of thirty-five houses in the midlands and the south; but this movement had not extended north of the Trent.

This situation changed within a few years of William I becoming king. In 1074 monastic life at Jarrow and Wearmouth was restarted by men, mainly English and led by one Aldwin, who came north from the West Midlands. It was from this initiative that monasticism was again to come into Northumberland. This said, it would be unfair to attribute revived interest in monastic life entirely to southern influences. Even before 1066 there was a renewed concern for the early Northumbrian saints, most of whom had been monks, and a great deal of excitement was generated by the discovery at Tynemouth in 1065 of the alleged body of St Oswin.

In fact it was at Tynemouth that monastic life re-entered Northumberland. Shortly after their arrival at Jarrow, Aldwin and his monks were given the ruins of the old monastery at Tynemouth by Earl Robert, who hoped and expected that they would extend their work north of the river. This did not happen until 1083, however. In that year, Bishop William of St Calais removed most of the monks from Jarrow and Wearmouth to Durham to be the new, reformed chapter of his cathedral in place of the hereditary, married priests, the Community of St Cuthbert. Some, however, under a monk named Turchil, were sent across the Tyne to reactivate monastic life at Tynemouth. Had this been a permanent development, Tynemouth would have been, like Jarrow and Wearmouth, a cell or outpost of Durham Cathedral Priory. That this did not happen was the consequence of a violent quarrel between Bishop St Calais and the earl of Northumbria, Robert de Mowbray, who in May 1085 repossessed the site, expelled Turchil and his monks, and entered into negotiations with the abbot of St Albans Abbey in Hertfordshire. The outcome was that, with a suitable endowment of land provided by de Mowbray, Tynemouth became a cell of St Albans Abbey and severed its more natural and local ties with Durham.

St Albans, and therefore Tynemouth, like Durham was a Benedictine monastery, that is, it functioned in accordance with the rule devised by St Benedict of Nursia (died c.548), which while strict was not immoderately harsh or demanding. It was the rule followed at that time by the large majority of west European monasteries. Adherence to Benedict's rule should have ensured uniformity of practice between monasteries, but since they were entirely separate and independent communities linked only by a

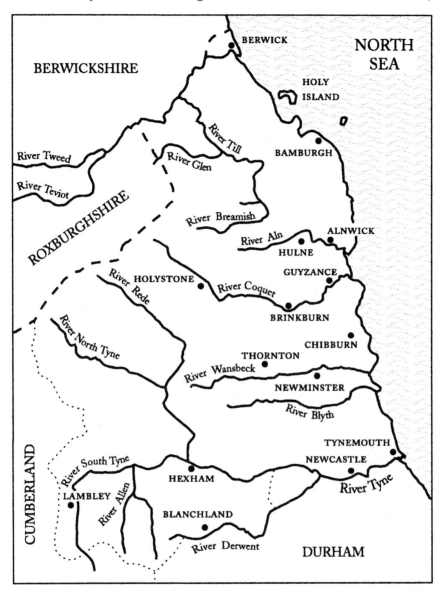

16: *Monasteries and Friaries*

ALNWICK: Premonstratensian Abbey
BAMBURGH: cell of Augustinian Priory of Nostell (Yorkshire) Dominican Friary
BERWICK: Cistercian Nunnery, Franciscan, Dominican, Carmelite, Augustinian and Trinitarian Friaries
BLANCHLAND: Premonstratensian Abbey
BRINKBURN: Augustinian Priory
CORHAM: cell of Augustinian Priory of Kirkham (Yorkshire)
CHIBBURN: preceptory of the Knight's Hospitaller
FARNE: cell of Durham Cathedral Priory
GUYZANCE: Premonstratensian Nunnery
HEXHAM: Augustinian Priory

HOLY ISLAND: cell of Durham Cathedral Priory
HOLYSTONE: Benedictine Nunnery
HULME: Carmelite Friary
LAMBLEY: Benedictine Nunnery
NEWCASTLE: Benedictine Nunnery, Franciscan, Dominican, Carmelite, Augustinian, Trinitarian Friaries
NEWMINSTER: Cistercian Abbey
THORNTON: preceptory of the Knights Templar
TYNEMOUTH: cell of Benedictine Abbey of St. Albans (Hertfordshire)

common heritage, local deviations and variations became common. This situation, however, was about to change. Enthusiasts for the monastic life were becoming increasingly dissatisfied with the black monk (from the colour of their habit) ways, which they were convinced were inadequate. While the monks from St Albans were restarting traditional monastic life at Tynemouth, men on the Continent were considering how that life could be made more rigorous and demanding. The thoughts of these men were in fact to have a profound impact on monasticism and monastic life in the course of the twelfth century. It was through their work and fervour that great enthusiasm for monastic life was engendered, which resulted in the foundation of hundreds of new houses in the course of the century.

During the reign of Henry I (1100-35), the years when Northumberland was finally Normanised, the most popular of the new monastic styles was that of the Augustinian or Black Canons. Their rule was based upon that devised by the great North African theologian of the early church St Augustine (died 430), the bishop of Hippo Regius (Annaba, Algeria). The attraction of this rule was that it brought priests together into regulated communities which would ensure, it was hoped, higher moral standards and deeper spirituality. At the same time, and in contrast to monastic rules, it allowed its members to go out from the cloister to work in the wider world. It was considered very suitable for large parish churches and for institutions such as hospitals. Most Augustinian canonries in England, however, were scarcely distinguishable in form and performance from conventional monasteries.

Two such houses were founded in Northumberland. The earlier was at Hexham, which like Tynemouth was an important religious site dating from the 670s. The origins of the new foundation went back to the early 1080s when Eilaf, the hereditary priest of Hexham, quit the Community of St Cuthbert, unwilling to accept Bishop St Calais' reforms, placed himself and his jurisdiction under the authority of the archbishop of York, and undertook to rebuild his church and engage in the recolonisation of the district. This commitment was continued by his son, also Eilaf, who succeeded him about 1086. This situation continued until 1113 when Archbishop Thurstan, a leading enthusiast for the Augustinian solution to the problem of clerical discipline, decided to replace Eilaf with a house of Augustinian Black Canons, headed by a man he brought from the canonry at Huntingdon. Eilaf was allowed to live out his time at Hexham, and upon his death in 1138 he bequeathed his possessions to the community that had superseded him. The other Augustinian Canonry, Brinkburn, was founded about 1135 and differed from Hexham in two respects: its founder was not an ecclesiastic but one of the most powerful members of the new Northumbrian baronage, William Bertram, lord of Mitford; and its situation on the banks of the Coquet was a greenfield site without previous religious associations. Like Hexham, however, its initial complement of canons came from the south, in this case from Pentney in Norfolk.

The Augustinian system continued to be popular throughout the twelfth, and indeed into the thirteenth, century so that by 1225 there were some one hundred and fifty Black Canon houses in England and Wales. At the same time, however, another and very different style had a meteoric rise to popularity. This was the order of White Monks or Cistercians, founded at the end of the eleventh century at Cîteaux (Latin = Cistercia) in eastern France. The Cistercians were strongly insistent upon puritanical simplicity and absolute uniformity, which were to be enforced by a system of inspection designed to make deviation and corruption impossible. To help in their search for a simple, ascetic existence they sought to found their houses in deserted areas away from centres of population. Their rigour and reticence should have militated against success and popularity. But successful and popular they became, partly because the quality of their life came close to representing the contemporary monastic ideal, but also through the influence of the dynamic and charismatic personality of their most famous member, St Bernard of Clairvaux.

St Bernard in fact made a significant contribution to the founding of Rievaulx abbey in Ryedale in the southern Cleveland Hills through the backing and encouragement he gave to the project devised by Archbishop Thurstan and Walter l'Espec, lord of Helmsley on whose land the house was to be built. Rievaulx was founded in March 1132, and two years later it admitted the man who was to be its most notable member, Ailred, the son of Eilaf II of Hexham: the father stood for an antique and discredited form of clerical life; the son exemplified the most avant-garde modernity. Also in 1132 the influence of Clairvaux drove a group of monks to leave the Benedictine house of St Mary at York and settle in a deserted spot provided for them by Archbishop Thurstan in Skeldale near Ripon. They too were admitted to the Cistercian order as Fountains Abbey.

There followed an avalanche of Cistercian foundations: by 1152, when a moratorium on new creations was imposed, no fewer than forty had come into existence in England and Wales. One of these, Newminster, was in Northumberland. Located on the banks of the Wansbeck a mile west of Morpeth, it was the work of the lord of that barony, Ralph de Merlay, who was fired with enthusiasm by a visit to Fountains in 1138. Newminster was in fact Fountains' first daughter house, and herself produced three daughters – Pipewell in Northamptonshire and Sallay and Roche in Yorkshire – within fifteen years of her own foundation.

Very similar to, and indeed inspired by, the Cistercians were the Premonstratensian or White Canons, an order founded early in the twelfth century by St Norbert of Xanten at Prémontré (Latin = Premonstratensia), like Cîteaux in eastern France. The order combined the strictness, simplicity and highly regulated ways of the Cistercians with the Augustinian licence to work outwith the cloister. They proved to be first-rate missionaries in the Slavic lands beyond the River Elbe which were being conquered by the Germans. This role was not available to them in England, and it is therefore not surprising that only thirty-three houses were founded. Two of these, however, were in Northumberland. The first was at Alnwick, founded in 1147 by the lord of Alnwick, Eustace son of John. The initial complement of canons came from Newhouse in Lincolnshire, the first Premonstratensian canonry in England. The other house, and the last house for men to be founded in the county, was founded in 1165 at Blanchland in the Derwent valley by Walter de Bolbec III, lord of Styford.

In addition to these monasteries and canonries, all male establishments, three nunneries were founded. The most prominent was that dedicated to St Bartholomew in Newcastle. Its origin is obscure, but the benefactions of Henry I of England and David I of Scotland point to an early twelfth-century foundation. The other two houses, Lambley and Holystone, were located in the wilder and poorer western areas of the county, and never managed to overcome that disadvantage. Virtually nothing is known of their origins, except that they were founded at some time before 1200.

Finally, four other monastic presences in the county need to be noted. Earliest in time were the two cells of Durham Cathedral Priory on Holy Island and Farne. Being the guardian of the uncorrupt body of St Cuthbert, the priory of Durham had an impeccable claim to the original properties of the Lindisfarne community. At an early date in their history the cathedral monks made good that claim by establishing the two cells, which thereafter housed Durham monks as did Jarrow and Wearmouth. In considerable contrast and later in time, the two military monastic orders acquired small footholds in Northumberland. The order of the Temple of Jerusalem (the Templars) had a house at West Thornton in Hartburn parish, while their rival, the order of the Hospital of St John of Jerusalem (the Hospitallers), had a preceptory at Chibburn in Woodhorn parish. The Templars were dissolved in 1312 by the papacy and their possessions were transferred to the Hospitallers.

It is clear that most of the monastic foundations in Northumberland were the work of the local baronage. What motivated them to go to such lengths? The clearest evidence is to be found in the opening statements of foundation documents. Thus, William Bertram in founding Brinkburn said that he was doing so 'for my soul and my parents, for the remission of my sins, for my lords living and dead, for my wife and sons and my faithful followers'. And very similar sentiments were expressed by the founders of Newminster and Alnwick. Although these statements have a conventional feel to them, there can be no doubt that the need for spiritual insurance was a powerful driving force. For certain, the founders of monasteries would expect the monks to remember them and their kith and kin specifically in their prayers, and they believed, or did not dare not to believe, that these prayers would be to their soul's advantage after death. Yet vanity and fashion must also have figured: monasteries were splendid and conspicuous edifices which patently demonstrated that a man could as well as would, and notably underlined his status this side of the grave as well as a concern for the life beyond.

This awareness of the here and now is revealed in the nature of the endowment founders provided for their creations. What they did not give by and large was well settled and cultivated land which was yielding them profit in terms of cash, produce and loyal followers. As we have seen, they readily parted with the advowsons of churches, and given the rising hostility to lay ownership of churches they lost nothing by so doing. Monasteries, however, could benefit greatly, either by imposing pensions on their rectors, or, more so, by appropriating. The value of churches to monasteries is well illustrated by the Premonstratensian canons of Alnwick, who were given their home parish of Lesbury by their founder, and subsequently acquired Shilbottle, Chatton, Chillingham, Alnham, Wooler and Fenton. At the end of the thirteenth century these seven churches were reckoned to be worth net over £250 a year. The Cistercians were the only order forbidden by their rule to acquire churches. Neverthless, Newminster acquired and appropriated Stannington and Kirkwhelpington in the second quarter of the fourteenth century; but by that time the heyday of monastic fervour was past and the Newminster monks were living with the harsh reality of diminished income as the consequence of Scottish raids and natural disasters.

What the Cistercians did accept, and indeed positively sought, was empty land devoid of settlement. This, it is quite clear, is what Newminster got from Ralph de Merlay: in his foundation deed he speaks of granting the monks all the valley of the Wansbeck as far as the territory of Mitford on the north bank and land bounded by the courses of certain burns on the south. At Brinkburn William de Bertram was even more specific, describing the land he gave to Brinkburn as being 'of my waste'; while at Blanchland the boundaries are so described as clearly to indicate empty land. Although such gifts did not diminish a baron's wealth, they did have potential, from which handsome profit could be realised, given the necessary inputs. Only Tynemouth and Hexham acquired well-settled townships, the former mainly from the estate of the old earldom of Northumbria while still under the control of Robert de Mowbray, while the latter benefited from the generosity of the lords of Hexhamshire, the archbishops of York.

Monasteries continued to require property, and not only from their founders' families. Other men of note seem to have preferred giving to existing houses rather than founding their own. Thus, Newminster acquired over 10,000 acres of high moorland at the head of Coquetdale known as Kidland from the powerful Umfraville family. Below baronial level, however, generosity was far less spectacular. Nor was it always generosity. Although the wording is often ambiguous, it is clear that some acquisitions were the result of purchase or mortgage foreclosure, not simple gifts. The range of transactions is revealed in the documents relating to Brinkburn's acquisition of land in Eshott, Felton, Bockenfield and Framlington. In 1244, Godfrey Manduit, the lord of Eshott, and his son Roger gave over 100 acres in Eshott, Bockenfield and Felton to the parish church of Felton, which Brinkburn owned, and appropriated a few years later. This clearly appears as a gift since it was specifically for the souls of Lady Constance, daughter of Walter son of William (and presumably Godfrey's wife) and both sets of ancestors. In contrast, Brinkburn's acquisition of three tofts and 26 acres of land in Low Framlington was a straightforward purchase for 20 marks (£13 6s. 8d.), while Richard Freman, who lived in Whalton, lost to the canons his right to a toft and 5 acres in Bockenfield as the result of an unsuccessful law suit. These examples also show how small individual acquisitions could be, a point underlined by Brinkburn's acquisition of an acre and a rood of land in Bockenfield, by purchase or gift, from a William Frankeleyn.

The flow of benefactions declined in the later middle ages, largely because the religious enthusiasm and generosity of the laity was channelled in other directions. Ironically, this happened as economic life was becoming more difficult and incomes were falling as the result of war and a declining population. One solution was to appropriate parish churches, a temptation to which, as we have noted, even the Cistercians were susceptible. But these too were a declining asset as falling population meant lower levels of production and consequently smaller income from tithes. Another solution was for a monastery to buy out its own freehold tenants, and then let their holdings at economic rents. Tynemouth Priory exploited this possibility to the full. In the course of the fourteenth and fifteenth centuries by means of nineteen licences to side-step the Mortmain ban, it made no fewer than 107 purchases, and in so doing it acquired almost 2,000 acres of land. Taken together, these changes and developments tended to alter the balance of a monastery's income between its spiritualities (churches) and its temporalities (land rents, sales of produce, court income), away from the former and towards the latter.

Very little of the great quantities of administrative record generated by monasteries has survived, and so it is impossible to discover the income enjoyed by each house during its existence. On the eve of the Dissolution, it is evident that Tynemouth was by far the most wealthy with an income of about £750. Well behind were Alnwick, Hexham and Newminster with between £250 and £300 each, and then Brinkburn and Blanchland, neither of which could hope to achieve £100. As elsewhere, the nunneries were abjectly poor: Newcastle had an income of about £35, while Holystone and Lambley were desperately poor with £11 and £5 respectively.

About the life of monks and nuns we know very little. Perhaps the most revealed house is Hexham, largely because, as was their right and duty, the archbishops of York from time to time conducted visitations (inspections) after which exposed faults and injunctions for improved performance were put on paper. From Henry Murdac in 1152 to Wiliam Lee in 1535 no archbishop seems to have been happy with what he found: discipline was lax; the rule was ignored; and some monks consorted with women. Whether the archbishops seriously expected their visitations to result in permanent reformation may be doubted. The only one who seemingly entertained unrealistic hopes was William Greenfield whose zeal led to unhappy confrontation. It began with his visitation in 1307 which was sufficiently aggressive to provoke a revolt of the canons led by one Robert of Whelpington, who had to be shipped off to a canonry at Gloucester to cool his heels. Greenfield clearly came to the conclusion that Hexham's problems would be cured only by firmness at the top. Consequently, when in 1311 the prior, Thomas of Fenwick, asked leave to resign (he claimed he was broken in health by age and stress), the archbishop attempted to intrude an outsider, Gilbert of Boroughbridge, a canon of Nostell. This was without doubt a flagrant violation of the community's rights, to which they responded by electing as their new prior none other than Robert of Whelpington. Angered by this insult, Greenfield applied the ultimate sanction: he excommunicated the entire community and sequestrated their property. In doing so he went too far, and on a petition to parliament the canons recovered their property. In the end Greenfield retreated. On 20th November he acknowledged the canons' right to elect their own prior, and accepted Whelpington as the new head of house. All he managed to extract from the débâcle was, rather spitefully, an annual pension of £20 for his thwarted protégé, Boroughbridge. This determination to control their own lives through the ability to choose their own leader was again demonstrated a hundred years later when, in 1409, the canons elected as prior William of Woodham, who at the previous visitation had been one of two canons condemned for having improper relations with women.

Another evident aspect is the attraction and vulnerability of monasteries to Scottish raiding parties. Hexham was burnt and looted in 1296, and again the following year when even William Wallace was unable to prevent the theft of the chalice during the celebration of mass. The house had become untenable, and to his credit Archbishop Greenfield found safe havens for the canons in other Augustinian houses in Yorkshire and Nottinghamshire. The Scots also came to Hexham during the Neville's Cross campaign in 1346, but this time the building escaped destruction. Blanchland too suffered considerably, and not only from the Scots: the presence of Edward III's army there in late July and early August 1327 was a sore trial. Tynemouth, however, managed to survive the Bruce period, partly because of its location, but also as the result of the good leadership of its prior, Richard of Tewing, although the six visits of royalty between 1292 and 1322 must have strained its resources. The priory did suffer, however, during the difficult years of the 1380s.

Tynemouth was also in a difficult situation in that it was the wealthiest house in Northumberland yet had least independence, which bred considerable resentment, aggravated no doubt by the knowledge that the mother house was so far away. All this led in the early 1290s to a concerted attempt to become an independent monastery. The move was led by the prior, Simon of Walden, and his cellarer, John of Throckley. The case they brought in the king's court, although not without some substance, was too weak to succeed. In April 1295 St Albans dramatically reasserted its authority when its dynamic abbot, John of Berkhamstead, aided by a small force raised by the Newcastle merchant, Henry Scott, tricked his way into the priory at night, arrested Walden and Throckley, and had them shipped south in chains.

Between 1536 and 1540 all monasteries were closed and their lands and other possessions taken into the hands of the Crown. Initially, houses with under £200 annual income were targeted. An attempt to include Alnwick, Hexham and Newminster in this category by falsifying the figures provoked resistance: Alnwick resorted to bribery, but Newminster and Hexham resisted physically. At Hexham, the approach of the King's Commissioners led by Sir Cuthbert Radcliffe on 28th September, 1536 led to hostilities in which the priory was shut and garrisoned with sixty armed men in addition to the twenty canons. In face of this defiance the Commissioners retreated. This incident, without intending to do so, helped to provoke the widespread uprising known as the Pilgrimage of Grace in 1537. With the failure of this campaign the monasteries were doomed.

Having closed the monasteries the government had the responsibility of providing for something like eighty six monks (Hexham 20, Alnwick 17, Tynemouth 15, Newminster 15, Brinkburn 10, Blanchland 9) and twenty-five nuns (Newcastle 11, Holystone 8, Lambley 6). The latter could be returned to their families, who would be expected to provide for them as for other single female members. The men, however, had to earn their living. Some found employment elsewhere in the church; but in addition all received pensions. The £80 awarded to Robert Blakeney, the prior of Tynemouth, was exceptional; but the £10 awarded to the prior of Blanchland and the £30 to the priors of Hexham and Newminster were reasonable and adequate. Likewise, the pensions of between £2 and £6 given to ordinary monks were not out of line with other stipends, particularly as they were paid regularly by the Court of Augmentations, the government department set up to handle the dissolution.

As regards the former monastic estates, contrary to what is often thought they were not rapidly and cheaply disposed of by a careless and profligate Crown. In fact, the history of most of these properties was lengthy and convoluted, as can be demonstrated by what happened to the demesne of Brinkburn Priory. Initially, this property, which amounted to 223 acres was not sold but leased, to Cuthbert Carnaby, a member of a Northumbrian family heavily involved in the dissolution process, for twenty-one years from 29th September 1536 for an annual rent of £7 4s. 4d. In 1546, with eleven years of this lease still to run, a second lease was granted, this time to George Fenwick, to run for forty years from 29th September 1557, the day Carnaby's lease expired. Not until 1550 was the freehold on the market. On 20th March that year the reversion of the freehold was granted to John Dudley, the guardian of the young Edward VI and soon to become duke of Northumberland. However, he fell from power and was executed when Edward VI died and Mary became queen in 1553. Four years later, in 1557, the reversion was awarded to Thomas Percy who was being restored to his family's estate and title as the seventh earl of Northumberland. Meanwhile, the lease had passed from George to Tristram Fenwick. Both Fenwick and Percy were attainted for their parts in the 1569 uprising (see Chapter 6) with the result that the land again reverted to the Crown. Finally, in 1562 the freehold with freedom to occupy was sold for £761 to Sir John Forster, the Warden of the Middle March and one of the government's chief agents in the county.

In the early thirteenth century the vogue for monasticism, which was already waning, was replaced by that for mendicancy. The concept of the friar, the cleric who lived by begging, was promoted by two men with very different aims and urges: Francisco Bernadone (St Francis of Assisi, died 1226), who had a mystical devotion to the ideal of utter poverty; and Domenico Guzman (St Dominic, died 1221), whose concern was the widespread heresy he found in southern France. The Franciscan order (also known as the Grey Friars and the Friars Minor), and the Dominican order (also known as the Black Friars or Friars Preacher) were the first and always the most popular orders, which in the end had sixty-five and fifty-eight houses respectively in England and Wales. Two other orders, however, did achieve significant popularity: the Carmelites and the Austin (Augustinian) Hermits with thirty-nine and twenty-four houses respectively. Another order, the so-called Friars of the Sack (the Friars of the Penitence of Jesus Christ), was founded in 1266, but ordered by the Papacy eight years later to merge with one of the other orders.

The friars had two distinguishing characteristics: they were essentially urban, revealing perhaps the inadequacy of the territorial parish to meet the needs of the rapidly growing towns; and they were prohibited from owning property. Although they circumvented this by the use of trustees, friaries did not become property owners except on a very minor scale. In contrast to monks, but less so to regular canons, their work was in the world, not in the cloister, although their houses were closely akin in form to monasteries, a fact amply demonstrated by the excellent remains in Newcastle and at

Hulne Park near Alnwick.

Being urban, it is not surprising that the friars were fully in evidence only in Newcastle and Berwick, all five orders establishing themselves in both towns and at an early date. The only other foundations were the Dominicans at Bamburgh and the Carmelites at Hulne. All friaries were the result of the support and sponsorship of the well-to-do, such as Sir Peter Scot, responsible for the Newcastle Dominicans, or Sir William Roos, lord of Wark, whose efforts created the Austin Hermit friary in Newcastle; and also King Alexander II of Scotland who settled both major orders in Berwick.

The house we know most about was the Dominican or Black Friary in Newcastle, which in the thirteenth century had twenty-six members. Its property comprised, in addition to the site of the house covering about seven acres, a mere two gardens and four small closes which yielded an annual income of £2 19s. 4d., a paltry sum for an institution that more than once in the fourteenth century accommodated the kings of England and Scotland and their retinues. In all, by the 1530s there were probably some forty-six friars operating in Newcastle, a greater number than the parish clergy. All the friaries were closed in 1539 as part of the dissolution of the regular religious orders in England.

At various times before the Reformation forty-six hospitals were founded in Northumberland. The earliest was that dedicated to St Giles near Hexham founded by Archbishop Thurstan of York shortly after 1114. Of the rest, three-quarters came into existence before the end of the thirteenth century. Probably none was founded in the fourteenth century, but after 1400 ten were created, all but two of them in Newcastle. In fact, hospitals were mainly an urban phenomenon, almost two-thirds of them being in or very close to boroughs. Indeed, Newcastle with thirteen and Berwick with five accounted for almost forty per cent of the total.

Virtually all of them were the products of lay piety. One, in Newcastle and dedicated to St Mary Magdalene, was a royal foundation (Henry I) and several others - Morpeth, Mitford, Wooler, Alnwick, Elishaw - were founded by baronial families. In Newcastle, however, wealthy citizens were responsible. Perhaps the most notable example was the Maison Dieu on the Sandhill and dedicated to St Katherine founded by the great merchant, Roger Thornton, early in the fifteenth century. It was to house nine poor men and four poor women, and was to be run by a warden in priest's orders. Similarly about a hundred years later, Elizabeth Nykson founded a more modest establishment for four poor women near All Saints chapel.

The use of the term 'hospital' is, however, misleading. None was engaged in curative medicine, and the only disease of concern was leprosy. In fact, sixteen foundations (thirty five per cent of the total) were wholly or partly leper houses. Their purpose, however, was not to cure but to care for the victims of the disease and to isolate them from the community.

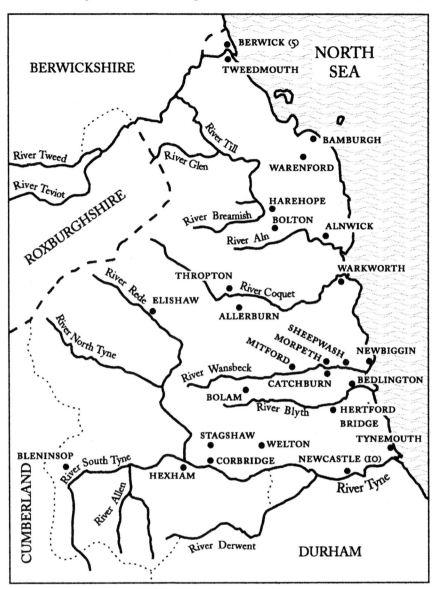

17: *Hospitals*

Nevertheless, the word in its modern sense can be justly applied to them. Virtually all the remainder were hospices for the care of the aged, infirm and indigent; while four were hostels offering shelter to travellers, especially pilgrims. All, however, were seen as ecclesiastical corporations since they were run by clergy, and many were also chantries with the duty of praying for the souls of their founders and benefactors. Consequently, virtually all of them fell victim to the measures taken between 1536 and 1547 to close monasteries, friaries and chantries. But not all of them

survived until that time. In fact, no fewer than eighteen appear to have
ceased to exist before the end of the fifteenth century. For this there were
several reasons, two of them biological. The first was the virtual
disappearance of leprosy in the later middle ages. Consequently, some
leper houses closed, while others survived by changing their role. St Mary
Magdalene in Newcastle, for example, was founded to care for lepers and
was still doing so in 1429; but by 1546 it had become an almshouse with
fourteen poor inmates. The other biological reason was plague, which after
1349 substantially reduced the population and thereby the demand for
hospice accommodation, although only the closure of Harehope can
confidently be attributed to the 1349 outbreak.

Another problem that affected the county's hospitals was war. Again
there is certainty about only one house: Welton was destroyed by the Scots
in 1296 and never refounded. But, the disappearance before 1400 of
hospitals at Bamburgh, Berwick, Capelford near Norham, Embleton,
Kirknewton, Warenford and Wooler was probably due in part at least to
their closeness to the Border.

In other cases, fragility was the result of inadequate funding. In contrast
to County Durham, where there were only sixteen hospitals but among
them three of the wealthiest in England (Kepier, Greatham and Sherburn),
Northumberland's hospitals were poor. Probably the richest was Bolton
near Edlingham, founded about 1225 by Robert de Roos, lord of Wark on
Tweed, for a master, three chaplains and an unspecified number of lay
brothers who were to care for thirteen lepers. Roos gave his foundation the
township of Bolton, land in Paston and Kilham, the mill at Mindrum, and
also properties in Lincolnshire and Yorkshire. Shortly after, the hospital
secured permission to enclose and cultivate 270 acres of moor and
woodland in Bolton; and before the middle of the fourteenth century it had
acquired land, grazing rights and rent charges in Shawdon, Branxton and
Middleton Hall. Its annual income at the time of closure was probably
between £30 and £35, no more than a third or a quarter of that enjoyed by
the wealthy Durham houses.

Nevertheless, Bolton's endowment was sufficient. The same could not be
said of many other houses. For example, Stagshaw (on the site of the
present Chantry Farm on the A68 between Corbridge and Portgate) was
founded in the thirteenth century by the Clavering family, the lords of
Corbridge, with an endowment of 24 acres of land and a few houses in
Corbridge market place. Since it acquired nothing further, and was
vulnerable to Scottish raids, it failed to flourish; and therefore in 1374 its
properties were transferred to a chantry being founded in the parish church.
Similarly, the hospital of St Giles in Hexham had only 32 acres of land and
rent charges from Hexham, Portgate and Fallowfield to support between
four and eight poor people or lepers. What made the difference was the
substantial quantities of bread and ale it received daily from Hexham Priory.

Being or becoming attached to a monastery or a friary in fact helped a large number of the twenty-eight houses which survived until the Reformation to avoid closure. Ironically, it was this very connection which sealed their fate after 1535. In fact, only four houses, all in Newcastle, managed to live through the revolution, largely because they were supported by the corporation, or in one case, Trinity House.

CHAPTER FIVE

Medieval Life: Government

Although the government and administration of Northumberland was basically the same as in other English counties, it did have two distinctive features. The first was the areas, known variously as regalities, franchises or liberties, where government was in the hands of private individuals or institutions. Such arrangements were to be found elsewhere in England, but those in Northumberland were very extensive in area covered and in the degree of independence. It must not be thought, however, that this was true or complete independence, but rather that in each case there were particular and peculiar reasons why the Crown granted or was willing to tolerate what at first glance look like states within a state. In fact, the Crown could, and on occasions did, repossess franchisal powers, and in the end did so permanently. Franchises should therefore be seen as peculiarities which the Crown accepted because it was useful or convenient to do so, or because there was no urgent reason for them to be abolished. Their existence, however, meant that Northumbrians differed in their experience of government. Even more distinctive were the special arrangements the Crown made to deal with distance between Northumberland and the seat of central government at Westminster. These three aspects – Crown government, franchisal government and Border government – need to be considered separately, although in reality they overlapped and interrelated to a considerable degree.

CROWN GOVERNMENT

Under this heading five aspects need to be discussed.

Parliament

Although it came into being in the thirteenth century, it was during the fourteenth century that parliament became a permanent and vital part of the English constitution. It comprised the lords spiritual and temporal who were summoned individually, and two elected representatives from each county and certain selected boroughs. It gradually became accepted that taxation and changes to the law (statutes) required parliamentary consent, and that in both matters the Commons (which after 1340 met separately from the Lords) had a central role.

Between 1295 and 1640 it has been calculated that there were 218 meetings of parliament, on average one every eighteen months. Although membership lists are not complete, we can be certain that Northumberland was represented on almost every, if not every, occasion. Until the mid-sixteenth century the county members were two men of knightly status who belonged to the relatively small group of substantial county landowners. In Elizabeth's reign, however, several members were incomers, although most were men who had married into Northumbrian families, such as Edward Talbot (who became earl of Shrewsbury on his brother's death in 1616), who was elected in 1584, was the husband of Jane, a daughter and co-heiress of Cuthbert, Lord Ogle.

Representing the most northerly county in England meant that Northumberland's knights had a long journey, especially if the parliament was summoned to meet at Westminster. Even though some parliaments were held nearer home, at York or Lincoln for example, and expenses of 4*s*. a day were paid, the business of being an MP was difficult and inconvenient, and it may have been for this reason that most men served only once: Sir Richard Horsley of Farnham, who represented the county in the parliaments of 1300, 1301 and 1307 was exceptional.

Being elected to parliament was not usually an isolated event in a man's life, but one incident in or aspect of a wide-ranging career of state service expected, indeed demanded, of men of knightly status, which implied possession of an appropriate level of wealth. Although each man had his own unique career, one example will serve as a representative illustration. Sir Thomas Grey of Heaton, with Sir John Mitford, represented the county in the parliaments of 1393 and 1397, each receiving £9 4*s*. 0*d*. and £7 12*s*. 0*d*. in expenses, indicating absences from home of forty-six and thirty-eight days. Sir Thomas was born in 1359 and succeeded his father in 1369 at the age of ten. His public career, therefore, did not begin until 1384 when he was in his mid-twenties. In that year he was made one of the county's tax collectors, and in the following fifteen years he served in a variety of capacities, including commissioner of array, justice of the peace, constable of Norham Castle and as a member of several commissions, such as that set up in 1393 to look into the water supply of Bamburgh Castle. Unfortunately, this useful career was cut short by his death in November 1400 at the early age of forty-one.

As regards the boroughs, in 1295 two burgesses each were sent by Newcastle, Corbridge and Bamburgh. Thereafter, however, only Newcastle returned members until the sixteenth century when Berwick secured representation in 1529 and Morpeth in 1553. The Newcastle members were almost invariably prominent and wealthy burgesses who had proved their worth in the offices of mayor, sheriff and alderman. Very few were knights, and very few also represented the county.

Taxation

Also from the reign of Edward I (1272-1307) direct taxation became a normal part of English life. The urgent reason for this was the Crown's need for money to finance its wars. Some people were exempt, most notably the poorest sections of the lay community, and also the clergy in respect of their spiritualities, that is, their churches. Unlike today, direct taxation was not levied on income, but on the assessed value of moveable goods, and was in fact known as a subsidy, not a tax. Not all possessions came into the reckoning, the most obvious exemptions being basic and essential household items and tools of the trade be it the farmer's plough, the weaver's loom or the knight's sword and armour. In reality for most people moveables meant what they had in their barns and byres, and hence valuations were usually made in late summer when these were at their fullest. The usual subsidy rates were $\frac{1}{15}$ for counties and $\frac{1}{10}$ for boroughs, but other fractions were used in the early years.

One of these exceptions was 1296, when the county rate was $\frac{1}{11}$ and the borough rate $\frac{1}{7}$. The details for Northumberland, which have been published in full, enable us to see how the system worked. The men in charge of the operation, who received their commission in December 1295, were a local knight, Roger Mauduit of Eshott, and a cleric, who may also have been a Northumbrian, Master Robert Merlay. Their role, in which they were entitled to the help of the sheriff (at that time Sir Hugh Gobyon of Shilvington), was to ensure that the exercise was properly and thoroughly conducted. The detailed work of assessment was carried out by a jury of twelve men from each of the eight wards into which the county was divided for this purpose: West Tynedale, East Tynedale, Tyne and Wansbeck, Wansbeck and Coquet, Bamburgh, Glendale, West Coquetdale, and East Coquetdale. (For an explanation of wards see pp. 161-2). The liberties or franchises of Norham and Holy Island, Tynedale, Redesdale and Hexham were not included, but Tynemouth was, although recorded separately, as was the barony of Embleton, probably because it was in the hands of the king's brother, Edmund, earl of Lancaster. Also recorded separately were eight boroughs: Newcastle, Corbridge, Bamburgh, Alnwick, Alnmouth, Morpeth, Newbiggin and Rothbury, although only the first three were charged the borough rate. Not recorded separately were four other boroughs: Wooler, Felton, Warkworth and Mitford. Missing altogether, although for no discernible reason, were twelve villages in the north-west of the county: Alnham, Branton, Caistron, Farnham, Fawdon, Glanton, Hedgeley, Little Ryle, Prendwick, Shawdon, Unthank and Wreighill.

Unfortunately, the detailed records of the assessments have not survived (as they have for some parts of the country) and so we cannot know exactly what goods were included and what values were assigned to them. However, we do have the names of those who paid the subsidy, the total value of their goods, and what they paid; and we also know the names of the jurors responsible for these figures. All in all, the county rate was paid by almost 4,000 people living in just over 400 villages and hamlets, and the borough rate by 358 persons in Newcastle, Corbridge and Bamburgh. The total value of goods assessed for the $\frac{1}{11}$ rate was £8,277 4s. $1\frac{3}{4}d$. and the tax paid came to £851 0s. $1\frac{1}{4}d$; the corresponding borough figures were £1,109 18s. $0\frac{1}{4}d$ and £157 0s. $1\frac{3}{4}d$. Even without the missing details, this document reveals a great deal about Northumbrian society at the end of the thirteenth century when population, and perhaps prosperity, were at their highest levels. Space does not permit a detailed analysis, but two basic facts stand out: one is that the wealthiest areas of the county were in the far north while the poorest were in the Tyne valley; the other is that Newcastle, with 297 taxpayers, was an urban community of considerable size and importance.

In 1334 the Crown drastically simplified the scheme, probably because of the frequency with which subsidies were being levied, but also because assessment was an immense and costly administrative task which almost certainly provoked considerable irritation and hostility. It therefore decided that each community would agree a global sum with the taxers, who would leave the leading members of the community to apportion and collect. This was a success, the subsidy yielding almost £37,500, an increase of over £3,000 on the previous occasion. In consequence, the new arrangements became standard until 1623, with communities having to petition for relief if they felt themselves to be over-taxed as a result of declining population and wealth.

Unfortunately, because of war devastation, Northumberland, along with Cumberland and Westmorland, was not included in the 1334 exercise, and it was not until 1336 that the new scheme was introduced. On this occasion the county was divided into five wards: Tynedale, Inter (that is between Tyne and Coquet), Coquetdale, Glendale and Bamburgh, plus the liberty of Embleton. In all some 319 settlements were listed, almost a hundred fewer than in 1296. Although some settlements may have disappeared, in most cases the missing places were subsumed under other names, as was the case with the twenty-three members of Tynemouth liberty recorded collectively in 1336, but individually in 1296. Also in contrast to 1296, Redesdale was included, but only one place, Newcastle, was classed as a borough. Although a detailed comparison has yet to be made, it seems certain that it will reveal a significant decline in wealth in the forty years between the two assessments. In the liberty of Embleton, for example, where a direct comparison can be made, in 1296 the value of the goods of 117 taxpayers amounted to £254, which yielded just over £23 in tax at the rate of $\frac{1}{11}$. It would have yielded less than £17 had the rate been $\frac{1}{15}$, which it was in 1336, when the total tax revenue from the thirteen settlements of the liberty was only fractionally over £9.

Law and Order

No attempt can be made here to describe the development of English law and legal institutions, but it needs to be recognised that both the law and the means of enforcing continued to expand and develop in complexity from the twelfth century. The system was headed by the central courts – King's Bench (criminal cases), Common Pleas (civil cases), Exchequer (cases concerning the Crown's revenue) – to which other courts such as Chancery, Admiralty and Star Chamber were added in the fourteenth and subsequent centuries. As well as being courts of first instance in the most serious matters, they heard appeals from courts operating in the provinces. It was with these that Northumbrians would normally have contact.

The means of bringing royal justice to the provinces also evolved gradually from the twelfth century. During the thirteenth century many cases were dealt with by commissions with precise and limited terms of reference. Until mid century these commissions were frequently composed of local knights, but thereafter professional judges were normally used. These were supplemented roughly every seven years by a general eyre (the word derives from an Old French word meaning journey). This was a commission of royal judges (usually three) charged not only with dealing with current cases, but also with examining the work of local administration since the previous occasion. The justices in eyre in fact had almost limitless powers to investigate and punish faults and abuses, and because of this they were much feared and hated.

In the late thirteenth and early fourteenth centuries more regular and less fearsome arrangements were introduced whereby the king's justices visited each county on a frequent and regular basis charged with 'hearing the assizes' (dealing with civil cases) and then 'delivering gaols' (trying criminals). From 1330 this new system became permanent with the establishment of the northern circuit in which Northumberland was linked with Cumberland, Westmorland and Yorkshire. In theory, the justices should have visited the county biannually; in practice visits tended to be biennial.

The law in action inevitably produced a growing volume of record which reveals not only the workings of the legal system but also the attitudes, habits and behaviour of men and women as individuals and collectively as communities. Much of this record has been lost, and much still remains unexamined. Consequently, a full and detailed account of law and order in medieval Northumberland is still a distant prospect. Nevertheless, there is enough available evidence to afford a glimpse of the range of legal problems and their solutions. Such is the record of the general eyre of 1256, which was held in the fortnight commencing on the Sunday after Easter. The venue was Newcastle, although exactly where was not stated. It was conducted by three royal judges headed by Roger of Thurkleby, who had been on the bench since 1240 and who enjoyed a high reputation for both knowledge of the law and concern for justice. He was accompanied by Nicholas of Hadlow and John of Wyville, and also by the abbot of Peterborough.

The opening session would have been attended by a very large gathering since the king's commission required all nobles (lay and ecclesiastical), knights and freeholders to be present, together with the bailiffs of the nine wards (four north and five south of the Coquet), a jury of twelve men from each of these two halves of the county and from the fourteen boroughs of Newcastle, Mitford, Morpeth, Warkworth, Newbiggin, Corbridge, Rothbury, Felton, Alnwick, Alnmouth, Bamburgh, Wooler, Wark on Tweed and Warenmouth, all of whose names were recorded, and four men (not named) from each township. In addition, the major officials of the county were required to attend: the sheriff (William Heron, lord of Hadston, and in the right of his wife, of Ford) and the coroners (Guy d'Arenes for south of the Coquet and William de Muschamp and Walter of Prendwick for north of the Coquet).

The first category of matters to be dealt with was what we would call civil cases, that is, between person and person. A total of 193 suits were heard, almost all concerned with the ownership of, or the right to occupy, land. Each case was unique, but one will serve to illustrate the sort of issue that arose between mid-thirteenth century Northumbrians. It concerned a woman of some standing, Isabel de Muschamp, the widow of Robert de Muschamp, lord of Wooler. He had died in 1250, and Isabel had subsequently married as her second husband a Richard Morin. She was accused by Alan of Harcarse and his wife, Agnes, of unjustly preventing them pasturing their animals throughout the year in a wood at Lowick, which they claimed the right to do as freehold tenants of the manor. The matter was put to the jury, who on oath were able to swear that Robert de Muschamp had not permitted Alan and Agnes to graze their animals in the wood, but that, after Muschamp's death, his estate was taken into the hands of the king's escheator (as was normal) who had allowed Alan and Agnes to have the use of it. However, the wood was assigned to Isabel as part of her dower (one third of a deceased husband's estate granted to his widow for life), and therefore she was within her rights to do as her former husband had done. Alan and Agnes, therefore, were found guilty of what was called a false plea.

The other category of business comprised felonies, that is, crimes that entailed the confiscation of property. The first problem was of course apprehending the suspect; and here the community was responsible, and was liable to be amerced if it failed to catch, or having caught, failed to hold, suspected criminals. In attempting to apprehend a criminal a community was entitled to the assistance of its nearest neighbours in the process known as the hue and cry.

Needless to say, few if any communities carried out these duties with any degree of enthusiasm, and so few criminals were ever caught. Most simply fled, usually to another jurisdiction, where they could not be pursued.

When this happened they were declared to be outlaws (if men) or waivers (if women) and as such could be killed on sight if they returned. The alternative escape route was to seek sanctuary in a church. There a criminal was safe, at least in theory, for forty days, during which time he was seen by the coroner to whom he had to confess his crime and who then gave him leave to abjure the realm, but with the loss of his goods.

On the rare occasions when criminals were caught in the act they were usually executed on the spot, either by hanging or beheading, although this act was supposed to have the coroner's approval. This being the case, it is not surprising that most criminals took to their heels. Only those who were truly innocent would readily stay and face a trial. This consisted of 'throwing him/herself on the country for good or ill', that is, a jury from neighbouring townships was empanelled to say whether the accused was guilty or not. In most cases the jury found for the accused. The 1256 record shows that no fewer than ninety-two persons were outlawed and another fourteen escaped via sanctuary. Only eighteen were executed, all but four by the axe. Two other ways existed of avoiding the fatal consequences of crime. One was to turn approver, that is, give evidence against one's accomplices. The other was prove oneself to be a clergyman, in which case the matter had to be transferred to the church courts.

The most common crime was unlawful killing, a term that must be used for the period before the reign of Henry VIII when distinction was made between murder and manslaughter. Some slayings seem to have been in pursuit of feud, as in the case of Gylmin of Elrington, who was attacked and killed while working in the fields at Langley by Adam of Harsondale and his two sons. In other cases, killings took place during the course of other criminal activities. Malcolm of Thirlwall, for example, already an outlaw, came with two accomplices to Redpath, robbed two men and killed a third, Thurkil of Blenkinsopp. That was his last escapade, however, for he was caught and beheaded. Some killings, as now, were family affairs. In temper, William Russell of Wardon threw a knife at his daughter, Cecily, wounding her in the side so that she died the following day. William fled to Hexham, the archbishop of York's jurisdiction, where he was joined by his wife, Isabel, who the court said was free to return since she was not suspected. Although most killings were by men, women too turned to physical violence on occasions. In one incident Susanna, the daughter of John the miller of Eshott, stabbed to death with a stake Agnes, daughter of Richard of Woodham. She was caught and imprisoned at Newcastle, but managed to escape into the liberty of Tynemouth. Wood in some form was in fact the commonest weapon in cases of killing, presumably because it was the instrument most readily to hand; but the knife, which almost everyone would carry, was frequently mentioned.

In contrast to the seventy-two cases of unlawful killing, only four cases of suicide were recorded, two women and two men, one of whom was the master of the Hospital of St Mary in Westgate in Newcastle. Both women hanged themselves. In one instance, that of Eda the wife of a Lucker man, the body was found by her son who cut her down, laid her on her bed and proclaimed to their neighbours that she had died of natural causes. Both he and his father, who colluded with this attempt at deception, were found guilty of concealing a felony, which of course entailed loss of goods which, in the case of the other female suicide, Beatrix of Roddam, who hanged herself in the tower at Newton on the Moor, were valued at £1 7s. 5d.

There were in addition fifty-five accidental deaths. These were supposed to be reported to the coroner before burial, rendering those who failed to do so liable to amercement. He or she finding and dutifully reporting such a death was specifically exonerated of any blame by the court. Of these deaths, a clear majority (thirty) were by drowning. This was sometimes a straightforward matter as in the case of Adam Bateman who was thrown from his horse while crossing the Till and subsequently found drowned by his daughter, Ada. More complicated was the case of three men loading stones on to a boat in Alnmouth harbour. Unfortunately, they did so carelessly so that it sank, and only one succeeded in swimming to shore. An even greater tragedy occurred at Alnmouth when a ship carrying twenty-six men tried but failed to make port in a violent storm which overwhelmed the vessel with the loss of twelve lives.

Other cases were tragic because of the youth of the victims. A seven-year-old, Nicholas the son of Michael, was killed instantly when run over by a cart at Ponteland, while another boy of the same age, William son of Adam of Lamesley, was scalded when a tub of boiling water overturned and died four days later. Working with animals also carried risks. Alexander Carter was gored by a cow at Fowberry and died after eight days, while a girl called Matilda was killed by a kick in the stomach by a horse. Finally, like guns today, bows could cause lethal accidents, as when Peter of Colwell in shooting at a dove managed to kill Uhtred the smith of Beuclay instead. Peter ran for his life, but later secured a pardon and permission to return home.

There were eleven cases of rape, attempted rape and alleged rape. In one instance the attempt had fatal consequences: Alice, the daughter of a man called Ivo of the dene, was attacked by Richard son of Gamel in the fields at Langley; in resisting his attentions she stabbed him with a small knife so that he died within the month. Her plea of self-defence was not entirely acceptable, and as a result her father had to pay £2 'for the king's peace'. In another case a married woman, Sywyna, the wife of John *le pater* of Pigdon, accused Ralph the messor (hayward) but was unable to find enough support for her case. Consequently, she was sent to prison in Newcastle, but managed to escape across the river into the bishop of Durham's liberty. False accusation could be used as revenge, as when Emma, the daughter of Dionisius of Weetwood, claimed that Thomas Pudding of Lilburn had tied her up and then raped her. He was found not guilty when it emerged that while working for William of Lilburn he had had occasion to drive sheep belonging to Emma's father off his master's land, and that the accusation of rape was then fabricated by Emma and her brother, Adam. Another case, however, apparently and hopefully had a happier ending. Jordan son of Robert, accused of raping a girl called Edith in Bradford (near Bamburgh), denied the charge, was found not guilty and subsequently secured the court's permission to marry the girl.

Only two cases of arson were recorded. One appears to have been a family tragedy, the cause of which was not noted. The culprit was John son of William Tod who killed three women: his wife, Helewysia; Tinnock the wife of a neighbour, Robert of Lilburn; and an unnamed female servant. He then set fire to the house, presumably to destroy the evidence, and fled; but he was caught and hanged. The other case was clearly one of revenge: a certain Adam of Paxton ejected one of his neifs named Gilemin, who came back the following night and set fire to the house.

Theft was very common, twenty-five burglaries and sixty-five robberies being recorded. The former crime, by definition, involved house-breaking, and in virtually all cases the burglars remained undetected. A rare exception was the attack on the house of William the miller of North Middleton who was wounded and the other members of his household tied up. In the course of the struggle, however, he managed to kill one of the intruders, John Payrecourt, whose chattels, worth only 2s., were automatically confiscated by the sheriff. John's identity being revealed, suspicion fell upon his known associates, Philip Payrecourt (presumably a close relation) and William of Foulden, who, doubtless with justification, fled and were declared outlaws.

Robbery, the more common crime, had several consequences. John of Errington, captured at Barrasford on suspicion of having committed a robbery in Hexham, was hanged on the spot. On the other hand, Roger Godman of Elrington, who was known to have stolen a cow, was detained by his community but allowed to escape, for which they were amerced £4 13s. 4d. by the sheriff. Another prisoner, Alan Grete of Thornton, was not so lucky. Accused of stealing two oxen, he was imprisoned at Newcastle where he died. In contrast, Simon of Pinchbeck, who stole some cloth at Morpeth, found sanctuary in North Gosforth chapel and was allowed to abjure the realm. Occasionally, those accused of theft asked for trial. The case of Nicholas *de Crawell*, Robert Loveles, Henry the Scot, Waldo *de Bremton*, Simon Jagg of Doxford, Costrick *de Brompdon* and Robert Joy is interesting in that the jury brought together from four neighbouring villages found five of the men innocent, but Nicholas guilty of stealing four sheep and Robert Joy of stealing a horse. Both were hanged, the Crown benefiting to the tune of £2, the value of their chattels.

This was a relatively small sum, but in total the eyre produced, as the Crown quite definitely intended and expected, a considerable financial return amounting to over £556. This was made up of four elements:

amercements (pecuniary punishments); fines (payments made for the court's permission to end a suit); deodands (literally gifts to god, that is, the value of any object that had caused accidental death which should have gone to charity); and the value of the chattels of convicted criminals.

The eyre of 1256 and its predecessors and successors dealt with local matters locally, but there were cases of national political importance which were moved to the central courts at Westminster. One such, in 1415, sprang from a variety of causes: the widespread discontent with the Lancastrian usurpation of 1399; the belief that Richard II was still alive and living in Scotland; the presence in England (as prisoners) of the Scottish king, James I, and Murdoch, earl of Fife who had been captured at Humbleton Hill in 1402 (he was the heir of Robert, duke of Albany, the ruler of Scotland during James I's captivity); and Lollardy, the radical religious movement hostile to the church establishment and its wealth. At the centre of this incident was a Yorkshire gentleman, Henry Talbot of Easington in Craven, who seems to have been one of a number of Lollards in touch with a group of Scottish nobles. He was also involved in the ambush and seizure of Murdoch of Fife as he was being taken north to negotiate his ransom. Murdoch was soon recaptured and the ransom negotiation fell through, but Talbot continued to make trouble by trying to foment rebellion in various parts of Northumberland in favour of the alleged Richard II. He clearly failed to do so, however, and was captured.

His case was eventually dealt with in 1417. The facts of the matter were established by means of inquests, that concerning his Northumbrian activities being held in Newcastle in April 1417 before the king's justices, Ralph Neville, earl of Westmorland, Richard Norton and James Strangeways. The following month Talbot was examined before the king. He admitted his part in the Murdoch incident, but denied that his intentions were treasonable. In answer to the second charge, that of conspiring with the Scots to overthrow Henry V in favour of 'Richard II', he was unable to make a coherent response: all he could say was that what he had done was for the best 'as God wills because God knows it'. Having repeated this several times, he was returned to the Tower, but brought back four days later for formal trial. He pleaded not guilty to the charge of treason, and claimed that at his earlier examination he was so terrified that he did not know what he was saying. However, he was unable to produce any significant defences and was found guilty and executed.

Military Service

Law and taxation could and did affect both men and women, but military service was exclusive to males. Throughout the period all men between the ages of sixteen and sixty bore the obligation of turning out to fight in defence of the country. Such a system was unlikely to produce a force of high military quality, and consequently armies were largely raised by other means. In the twelfth and thirteenth centuries fighting in the field was dominated by heavily armed cavalry, raised from those tenants of the Crown owing military service who produced either their quota of knights or cash in lieu (known as scutage from the Latin scutum = shield).

From the late thirteenth century, however, infantry became steadily more important with the development of the long bow, which was effective against even the most heavily armoured troops, and the demand for foot soldiers increased as war between England and her neighbours, Wales, Scotland and France, became almost continuous. Consequently, the Crown looked to this ancient obligation to provide enough archers to meet its requirements. Thus, in February 1339 Gilbert Umfraville, Henry Percy and Ralph Neville were commissioned to array the fighting strength of Northumberland and from it produce a force of 500 archers (half of them mounted) as well as 70 men at arms (heavy cavalry).

This method, however, did not prove entirely satisfactory, and increasingly royal armies were raised by contract: the king contracted professional captains to raise and lead agreed numbers of troops of various sorts at set wages for a specified length of time. Nevertheless, from time to time men were arrayed to establish the size of the reservoir of military capacity. The musters held in the spring of 1538 and 1539 give a good idea of how the business was organised and what it revealed.

In the former year records have survived of musters held on Abberwick Moor by Sir Cuthbert Radcliffe (constable of Alnwick castle), Robert Collingwood and Robert Lowes, on Coldmartin Heath and at Mitford by Sir Ralph Ellerker and Lionel Grey, and on Fleetham Moor by Sir William Eure (captain of Berwick) and John Horsley (captain of Bamburgh). What they had to discover was the number of men capable of military service, and who of them were 'able with horse and harness'. This phrase was not defined, but it is reasonable to assume that, in addition to a suitable horse, the men in this category had a sword and a spear and adequate protective gear for head and body.

In all, these musters involved 154 settlements and were attended by 3,355 men, of whom only 1,220 or thirty-six per cent were considered adequately equipped. The following spring a large muster was held (where was not recorded) in Tynedale ward by Sir Reynold Carnaby, Sir John Fenwick and John Swinburne. The men, who came from 97 settlements numbered 2,841, of whom 1,740 or sixty-one per cent were classified as satisfactory. A closer look at the figures reveals that military preparedness was markedly greater in the western upland parts of the county than in the coastal lowlands. The clear majority of able men in 1539 was due to the presence of 392 men described as 'North Tynedale thieves', while the 185 able men from Redesdale at the Abberwick muster of 1538 turned what would have been a minority into a majority. Even if these very distinctive districts are ignored, the east-west contrast is still obvious: in 1539 the small hamlets of Stocksfield, Ridley, Hindley, Broomley, Fotherley, Cronkley, Healey and Slaley produced 41 men all 'able with horse and harness'; in contrast in the previous year only 27 of the 423 mustered on Fleetham Moor from sixteen places in Bamburgh and Embleton parishes were so described, and half of them were the retinue of John Horsley. Even closer to the Border, in the townships of Wark on Tweed, Carham, Mindrum and Learmouth, under a quarter of the 186 fit men were equipped to fight. Clearly, social and well as security factors were at work.

Inadequacy was not the case in Newcastle, however, where the muster was held on 27th March 1538, probably at Shieldfield, under the supervision of the mayor (Thomas Bewick), the sheriff (George Selby) and the six aldermen (Henry Anderson, Thomas Baxter, Robert Brandling, Thomas Horsley, James Lawson and Gilbert Middleton) who were assisted by the two constables from the twenty-four wards into which the town was divided, each ward being responsible for manning one of the eighteen wall towers and six gates. At this muster the equipment brought by each man was noted. Being townsmen, Novocastrians were foot soldiers, and it is clear that each was expected to furnish himself with a sallet (a light helmet) and a jack (a thick leather coat) for protection, and to be armed with a halberd, a bill or a bow. Some of the better-off had acquired superior protective gear such as steel bonnets and plate armour, while a Thomas Cromer had provided his servant with a 'hand gowne'.

In all 806 men were classed as 'able' and a further 64 sailors and 8 artificers (5 of whom were shipwrights) promised to become so. There were, however, 249 men, twenty-two per cent of the total, who had nothing or an incomplete accoutrement, and who were deemed too poor to afford it.

Local Officers

The effectiveness of government was to a considerable extent dependent on the efforts of its county-based officers and organisation. In this respect Northumberland was distinctively different in several ways from most other English counties.

Wards. Well before the Conquest the midland and southern counties of England were divided into hundreds or wapentakes, the latter word (meaning weapon take) being adopted in those counties that had been subject to heavy Norse or Danish settlement. These districts were not only for administrative purposes, but had a judicial function: there, every male over the age of twelve was required to belong to a tithing, a group of ten whose members were mutually responsible for each other's conduct. These arrangements were inspected twice annually by the sheriff (the occasions were known as the sheriff's tourn or the view of frankpledge), who used the opportunity to deal with petty crime and prepare more serious cases for the king's justices.

This system did not obtain in Northumberland. Never a county until late

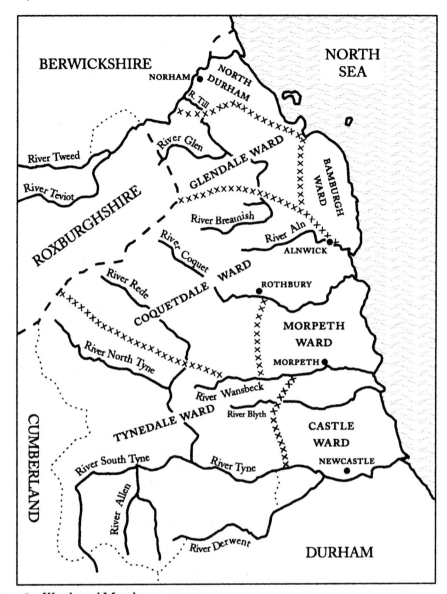

18: *Wards and Marches*

EAST MARCH: North Durham and Glendale and Bamburgh Wards
MIDDLE MARCH: Castle, Morpeth, Tynedale and Coquetdale Wards

in the eleventh century, like Cumberland, Westmorland and Durham it did
not acquire hundreds of wapentakes (the exception was the small enclave in
southern Durham where Danish settlement had occurred, known as the
wapentake of Sadberge). Instead, Northumberland was divided for
administrative purposes into two halves, north and south of the Coquet,
each in the charge of a king's reeve based respectively in Bamburgh and
Corbridge. Early in the twelfth century these were replaced by a single

officer, the sheriff. Although the bipartite division continued to be used, at some stage before the end of the thirteenth century the county was divided into districts known as wards. As we have seen, the subsidy records of 1296 and 1336 show the existence of eight and five wards respectively, perhaps indicating that the scheme was still fluid. In the end, however, the county had six wards: Castle, Morpeth and Tynedale roughly south of the Coquet; and Coquetdale, Glendale and Bamburgh roughly north of that river. Unlike hundreds and wapentakes, however, wards were solely for administration, not for legal purposes.

Sheriff. The sheriff was the king's chief officer in each county. In the twelfth century the role was performed by powerful men who held office for many years. For example, Northumberland's sheriff between 1170 and 1185 was the Yorkshire baron, Roger de Stuteville. During the next century, however, it came to be the norm for sheriffs to be drawn from county families of knightly status. This development was related to the process known as 'distraint of knighthood', whereby any man with land worth more than £20 a year was required under financial penalty to become a knight. The Crown had various reasons for taking this line, the chief among them being the need to expand and maintain a body of local men of sufficient substance to undertake the ever-growing amount of local administration. Legislation by Edward III and Richard II laid down that no-one should serve as sheriff for more than one consecutive year, and should not be reappointed in under three years. This clearly helped to limit the sheriff's power, which in any case was being steadily eroded by the increasing use of itinerant justices, local justices of the peace and special investigatory commissions. The sheriff did not disappear, however. He continued to occupy his high position as titular head of the county, as well as being required to organise the work of the county court and the visiting justices, and to deliver writs and summonses, arrest and hold suspects and collect fines, amercements and deodands; and he was appointed to many of the commissions set up to deal with specific problems.

Indeed, men who served as sheriff usually performed many other roles in local government. One such was Sir Thomas Grey of Heaton, who was sheriff in 1408/9. He was the son of Sir Thomas Grey who was MP in 1393 and 1397 and who died in November 1400. The younger Grey was born in November 1384 and was thus in his mid-twenties when he served as sheriff. He was also for many years a justice of the peace, constable of Bamburgh castle from 1404, and commissioner of array in 1410. In 1415, however, he achieved national notoriety by joining the conspiracy to murder Henry V at Southampton as he prepared to invade France, and to replace him with his cousin, Edmund, earl of March. The plot was masterminded by Richard, earl of Cambridge, to whose daughter, Isabel, Grey's son, Thomas, was betrothed (at the age of seven) in 1412. Grey, together with Cambridge and Lord Scrope of Masham, was executed on 2 August 1415, an incident portrayed by Shakespeare in Act II, Scene II of *Henry V*.

Coroner. The office of coroner was created in 1194 and was intended to be part of the eyre system. Coroners were local men, elected in the county court, who were to be responsible for investigating, by means of inquests of local juries, all cases of sudden or accidental death.

The history of the office in Northumberland is distinctive in that initially coroners were hereditary; not until after 1246 were they elected in the county court. Thereafter, the county had four coroners, two north and two south of the Coquet. Northumberland's coroners were also distinctive in that, in addition to sudden death, they also investigated all other felonies and cases of wreck and treasure trove, elsewhere dealt with by the sheriff. The reason for this enlarged role was the absence of the sheriff's tourn. The records of their activity were presented to the king's justices for scrutiny and confirmation. An extant record shows William Hedwin, one of the southern coroners, holding an inquest in January 1357 into fifteen thefts of animals in Tynedale ward that had occurred since 1348. In the later fourteenth and fifteenth centuries the coroner's role declined in importance.

Escheator. One reason for this was the development of the role of the escheator. The Crown was always keen on its right to repossess the estates of its deceased tenants, which from the late thirteenth century were investigated by inquests *post mortem* to determine their annual value and the person and age of the legal heir. If that person were under age, he or she became a royal ward until they attained their majority; in the meantime the estate was managed for the king's profit by his escheator. Like the coroners, these men were initially landowners below knightly rank, but as the office grew in importance and acquired functions previously performed by sheriffs and coroners, so the status of the holders grew. Thus the king's escheator between 1424 and 1426 was Sir John Middleton of Belsay, who had already served as an MP in 1414 and sheriff in 1423.

Justices of the Peace. Also of rising importance were the members of the peace commission. The beginnings of the system go back to the early fourteenth century, but it is the statute of 1361 which is regarded as the true foundation of what was increasingly the mainstay of English local government until modern times. Further legislation of 1390 imposed a maximum of eight justices per county, but by 1500, Northumberland had twenty-eight, a testimony to the ever-growing range of work the justices of the peace were required to undertake. Like all the other local offices, that of justice of the peace was filled by members of the county's gentry families.

FRANCHISAL GOVERNMENT

Royal administration did not directly or immediately affect the whole of Northumberland in that there were regalities, liberties or franchises where administration was the responsibility of other persons or institutions. It cannot be emphasised too strongly that these enclaves were not truly independent, and that their continued existence was conditional upon the goodwill of the Crown. Their essentially subordinate quality was made plain in many ways. The law they administered was that of England, which they had no power to alter; and although the Crown's officers were normally excluded, there were exceptions when the Crown so wished. For example, the Statute of Treasons of 1352 specifically overrode franchisal independence, which was also entirely absent in the matter of policy towards foreign states. Most significantly, perhaps, they automatically reverted to the Crown upon the death of their holders pending the acknowledgement or appointment of a successor; and on other occasions they were seized into the king's hands if they incurred royal displeasure. In all, there were six major liberties in Northumberland, each with its own history.

NORTH DURHAM

Pride of place must be given to North Durham since it was part of the largest and most complete English liberty, that of the bishops of Durham. This liberty comprised all County Durham as it was before 1974, the manor of Crayke in Yorkshire, and the parishes of Norham, Holy Island and Bedlington in Northumberland. The Durham part was not complete until 1189 when Bishop Hugh of le Puiset (1154-96) bought what was known as the wapentake of Sadberge from Richard I for 600 marks (£400). Before that the wapentake (which was made up of three separate areas of land along the north bank of the Tecs) was counted as part of Northumberland. This gives a clue to the origins of the franchise. Originally, the land between the Tees and the Tweed had been ruled by an earl with vice-regal powers. Robert de Mowbray had conceded to William of St Calais that the bishop should exercise these powers in the lands of St Cuthbert, and this arrangement was allowed to continue after 1095 when Mowbray was deposed by William II and the earldom went into abeyance. Thus, the bishop's powers were essentially those of the earls which he retained after the earldom was discontinued. However, the Crown was unlikely to have allowed this in the case of a layman, but there the powers were deemed to belong to St Cuthbert, a powerful and feared saint, whose guardian, trustee and champion the bishop was. To leave well alone, therefore, was good politics, especially as the Crown controlled the appointment of the bishops, and had the right at any time to retrieve what after all was royal authority in matters secular.

As the systems of royal administration and law enforcement developed, so they were adopted or imitated by the bishops, although not always with the king's instant approval. In the end the government of the palatinate or bishopric was a miniature, and for practical reasons, simpler version of that of the kingdom.

It was in this arrangement that the territories of Norham and Holy Island, which covered 61,000 acres and included thirty-two townships, and

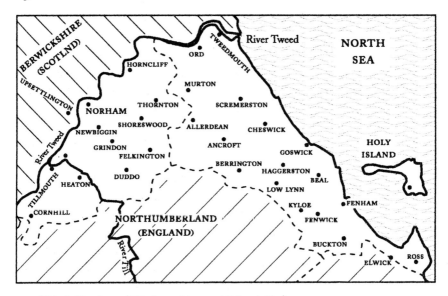

19: *North Durham (Norhamshire and Islandshire)*

which became known as North Durham, functioned (Bedlington, however, was treated for administrative purposes as a detached member of Chester Ward in Durham).

The focal point of the episcopal administration was Norham where Bishop Ranulf Flambard had built a castle in 1121 on the orders of Henry I. The bishop's chief officer was the sheriff of Norham, who was normally also the constable of Norham Castle. Little record of the administration of North Durham has survived, but it seems clear that by 1400 the bishop's ordinary revenues were collected by a receiver responsible to the bishop's exchequer in Durham, but that the revenues of estates of episcopal tenants in the bishop's hands through the minority of heirs or confiscation for misdemeanour were the responsibility of an episcopal escheator. By that date also North Durham had its own commission of the peace headed by the sheriff and including several leading tenants of the liberty, but not professional lawyers. These justices met between three and five times a year and dealt with matters civil and criminal. In virtually all matters, including most importantly taxation and the arraying of troops, the king's officers in Northumberland were excluded and the bishop's officers were deemed competent.

TYNEMOUTHSHIRE

The liberty of Tynemouth belonged to the abbey of St Albans but was administered through its cell at Tynemouth. It comprised twenty-eight townships or parts of townships, but unlike North Durham they were not contiguous but in four separate clusters. The largest of these was in the area between the rivers Tyne and Blyth and it included Tynemouth, North Shields, Preston, Murton, East Chirton, Balkwell (Middle Chirton), West

Chirton, Flatworth, Whitley and Monkseaton (in Tynemouth parish), Earsdon, Backworth and Seghill (in Earsdon chapelry) and Hartford, Cowpen and Bebside (in Horton chapelry). Further up the coast, in Warkworth parish, were Amble and Hauxley, and in the Tyne valley South Dissington, West Denton and Woolsington (in Newburn parish), Wylam and Welton (in Ovingham parish) and Elswick and Benwell (in Newcastle St John's chapelry). The fourth cluster was in far distant Eglingham parish: Eglingham, Old Bewick, New Bewick, East Lilburn, Wooperton and Harehope.

The liberty owed its existence to Earl Robert de Mowbray who in the mid-1080s reactivated the monastery at Tynemouth and handed it over to St Albans Abbey with an endowment comprising Tynemouth and Preston, Amble and Hauxley, over which the monks were to have comital authority. This was confirmed by William II when he repossessed the earldom in 1095: as at Durham he chose not to disturb Mowbray's arrangement, and possibly for the same reason, the presence of a powerful saint, in this case St Oswin. In the course of the twelfth century additional properties and rights were acquired, Henry I and his queen, Maud, being notably generous; and in 1189 the gains of the previous hundred years were confirmed in a comprehensive charter issued by Richard I.

Tynemouthshire was never a totally exclusive liberty. As we have seen, its inhabitants were liable to royal taxation, even though assessment and collection were self-administered. And they were liable for military service, although they formed a separate unit, which, alas, disgraced itself at Flodden in 1513 by running away at the first shot. Also, it was clearly understood that anyone not satisfied with justice in the court of the liberty could apply to the king for redress.

The administrative personnel comprised a bailiff, equivalent to the sheriff in the county, and a constable to command the castle. Both were appointed by the prior, but the coroner was elected in the court of the liberty, which met every three weeks and was attended by the free tenants. As the system of itinerant royal justices developed, Tynemouth was incorporated into it. When the king's justices approached, they were met at Gateshead (if coming from Durham) or Fourstones (if coming from Carlisle). There the prior proved his right to the liberty, appointed two men to be justices and asked the king's judges to name a third. The court then met, usually at Elswick, to hear the assizes and to deliver the gaol of the liberty, all profits going to the priory.

This all seems very impressive. In fact, the liberty appears to have ceased to function well before the dissolution of the priory. Consequently, it was never formally abolished; it simply ended with the house. The likely reasons for this failure to sustain a vigorous life were the dispersed nature of the liberty and distance between Tynemouth and St Albans.

HEXHAMSHIRE

Like North Durham and Tynemouthshire, Hexhamshire was a late eleventh-century creation in favour of an ecclesiastic, in this case the archbishop of York. Unlike Tynemouthshire, however, it was a single block of territory comprising the valuable land north of the Tyne as far as Erring Burn (the chapelry of St John Lee) and a much larger upland area south of the Tyne almost as far as the Nent (the chapelries of Whitley and Allendale). In all, it covered some 80,000 acres. Its origins can be traced to the grant of the secular lordship by the provost, Uhtred, to Archbishop Thomas I of York in 1071. It is almost certain that this grant included very extensive administrative powers, which were confirmed by Henry I. The Crown's officers were excluded and the archbishops had the right to deal with all legal matters, civil and criminal, and to keep all the profits of justice. The only rights retained by the Crown were taxation and the licensing of markets and fairs.

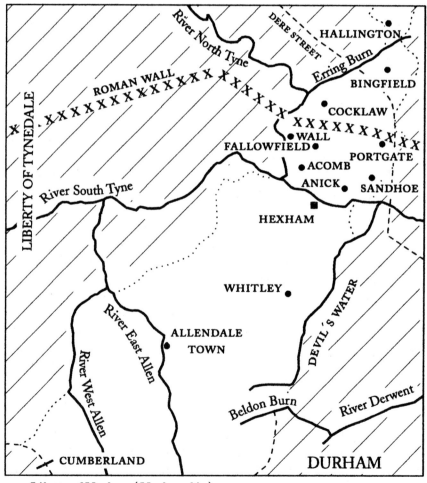

20: *Liberty of Hexham (Hexhamshire)*

For administrative purposes the shire was divided into six districts: the borough of Hexham, Newlands and Rowley Ward, and the grieveships of Acomb and Wall, Park and Forest, Allenton and Catton and West Allen and Keenley. The archbishop's chief executive officer was called the bailiff, but was in effect the sheriff. The court of the liberty was held twice a year when juries (usually fifteen strong) from each ward or grieveship presented suspects. As in the county, however, the main burden of law enforcement was gradually assumed by justices of the peace, of whom there were usually three, all local gentry.

In contrast to Tynemouthshire the liberty survived the dissolution and continued to function until 1572 when it was formally abolished by act of parliament. Thereafter, Hexhamshire was part of Northumberland, although ecclesiastically it continued to be in the diocese of York until 1837.

TYNEDALE

Tynedale was the largest liberty covering more than 200,000 acres in the valleys of the North Tyne, South Tyne and Allen. It was not quite so neat as its neighbour, Hexhamshire, in that the lands of Langley barony in Haltwhistle and Wardon parishes intruded. Unlike the three ecclesiastical liberties, it was of late origin, created by Henry II shortly after 1157 to compensate William, the younger brother of Malcolm IV of Scotland, for the loss of the earldom of Northumberland. Thereafter, until the death of Alexander III in 1286, it was administered by the Scots kings, although in accordance with English not Scottish law. Their powers were complete, except that they were denied the right to license markets and fairs or to grant permission to crenellate, the one being of commercial, the other of military, significance.

How the regality was administered, at least in its latter days, is clearly revealed in the record of the eyre conducted by four royal justices – Thomas Randolph, Simon Fraser, Hugh *de Peresby* and David of Torthorwald – in 1279 and 1280. The sessions were held at Wark on Tyne, the capital of the regality where the king of Scotland had a castle and a substantial demesne. As in the county, the chief executive of the regality was the sheriff, assisted by three coroners and two bailiffs, all of whom were drawn from the landowning class of the liberty. In addition to scrutinising the work of these men, the justices heard civil cases brought by plaintiffs and criminal cases presented by a jury of twelve men for the regality and separate juries, also twelve in size, for the borough of Haltwhistle and the 'new borough' (Newbrough).

In all fifty-four civil cases, almost all involving rights of ownership or occupancy of land, and involving forty-seven persons, were heard. Most notable was a series of issues between one of the leading landowners of the regality, William of Bellingham, who had recently served as sheriff, and

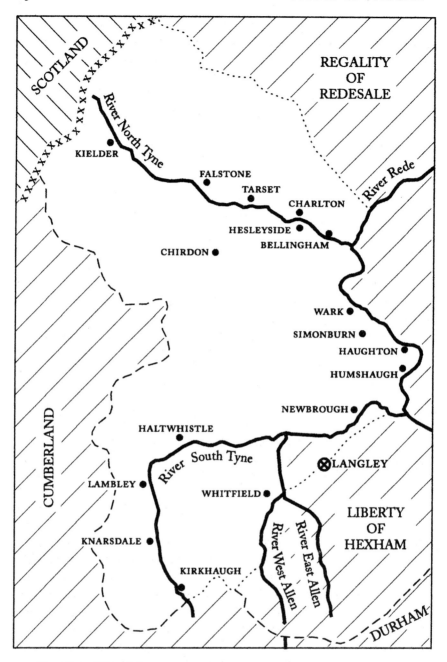

21: *Regality of Tynedale*

Nicholas of Plenderleith, the abbot of the Augustinian Canonry at Jedburgh. The trouble between them stemmed from the fact that they were neighbours: Bellingham was well established at Hesleyside, while Jedburgh had acquired property and pasture rights in Ealingham. The issues were varied: failure to maintain boundary hedges and ditches; failure to pay a certain rent in cash and flour; pasture rights in Ealingham common; and the failure of the abbot of Jedburgh to return a legal document to Bellingham. In the end the two parties came to a compromise: Bellingham agreed to maintain the hedges and ditches between Hesleyside and Ealingham and to give up his claim to the rent and to pasture rights in Ealingham common; and he also conceded the abbot's demand for pasture rights in Hesleyside common. In return, the abbot returned to Bellingham pasture rights in Bellingham, Wardlaw and Greenacres, which Bellingham's grandfather had given to Jedburgh. Who got the better of whom is not clear, but it is not difficult to suspect that Bellingham got what he was after from the start.

The pattern of criminal cases was broadly similar to that in the county in 1256. Of the eighty-seven cases dealt with, twenty-five were of unlawful killing and twenty-two of accidental death. In contrast to the county, burglaries (twenty-nine) far exceeded robberies (seven), but the numbers of suicides (three) and cases of arson (one) were equally few. Thirteen executions took place, eight by the axe and five by the rope; and one thief, caught stealing four geese at Newbrough, was punished, with the coroner's approval, by the amputation of an ear, said to be worth 1*d*. Again in some contrast to the county a relatively large number of people (fifty-two) elected to stand trial, and in all but four cases their faith was justified by not-guilty verdicts. On the other hand sixty-nine people, including six women, fled and were declared outlaws or waivers. In a few cases fear drove the innocent to run, as with John of Keepwick who, having accidentally killed Alan son of Gunn, took to his heels. The court declared him innocent, and allowed him to return; but he still lost his chattels for having fled.

Like the king of England, the king of Scotland found that justice filled the coffers, the total receipt for this eyre being in excess of £250. Of that sum, nearly forty per cent was derived from the chattels of convicted felons, and a further sixteen per cent from the amercement of those who purposely undervalued goods forfeit to the Crown. The remainder was made up of fines for permission to settle out of court and amercements for failing to pursue a prosecution, to appear in court and unjust detention of goods.

Shortly after the death of Alexander III the liberty came into the hands of the empire-building bishop of Durham, Antony Bek, who retained possession until his death in 1311, except for a brief period in 1307 and 1308 when it was confiscated by the Crown. After 1311 it passed rapidly through the hands of five people until about 1336 when it was acquired by Edward III's wife, Philippa. From her it descended to her fourth son,

Edmund, duke of York, and it remained in that family until it was merged with the Crown estate in 1484. It continued to be royal property until 1604 when James VI and I handed it over to one of his Scottish favourites, George Hume, who later became earl of Dunbar. On his death in 1611 it passed through his daughter to her husband, Lord Howard deWalden.

REDESDALE

Immediately to the north-east of Tynedale was the liberty of Redesdale comprising the parishes of Elsdon, Corsenside and Holystone, and part of Alwinton, and covering about 150,000 acres. If the origin of Tynedale is clear, that of Redesdale is not. Originally it was thought that the liberty was granted by William I to a Robert de Umfraville, known as Robert with the beard. The document recording this gift is a proven forgery, and the origins of the liberty probably lay in the early twelfth century. The earliest reference to Robert de Umfraville is in 1130, and he is known to have lived until about 1145. Henry I may therefore have granted Redesdale to him about the same time that he made him lord of Prudhoe; but Percy Hedley thought it possible that the Scottish Earl Henry was the grantor sometime after 1139, and given Umfraville's known friendship with Henry's father, David I, this is not implausible. Whatever the truth, the Umfraville family were in possession by 1158 when Henry II ordered Odinel de Umfraville to build the castle at Harbottle, which henceforth was the capital of the liberty.

Redesdale continued in the Umfraville family until the death of the last male Umfraville in 1436, when it was inherited by Sir Walter Tailboys, who traced his descent from Gilbert de Umfraville, earl of Angus, who died in 1381. The tenure of the Tailboys family lasted until 1541 when again failure to produce a male heir intervened. The new owner was Thomas Wynbyshe, who had married Elizabeth, the sister and sole heir of Robert, Lord Tailboys. She and her husband restored Redesdale to the Crown in return for lands in the West Midlands. Redesdale remained in royal hands until James VI and I gave it to George Home, together with neighbouring Tynedale.

NEWCASTLE UPON TYNE

The sixth franchise or liberty, Newcastle upon Tyne, is not normally classed as such, yet this is what in effect it was, in that like other liberties it was an area of land which was self-governing and from which the Crown's officers were normally excluded. The journey to this condition was, however, long and difficult.

The beginnings of Newcastle must be dated from the building of the castle by William I's son, Robert, above the site of the Roman bridge, *Pons Aelius*, in 1080. Assuming there was no significant settlement there at that time – and there is as yet no evidence that there was – the growth of the

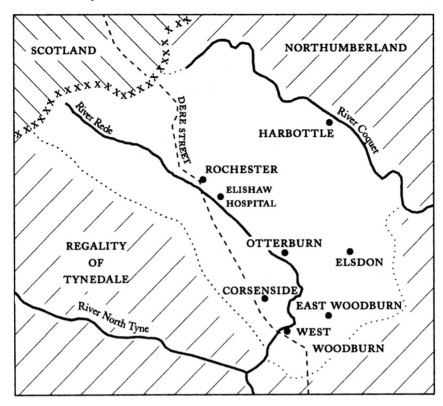

22: *Regality of Redesdale*

town was rapid. Although there is no substance in the claim that William II granted it borough status, it seems likely that his successor, Henry I, did. His grandson, Henry II, certainly did; and it is probable that he conceded to the burgesses the right to compound for the rents and dues they owed the Crown by a fixed annual payment known as the 'farm of the borough' payable at Michaelmas (the original meaning of the word farm was a fixed sum in lieu of variable dues, in effect, a lease). This we know from the negotiations between the burgesses and Henry II's grasping and unscrupulous son, John, between 1201 and 1216, one consequence of which was that what was called the 'ancient farm' was doubled to £100. In return, John conceded a number of privileges which diminished the influence of the sheriff of Northumberland in the town's affairs.

Nevertheless, the sheriff continued to be a powerful and threatening presence, and it was towards his removal that Newcastle, like other leading towns, constantly strove. But progress was slow. In 1251 the town acquired the right to elect a mayor as well as its four bailiffs, and in 1276 its own coroner. In 1318 the Crown conceded to the burgesses the right to hold their own court to deal with such matters as did not affect the Crown; and fifteen years later in 1333 Edward III decreed that the mayor should be the king's escheator in the town. Full emancipation came in 1400 when the town was elevated to county status. As a result, Newcastle had the right to elect its own sheriff who replaced the four bailiffs and who had full shieval powers, including the right to hold a monthly court and to answer direct to the king's exchequer for the monies he collected. The town also acquired the right to elect six aldermen (raised to ten in 1550), who with the mayor were to be justices of the peace for the borough. Newcastle was now entirely severed from Northumberland, and henceforth it would be a self-governing community. It was a measure of Newcastle's size, wealth and importance that it was only the fourth English town to be granted such a privileged status after London (c.1120), Bristol (1373) and York (1396).

Almost two hundred years later, in 1589, Queen Elizabeth granted (without charge) a charter whereby the mayor and burgesses became a corporation. The town had long acted as though it were a corporation, having and using a common seal and passing and enforcing byelaws. The charter legalised these practices, and in particular ensured that henceforth the town could corporately own, buy and sell property. At the same time the Crown handed over to the town the castle (except for the part used as the Northumberland county gaol and the Moot Hall) which for many years had been a refuge for criminals. The town was also promised the right to hold its own Admiralty Court to deal with such matters as piracy, wreck, and flotsam and jetsam upon the death or resignation of the then Lord High Admiral, Lord Howard of Effingham. This became effective upon Effingham's retirement in 1606.

Newcastle's civic liberties were made complete in 1600 when, for a fee of £635 10s. 0d, the queen granted to the borough what came to be known as the Great Charter which vested the government of the borough in a Common Council comprising the mayor, ten aldermen, the sheriff and twenty-four annually elected members. The electoral process was extremely convoluted and intentionally designed to ensure that political power was retained in the hands of the aldermen: although apparently democratic, Newcastle's government was narrowly oligarchic. The arrangements were in fact a variant of those formulated in the 1340s which were the consequence of a power struggle between the established Merchant Adventurers' Company comprising the Drapers (cloth merchants), Mercers and Boothmen (corn merchants) and the newer craft guilds: Bakers, Butchers, Cordwainers, Fullers, Saddlers, Skinners, Smiths, Tailors and Tanners. The arrangements agreed in 1342 gave all twelve organisations a role. However, the turbulent and violent politics of the town which resulted in the judicial murder in 1344 of one of its leading citizens and former mayor, John of Denton, forced Edward III to intervene. The outcome was a new and safer scheme in which the initiative in choosing the town's officers was given to the outgoing mayor and bailiffs. The 1342 constitution was restored in 1371, but was again modified in 1518 so as to shift political power more completely into the hands of the aldermen and former mayors and sheriffs.

The history of Newcastle's struggle for municipal independence demonstrates perhaps more clearly than that of other franchises the essential quality of the medieval liberty. Very obviously a liberty was a privilege conceded and defined by the Crown which could be, and was, suspended whenever the Crown felt that power had been abused. At the same time it reveals the usefulness of delegating the work of government, and also the wisdom of placating or indulging powerful men or institutions without, of course, allowing them true independence.

BORDER GOVERNMENT

In addition to normal royal and franchisal government, Northumberland experienced another layer of authority made necessary by its location on the frontier between two nations. The concept of the march as a frontier line and frontier zone was formalised in 1249 when a joint Anglo-Scottish commission perambulated the Border to establish an agreed boundary and gave recognition to the existence of March Laws. In fact the frontier had been long established and had been the subject of recent perambulations in 1222 and 1246; and the Laws governing cross-border homicide and theft were even older, originating in the twelfth century or even earlier.

The administration of these Laws and the handling of Border problems generally might well have remained part of the sheriff's duties had not war become endemic after 1296. The consequence was the emergence in the first third of the fourteenth century of two clearly defined marches, the West March covering Cumberland and Westmorland, and the East March covering Northumberland. In charge of each was a warden with a twofold responsibility. The more urgent was defence, for which he had the command of royal castles and the power to array troops. In between bouts of fighting he was charged with seeing that truces were observed on his side of the Border, and with arranging with his Scottish counterpart March Days when disputes between individuals of the two nations could be settled in accordance with the March Laws.

Initially, the wardens were temporary commissioners, but because of the almost constant warfare they became permanent officers in the middle decades of the century. The arrangements achieved a standard form in 1389. Thereafter a warden held a contract for a year or more to command the royal fortress (Berwick in the East March, Carlisle in the West March) and to defend the frontier in peace and war, at rates of pay specific to each condition. How many men he retained for this purpose was a matter of his judgement and discretion so that, in Robin Storey's succinct words, he had a licence 'to maintain a private army at the king's expense'. In time of war they also could command all castles and towers and could direct the civil officers of the Crown in matters of defence; and they had the right to appoint deputy wardens. They had to respect liberties, however, and to seek support and co-operation of the franchise holders.

The system established in the last quarter of the fourteenth century was the product of three factors. The first was the renewal of war in the late 1370s; the second was the evident failure of an attempt to make John of Gaunt, duke of Lancaster (Edward III's third surviving son and the uncle of the young Richard II), the king's lieutenant in the north, a role he found impossible to sustain because he lacked a sufficient power base in land and followers. The third factor was the political impossibility of ignoring or subordinating the Neville and Percy families. The Percy domination of Northumberland, already substantial, was underlined by the award of the title of earl of Northumberland in 1377; and their acquisition of the lands of the Lucy family based upon Cockermouth bade fair to make them equally powerful in the West March. To counter this, the Nevilles, already powerful in South Durham and the North Riding of Yorkshire, were given the estates formerly belonging to the Scottish kings around Penrith, and the title of earl of Westmorland.

As a result, from the late fourteenth century the West March was normally held by a Neville and the East March by a Percy. This arrangement lasted until the 1480s when first Richard III and then Henry VII took a major step towards establishing greater Crown control. Richard III, as duke of Gloucester, had been made warden of the West March by his brother, Edward IV, and he retained the post after becoming king. His successor, Henry VII, continued this policy, and added the wardenship of the East March in 1489 when the fourth earl of Northumberland was murdered, leaving an eleven-year-old heir. The work, of course, was done by deputies, but they had less power and much smaller rewards. In some respects this change was not as great as it seemed, since both Neville and Percy wardens were great magnates involved in national politics, and consequently they too were to a large extent absentees working through deputies. The crucial difference, of course, was that the deputies now answered to the Crown, not to a local magnate.

The policy of having a supremo on the Border was maintained for most of the next eighty years until the 1550s. Henry VII appointed his under-age sons, Arthur and then Henry, to be Warden-General. When the latter became Henry VIII, he used Thomas Howard, earl of Surrey, the victor of Flodden, and then his own illegitimate son, Henry Fitzroy. After a break between 1527 and 1542 the role was undertaken by Edward Seymour, duke of Somerset, and then by John Dudley, duke of Northumberland, the successive guardians of the young Edward VI. Although all of these men and boys worked through local deputies, the principle of Crown control was firmly established.

Also during this period the East March was split in two, the East March and the Middle March. The dividing line ran from the mouth of the Aln via Alnwick to Bewick and thence across country to the Border near The Cheviot. The effect was to assign the lowland district bordering the Tweed and the North Sea to the East March, and the upland areas of Redesdale and Tynedale to the Middle March. This division was made possible by Tynedale becoming part of the Crown estate in 1484, and Redesdale likewise in 1541.

During Elizabeth's reign the policy of having an overall commander or warden-general was discontinued, probably because it was no longer necessary. Throughout most of her reign the East March was in the hands of southerners, notably Francis Russell, earl of Bedford 1563-67, and Henry Carey, Lord Hunsdon, her cousin, 1568-96. In all that time the warden of the Middle March was Sir John Forster, a local man but one who had proved his commitment to the Crown's interest (and, it must be added, to his own) since the 1540s. When the office of warden was abolished after the accession of James I in 1603, the two posts east of the Pennines were held by Lord Hunsdon's sons, Sir Robert Carey in the Middle March and Sir John Carey in the East March.

During the reign of Henry VIII, Crown control was further extended by two other measures. In 1536 the Act for the Resumption of Franchises and Liberties effectively terminated the bishop of Durham's supreme authority: henceforth government was conducted in the king's name, not the bishop's, although in practice the administrative and legal machinery continued to function much as before. With Tynedale already in royal hands, Tynemouth moribund and Redesdale and Hexham shortly to be surrendered, the inconvenient and often inefficient franchises were at last removed. The following year saw the setting up of the King's Council in the North Parts, usually known as the Council of the North, which in effect was a regional government. Composed of roughly equal numbers of full-time professional legally-trained officials and part-time nobles and gentry, it was based at York but expected also to hold sessions at Hull, Durham and Newcastle. In fact, within twenty years it had ceased to be peripatetic, business going to it, not vice-versa. This influence was further reduced by its failure to secure the subordination of the wardens of the marches. This was the intention of the original scheme, but it was found that in defence matters the wardens needed to have direct access to the Crown. Nevertheless, the Council was there, and until its abolition by the Long Parliament in the 1640s it was a factor in Northumberland life.

If anyone alive in 1603 had looked back to the late fifteenth century and analysed the changes in the way Northumberland was governed, they would have instantly recognised a considerable extension of the direct power and influence of the English state and a corresponding reduction of local influences, a theme that we shall return to in the last chapter.

CHAPTER SIX

Northumberland and National Conflicts

Being part of England, Northumberland was bound to be influenced and affected to a greater or lesser extent by events of national importance. This chapter will attempt to examine the nature and extent of this involvement on five occasions between the early thirteenth century and the mid-seventeenth century. Although each was separate and had its own causes and personalities, one feature was broadly common to all: Northumberland was in northern England, which differed in many ways from the country south of the Trent, and within that region the centre of action was, or was in, Yorkshire. Consequently, the studies will reveal not only the impact of national events on Northumberland, but how that impact was affected by what happened around York.

MAGNA CARTA 1212–1216

Everyone knows that in June 1215 King John was forced by his rebellious barons to agree to the document known as Magna Carta; and it is commonly thought that his concessions were the foundation and embodiment of the liberties since enjoyed by English men and women. While it would be false and foolish to dismiss out of hand this idealistic view, it has to be recognised that the political reality of the time was harsher and more basic. John and his baronial opponents were far less concerned for political ideals or principles than with material self-interest.

Also not widely recognised is the extent to which the revolt against John was led by barons whose centres of power were in northern England. The hostility towards John of so many northern barons had its roots in the reign of this father, Henry II. Until the brief civil war in 1173 and 1174 between Henry and his eldest son northern England had been only lightly controlled by the Crown. In the four northern counties particularly royal control was virtually non-existent before 1100, and between 1135 and 1157 the area was dominated by the Scottish king, David I, as a result of the disturbed conditions during the reign of King Stephen. In the last quarter of the twelfth century, however, the pressure of English royal authority in the north began to increase, although to nothing like the extent to which it was to be applied by John.

There is no doubt that King John (1199–1216) was a highly intelligent man with a very considerable flair for administration. But he had two fatal flaws. In his dealings with men he was totally partial: those he favoured, he favoured fully; but those he considered his opponents, he treated harshly. There was no doubt as to who was 'in' and who was 'out'. Thus his policies and their implementation were therefore politically divisive. Allied to this was an obvious and self-assured cunning and cleverness which, combined with a willingness to be ruthless, engendered fear and mistrust.

What did John do to arouse such hostility in the north? It is worth noting that he was a frequent visitor, coming north of the Trent in all but four years of his reign. In doing so he acted in complete contrast to his predecessors, his brother, Richard II, and his father, Henry II; and through his visits he acquired the direct knowledge of men and situations which enabled him to act with confidence and certainty. More significant, however, was his introduction into important administrative posts of men of lower social origin and status. These were his creatures and worked for him, and, with his support or acquiescence, for their own advancement. Thus, the favours that the baronage had hitherto received, and expected to receive, now went into the hands (and pockets) of their inferiors: no longer were they granted the wardships of minors, the marriages of widows and heiresses, and the estates of churches during vacancies, but had to see men of lesser standing gain from these perks. In Northumberland, for example, Philip of Oldcotes, a man from a modest knightly family in north Nottinghamshire who had gained a reputation in Normandy, was made keeper of the estates of the bishopric of Durham following the death of Bishop Philip of Poitou in 1209, sheriff of Northumberland in 1212, and was granted the estates of Roger Bertram of Mitford, one of the rebels against John. With the income from these estates be could afford to build his own castle at Nafferton, which was not pulled down until after his death in 1221.

John not only denied the baronage their natural expectations, he virtually declared financial war on them. He amerced them heavily for every possible offence, charged them large sums for regaining his goodwill, imposed huge reliefs (the sums heirs were required to pay for the right to succeed to their fathers' estates and titles), and bought up their debts, particularly those to the Jews. This pressure increased markedly after 1204 when John was ejected from his French possessions in Normandy, Anjou and Maine. The issue on which baronial hostility came to focus was military service. They became increasingly reluctant to serve overseas, either in person with their quota of knights, or by paying scutage (money paid per knight in lieu of service). This was not the real issue, however. Behind the dispute were the years of harsh and hostile treatment in a wide range of matters in which the king had interpreted his rights vis-a-vis the barons in such extreme form as to deprive them of theirs.

Although the baronial opposition included men from all parts of northern England, John's most implacable enemy was a Northumbrian, Eustace de Vesci, lord of Alnwick, the largest of the county's baronies created between 1095 and 1135. Vesci also had large estates in Yorkshire around Malton, and it has been calculated that only thirty-eight per cent of his income derived from Northumberland while fifty-one per cent came from his lands in Yorkshire. This pattern of land holding was not uncommon so that it has been argued that the epicentre of the revolt was in the North Riding where many of the leading rebels had their chief estates. This said, however, the Vesci family had been established in Northumberland for three generations, and also had interests in Scotland as the result of Eustace's marriage to one of King William's illegitimate daughters.

Vesci was one of the leaders of the plot hatched in the summer of 1212 to murder John during the campaign against the Welsh, and perhaps offer the throne to Simon de Montfort (Montfort was the leader of the successful crusade by the French Crown against the heretics of Provence and the father of the famous Simon de Montfort who led the unsuccessful revolt against John's son, Henry III, in the 1260s). The plot became known, however, and Vesci fled to Scotland. Although the evidence is not conclusive, it points to the involvement of several other Northumbrian barons: Richard de Umfraville (Prudhoe and Redesdale), Roger de Merlay (Morpeth), Robert de Muschamp (Wooler) and Gilbert de la Val (Callerton). Vesci fled in August 1212, but by May 1213 he was back in England making his peace with the king. This very fact indicates the breadth and depth of the opposition and the underlying weakness of the king's position: had John felt stronger, he would have dealt harshly with Vesci.

The tensions between king and barons remained unresolved. What brought them to a head in open revolt was the defeat of John's continental allies by Philippe II of France at the battle of Bouvines in August 1214 which ruined any chance John had of recovering his French possessions. Had his continental scheme prospered, he would have been able to crush the opposition at home. Its failure was bound to give that opposition the encouragement it needed. The breaking point came at Easter 1215 when the king's leading opponents assembled in arms at Stamford; and after they had seized control of London in May, John had to capitulate.

Magna Carta did not bring peace but civil war. Like all such agreements, it was a compromise. To John it was totally unacceptable: he would never willingly accept permanent curtailment of his powers as king. On the other hand, to men like Vesci its terms were too moderate and did not sufficiently tie the king's hands. Consequently, there was a drift to war in which all the barons of Northumberland except two – Hugh de Balliol (Bywell) and Hugh de Bolbec (Styford) – were opposed to John and did homage to Alexander II of Scotland who crossed the Tweed in October 1215 to renew his claim to the earldom of Northumberland. This forced John to come north during the winter of 1215/16, and although he reduced the castles at Mitford, Morpeth and Prudhoe, he was unable to stay long enough to subjugate the area completely. In the spring of 1216 John was assailed on all sides. A French army commanded by Louis, the son of Philippe II, landed on the south coast at baronial invitation; while Alexander II of Scotland captured Carlisle and advanced across Stainmore. With him was Eustace de Vesci, who was killed in a skirmish outside Barnard Castle. He therefore did not live to see the end of John, who died a few months later of dysentery, leaving an under-age heir and the problem of restoring normality.

WARS OF THE ROSES 1455-1487

Thanks to William Shakespeare, the so-called Wars of the Roses (the earliest known use of the term was by Sir Walter Scott) are one of the best-known yet most misunderstood episodes in English history. In military terms the wars amounted to sixteen battles fought in eleven years between 1455 and 1487. Although there were links between the bouts of fighting, and the leading characters were involved in several incidents, each episode had its own causes and was not simply a continuation of its predecessor.

The first outbreak was short in time and small in scale. On 22nd May 1455 a brief scuffle involving a few hundred armed men took place in St. Albans ending with about fifty dead. It was the product of political tensions that had been building for almost twenty years, the underlying cause of which was the king, Henry VI, who had succeeded his father, Henry V, when only nine months old in 1422. Henry's personal rule began in 1437, and he very rapidly demonstrated his total inadequacy. The first consequence of his ineptitude was military: between 1437 and 1450 all of Henry V's French empire was lost, except for Calais and its immediate hinterland. This was a severe blow to national pride for which Henry was largely to blame. Not only did he have no interest in, or capacity for, war, he appointed poor commanders. Worse still, he even gave back Anjou and Maine to please his wife, Margaret, the fifteen-year-old daughter of Duke Réné of Anjou (and niece of the French king, Charles VII), whom he married, without a dowry, in 1444.

He proved equally incapable of handling domestic affairs, with the result that power fell into the hands firstly of William de la Pole, earl of Suffolk, and then after 1444 of Edmund Beaufort, duke of Somerset. Both men were exclusively concerned to promote their family interests, and so broke the cardinal rule of medieval kingship, namely, the need to maintain some sort of balance between the conflicting ambitions of the various contending and contentious families and family groups. It was a difficult task, but it could be done, given strength of character and a good degree of perception and subtlety. Not only did Henry lack these essential attributes, he allowed his minders to exclude from the king's council the most powerful English magnate, Richard, duke of York. York was descended from both the second and fourth sons of Edward III, was the richest man in the country, and until the birth of Henry's son, Edward, in 1453, the heir to the throne. By all custom, as well as common political sense, York was entitled to belong to the central policy-making body of the realm, and he knew it.

In the skirmish at St. Albans, York and his supporters killed the duke of Somerset and imposed themselves on the king. But at this point there was no question of replacing him; nor could they expect to control him indefinitely. In the following four years, the queen emerged as the leader of the court party. As she matured, Margaret developed into a woman of intelligence and determination, who after the birth of her son, Edward, had a cause to fight for.

As a result, the problems of York's exclusion and the partiality of the Crown continued. They were finally resolved in the years 1459-61 when in a nineteen-month period seven battles were fought, ending with that at Towton between Ferrybridge and Tadcaster in Yorkshire. On 28th and 29th March 1461, in one of the largest battles ever fought in Britain, the Yorkist army won a total victory in a blinding snowstorm. Henry VI became a deposed fugitive, and the Crown was placed on the head of Edward, earl of March, the son of York, who had been killed in battle near Wakefield late in the previous year.

The next bout of fighting took place between 1469 and 1471. Its underlying cause was the wealth, power and inordinate ambition of Richard Neville, earl of Warwick. Known as the kingmaker, Warwick was not content to be that, but sought and expected to be the power behind the throne, formulating and directing its policy. Edward IV was too strong a character to allow this, but he compounded his problem in May 1464 by secretly marrying Elizabeth Woodville, the daughter of a minor gentleman and widow of a Lancastrian knight, Sir John Grey. This was certainly an act of personal indulgence, but there may also have been political calculation: by favouring his wife's connections he would be able to build up a party dependent upon himself which would be a counterweight to the mighty Nevilles. It certainly alienated Warwick, whose rebellion five years later was initially successful, forcing Edward to flee abroad. There he managed to raise a small force and return to England where he attracted sufficient troops to defeat and kill Warwick at Barnet in April 1471.

The last of the Wars of the Roses, between 1485 and 1487, stemmed from Edward IV's premature death in 1483, leaving two under-age sons, Edward V and Richard, duke of York. This prompted Edward IV's younger brother, Richard, duke of Gloucester, to usurp the throne, an act that cannot be dismissed simply as the product of a warped and evil nature. Richard was in fact in a dire political situation: the boy king was in the hands of his mother's family, the Woodvilles, who controlled London and the organs of central government, and who would almost certainly seek to destroy him. The usurpation, therefore, was an understandable, although not entirely necessary, pre-emptive strike. What turned the political nation against Richard III was his excess. Not only did he murder his own nephews and erstwhile supporters like Lord Hastings, he was prepared to have acts of attainder passed against no fewer than one hundred opponents. No-one could feel safe, and consequently few chose to support him when Henry Tudor, earl of Richmond, the Lancastrian claimant, returned from exile in August 1485. Richard's defeat and death at Bosworth, which put Richmond on the throne as Henry VII, did not end the fighting. The final battle was fought in June 1487 on the banks of the Trent at Stoke in Nottinghamshire when a small and feeble force supporting Richard III's nephew, John de la Pole, earl of Lincoln, was routed and its leader killed.

How did Northumberland figure in these events? There are in fact two distinct questions. One concerns the role of the earls of Northumberland; the other relates to the fighting that took place in the county between 1461 and 1464 following Edward IV's victory at Towton. The brief answer to the first question is that the activities of the Percy family, although of major significance nationally, did not involve the county of their title. The importance of the Percies lay in their ongoing rivalry with the other great northern family, the Nevilles. Indeed, it can be shown that the outbreaks of warfare in 1455 and 1459 stemmed from this rivalry which developed a national dimension as the Nevilles joined forces with Richard of York and the Percies allied themselves to the Crown. In this rivalry two individuals were important: Neville power was clearly expanding under the thrustful leadership of Richard Neville, earl of Salisbury; while on the Percy side, the lead was taken by the second son of the second earl, Thomas Percy, Lord Egremont, a violent and hot-headed individual.

The stage on which the two families clashed was not Northumberland but Yorkshire, and to a lesser extent Cumberland. Although the Nevilles had acquired properties around Bywell and Styford in the late fourteenth and early fifteenth centuries, they had insufficient presence in Northumberland to loosen the Percy grip. In contrast, in Yorkshire the two families were evenly matched in wealth and possessions, which were closely interwoven. Neville power was concentrated around their castles at Richmond and Middleham, and Sheriff Hutton, between which lay the Percy properties around Topcliffe. Further south the Percies had a large block of land based upon Spofforth, between Harrogate and Wetherby, and substantial holdings further east around Pocklington and Leconfield, between which were the Neville estates in the Derwent valley near Stamford Bridge. It was in Yorkshire, therefore, that the rivalry was intense, although it extended into Cumberland where Lord Egremont built up a following and secured the election of his brother, William, as bishop of Carlisle.

When the two sides came to blows, however, it was in Yorkshire. On 24th August 1453 a force of over seven hundred armed men led by Egremont and one of his younger brothers waylaid the earl of Salisbury and his retinue at Heworth Moor near York. Until that point Salisbury's journey had been pleasant and profitable. He and his family were returning from Tattersall Castle in Lincolnshire after attending the wedding of his son, Thomas, and Maud Stanhope, widow of Robert, Lord Eresby, and heir of Tattersall's owner, Ralph, Lord Cromwell. Percy's anger was inflamed by this marriage because among Lord Cromwell's properties were two manors, Wressle in Yorkshire and Burwell in Lincolnshire, which had belonged to the first earl of Northumberland but were lost when he forfeited his title and estates for rebellion against Henry IV. Although the bulk of the estate had been restored to the second earl in 1416, Wressle and Burwell had been given to Lord Cromwell. Thus, by this marriage two Percy properties were destined shortly to end up in Neville hands. The clash was violent and bloody, but inconclusive, presumably because the two parties were evenly matched. Consequently, Neville reached the safety of Sheriff Hutton without damage to his family. The essentially Yorkshire nature of this incident is underlined by the fact that of Egremont's seven hundred men, all but fifty Cumbrians were from Yorkshire.

It was from this point that the Neville-York alliance developed and the Percies drew closer to the court. When the two enemies clashed again, it was with more serious consequence. At St Albans two years later, while York took care to see that the duke of Somerset died, Salisbury made sure that the earl of Northumberland did not survive. As was said by a contemporary commentator, when these two were dead, the fighting stopped: St Albans was not so much a battle as a disguised murder.

This pattern of allegiance continued. In 1461, Henry Percy, third earl of Northumberland (Lord Egremont's elder brother), was killed at Towton fighting for Henry VI. His son, also Henry, was captured and imprisoned in the Tower. In 1470, however, he was released and restored to his inheritance as the fourth earl when Edward IV fell out with Warwick. Edward's reward was Percy's neutrality when in March 1471 Edward landed on the Yorkshire coast in his bid to recover the throne. Had Percy remained true to his family's traditional Lancastrian attachment, he could easily have prevented Edward's progress through Yorkshire and into the Midlands. Sixteen years later at Bosworth the fourth earl again remained neutral, but this time with fatal consequences for the Yorkist cause. Summoned by Richard III, he turned up with his retainers; but he did not enter the battle. Had he done so, it is very likely that Richard III would have won and retained his throne.

From this brief survey it is clear that the Percy family at all stages played a crucial part in the political and military conflicts of these years. But it is equally clear that their concern was with their family's fortunes, not those of the Crown, and that the centre of their fortunes was in Yorkshire, not Northumberland.

This said, Northumberland was for three years the very heart of the conflict. On learning of the disaster at Towton, Queen Margaret fled from York with her husband and her son and with a number of loyal supporters, notably Henry Beaufort, duke of Somerset (son of Edmund Beaufort, killed at St Albans in 1455). They reached safety in Northumberland where the castles of Alnwick, Bamburgh and Dunstanburgh were held by friendly garrisons. Edward IV came after them, but after seeing to the execution of the earl of Wiltshire at Newcastle, left for the south in order to attend to his coronation, take control of the central government offices at Westminster and in the Tower, and to prepare to deal with a possible French invasion.

Once established in Northumberland, the queen negotiated Scottish help in return for surrendering Berwick and a promise to hand over Carlisle. Carlisle, however, was saved by a relieving force led by John, Lord Montague, the brother of the earl of Warwick, and a Lancastrian advance through Northumberland and as far as Brancepeth in Co. Durham failed to produce any reaction in favour of Henry VI. Scottish help, although of some use, was unlikely to be enough since in August 1460 the king, James II, had been killed besieging Roxburgh, leaving his widow, Mary of Guelders, to sustain as best she could a government on behalf of their eight year old son, James III. Margaret turned to France, where in July 1461 Charles VII had died and been succeeded by her cousin, Louis XI. Louis, however, was at this stage inclined to the Yorkist cause. Meanwhile, the castles at Alnwick, Bamburgh and Dunstanburgh were surrendered by their garrisons.

In 1462, however, Lancastrian fortunes revived. A second approach to Louis XI produced a positive result: in return for a promise to hand over Calais, Margaret acquired a small army of between two and six thousand men commanded by an old friend and able soldier, Pierre de Brézé. This force landed at Bamburgh in October and quickly retook all three major castles. The only setback was the wrecking of the queen's small fleet off Holy Island as it sailed north to allow Margaret and some of her troops to link up with the Scots.

Edward reacted quickly to this renewed threat. By early November he had collected sufficient troops and advanced north. At Durham, however, he was forced to retire to bed with measles, leaving the business of the campaign to be dealt with by the earl of Warwick. From his base at Warkworth, Warwick secured the conditional surrender of Dunstanburgh and Bamburgh on Christmas Eve. The commander of Dunstanburgh, Sir Ralph Percy (the third earl's younger brother) agreed to change sides, provided he was allowed to retain his post and also have command at Bamburgh, while the duke of Somerset agreed to do homage to Edward as the price of retaining his estates. The Alnwick garrison, however, held out until early in 1463 when a relief force came down from Scotland. Neither side dared risk a battle, and Warwick allowed the garrison to return to Scotland with its allies. Alnwick was then given a Yorkist garrison under the command of Sir John Astley, a Suffolk knight, with Sir Ralph Grey as his deputy.

All these arrangements were based upon false hopes. In March, Sir Ralph Percy changed sides again and admitted French and Scottish troops to Bamburgh and Dunstanburgh; and in the following month Grey made Astley a prisoner and handed over Alnwick to a Lancastrian commander, Lord Hungerford. Grey, the grandson of Sir Thomas Grey, the executed traitor of 1415, and a long-time Yorkist, was aggrieved as being passed over in favour of a man with no local standing. Two months later, in July, the Scots laid siege to Norham Castle. This brought the earl of Warwick to Northumberland yet again. He easily drove off the besiegers and then conducted a retaliatory raid into the Scottish lowlands. With this failure, Queen Margaret appears to have lost heart and returned to France, taking her son but abandoning her husband.

The rest of 1463 was taken up with diplomatic moves of considerable significance. Early in October Edward negotiated a year's truce with Louis XI, and in December a truce with the Scots to last until the following October. Both agreements included an important clause whereby the French and the Scottish governments promised to withdraw aid from the Lancastrians. Edward's one diplomatic failure was with the duke of Somerset, who in spite of many blandishments returned to his Lancastrian allegiance. Just before Christmas he slipped away from his estates in South Wales, and although spotted at Durham, managed to reach Bamburgh.

There he breathed new life into the Lancastrian cause, which had become dormant without Scottish support or the leadership of Queen Margaret. Early in 1464 he went on to the offensive, capturing the castles at Bywell, Prudhoe, Langley and Hexham in Tynedale, and thereby threatening Newcastle and cutting communications with Scotland. This last point was important in that a Scottish delegation was heading south to discuss the possibility of extending the truce. The situation was retrieved by Lord Montague. Coming north from York with a small retinue to meet the Scottish envoys at Norham, he narrowly missed being ambushed near Newcastle. He thereupon assembled a larger force numbering about 4,000 and advanced towards Norham. On 28th April he was intercepted by a Lancastrian army of about the same size led by the duke of Somerset, Sir Ralph Grey and Lord Hungerford at Hedgeley Moor six miles south of Wooler. The outcome was a Yorkist victory, in which Ralph Percy was killed, sufficiently conclusive to allow Montague to collect the Scottish envoys at Norham and return south to York unscathed.

The Lancastrian situation was now more desperate, but rather than wait to be attacked Somerset moved his forces into the Tyne valley, hoping to gain recruits and win a victory to retrieve the advantage lost at Hedgley Moor. Montague, however, did not give him time to develop this strategy. Collecting what forces he could, he left Newcastle on 14th May, advanced up the Tyne valley and found the Lancastrian army the following day drawn up on the banks of the Devil's Water near Linnels Bridge. The ensuing battle, in which again about 4,000 men were engaged on each side, was quickly over and ended in a complete rout of the Lancastrians. Somerset was captured and executed immediately; and a further thirty prominent Lancastrians met the same fate in the days that followed, including Sir William Tailboys, who was found hiding in a coal pit near Newcastle with £2000 of Henry VI's money which Montague used to pay his troops. Meanwhile, Henry VI escaped from Bywell Castle, probably before the battle, leaving behind his sword and crowned helmet. He was eventually captured in July at Clitheroe in Lancashire. The fight on 15th May came to be known as the battle of Hexham. This is curious if, as Dorothy Charlesworth believed, it took place at Swallowship Hill, which is on the eastern side of Devil's Water in Dilston. If it took place on the western bank, however, the title would be accurate.

There remained the task of reducing the castles at Alnwick, Dunstanburgh and Bamburgh, and for this siege guns were needed. Three were supplied by the royal army under the earl of Warwick which arrived too late for the fighting. Each gun had a name: 'London', 'Dijon' and, appropriately, 'Newcastle'. Alnwick and Dunstanburgh were surrendered without delay on 23rd and 24th July. Bamburgh, however, put up a resistance largely because its commander, Sir Ralph Grey, was excluded from all offers of pardon on account of his earlier betrayal. Consequently, the castle had to be stormed after a preliminary bombardment. Grey was captured and taken to Doncaster where he was tried and executed.

The campaign which saw the Crown change hands was now over. It is tempting to dismiss the events in Northumberland as a sideshow or mopping up operation. To do so, however, is to see certainty of outcome before the event. While Queen Margaret and others were active and the French and Scottish governments prepared to back them, the Lancastrian cause was not dead. And, as any reading of the Wars of the Roses makes evident, fortunes changed dramatically as the result of single battles. The Lancastrian forces in Northumberland had to be defeated, the castles captured and the Scots and French threats neutralised before Edward IV could claim to have truly won his kingdom.

PILGRIMAGE OF GRACE, 1536-1537

The uprising known as the Pilgrimage of Grace took place between the beginning of October 1536 and the end of February 1537. Initially it was a spontaneous protest against the ecclesiastical and doctrinal changes being imposed and proposed, taxation, and what was felt to be undue royal influence over parliament. It began at Louth in Lincolnshire and spread rapidly through the East and West Ridings of Yorkshire. At its height some 30,000 men were 'out', headed by Robert Aske, a pious lawyer from Aughton near Selby. The rebels dispersed early in December after a meeting at Doncaster when the king's representative, the duke of Norfolk, promised a general pardon and parliamentary consideration of their demands. Unfortunately, there was a renewed uprising in January 1537 in the East Riding led by Sir Francis Bigod, and also in Cumberland and Westmorland where the grievances were essentially economic, relating to such matters as land rents and the enclosure of common land. This second revolt gave the government an excuse to crack down on the northern counties and several hundred men were executed.

Clearly this brief account suggests a complete lack of Northumbrian involvement. However, the earl of Northumberland and his family were engaged, and they used the opportunity to deal with a situation in Northumberland caused by a family problem. The problem was in fact the sixth earl himself, who had succeeded to his inheritance in 1527. Even at this point he was a pathetic and rather tragic figure. He appears to have suffered from ill-health most of his life as the result of a disease or condition which killed him at the early age of thirty-five. On top of this he had a reputation for being incompetent. Certainly his father, the fifth earl, considered him so, describing him as 'a thriftless waster', and writing to him complaining that 'of thy natural inclination thou art disposed to be wasteful and prodigal and to consume all that thy progenitors have with great travail gathered together and kept with honour'.

This opinion was shared by Cardinal Wolsey, who refused to allow him to attend his father's funeral in 1527, and considered him unfit to take charge of his inheritance, even though he was twenty-five years old. And Wolsey knew him well since he had been brought up in the cardinal's household. Also, Wolsey had been responsible for forcing Percy to break his privately contracted engagement to Anne Boleyn (who had aroused the king's interest) in 1524, and for arranging his marriage to Mary Talbot, the daughter of the earl of Shrewsbury. The evidence clearly indicates that certainly Percy and probably Anne had a genuine attachment and positively wished to marry. What is indisputable is strong mutual antipathy between Percy and Mary; their marriage was a disaster and ended in separation.

From the outset the new earl proceeded to live up (or rather down) to the low opinion of his elders, although whether his actions were the consequence of the incompetence they discerned, or of some deliberate and perverse decision on his part, is not fully clear. What is entirely evident, however, is that between his accession in 1527 and his death in 1537 he divested himself (and thereby his successors) of his entire estate. The process had two aspects. One was the earl's dealings with the Crown, which culminated in two extraordinary agreements in 1536 and early 1537. By the former he made the king his heir; but a few months later this was replaced by an agreement to hand over immediately what was left of his estates in Yorkshire, Cumberland and Northumberland to the Crown in return for an annual pension of £1,000. Earlier he had handed over most of his southern and midland properties to discharge a debt of over £10,000. Some of this he had inherited from his father, but the bulk of it was the result of his agreeing, unwisely, indeed recklessly, to underwrite a loan of £8,000 from the Crown to an Italian financier, Antonio Bonvisi, who defaulted. But, although substantial, this debt was not large enough to warrant the complete disposal of property. There is as yet no fully satisfactory explanation of the earl's bizarre behaviour; but ill-health, a disastrous marriage, lack of children and family discord all may have contributed. The Crown, if surprised, was not unhappy. It was only too pleased that an act of self-destruction got rid of a powerful magnate family who traditionally commanded strong regional loyalty.

The other aspect was the earl's gifts or favourable leases of land to a number of favourites. The most notable of these was Sir Reynold Carnaby, whose father was the lord of Halton near Corbridge where his family had become established in the late fourteenth century. Between 1530 and 1535 Reynold obtained a number of beneficial grants, including a ninety-nine year lease of the fish weir at Ovingham, reckoned to be worth £60 to £80 a year, at an annual rent of £3 6s 8d, the demesne at Langley and the manor of Corbridge. He was also given the Percy properties in Kent, which he promptly sold to the king's minister, Thomas Cromwell, and used the proceeds to buy other properties in Northumberland. Carnaby also secured favours for his brothers: Cuthbert was appointed to the posts of earl's receiver in Northumberland and constable of Warkworth Castle, both excellent opportunities for personal enrichment; while Lionel was granted the manor of Byker. Reynold Carnaby was a man on the make who supported royal policy towards the monasteries and was rewarded with Hexham Abbey and some of its properties.

These two events, the earl's disposal of his estate and the Yorkshire uprising, became entangled. Throughout the rebellion the earl refused to leave Wressle (which the Percies had managed to recover), and in spite of urgent pleas, declined to give his support to it. This may have been due in part to genuine opposition to the rebels' conservative programme, and perhaps to a sense of loyalty to the Crown; but what also must be taken into account was that he was seriously ill (the symptoms were a bloated stomach and yellow skin) and in fact had less than a year to live.

In contrast, his two younger brothers were very much involved. The elder, Sir Thomas Percy, was conservative in religion and aggressive in temperament; and he had a huge sense of grievance arising from the king's refusal to recognise him as his brother's heir, which in law he was. Not surprisingly he became one of the leading figures of the revolt and was among those eventually executed at Tyburn. The younger of the two, Sir Ingram Percy, was more involved with Northumberland, where he was the earl's vice-warden of the East March and constable of Alnwick castle.

Both brothers were convinced that the author of their troubles was Sir Reynold Carnaby, who, according to Sir Thomas, 'hathe beyn the destruction of all our blude, for by his means the kyng shall be my lorde's heyr'. This was an over-simple analysis of what was happening, but it does convey the depth of animosity felt by the effective head of a proud and long-dominant clan towards an upstart gentleman who was advancing his own fortunes at his expense. The upshot was a conference held at Alnwick Castle on 22nd October 1536 attended by most of the county's leading gentry. The ostensible purpose was to rally support for Aske's programme. The real reason, however, was to organise a campaign of persecution of the Carnabies. This was effective enough to force Reynold to take refuge with Sir Ralph Ellerker in Chillingham Castle.

The end of the rebellion, with the execution of Thomas Percy and the imprisonment of Ingram, did not bring relief to the Carnabies. The feud against them was pursued with great vigour by Sir John Heron of Chipchase, who also feared their growing influence in Tynedale and resented Reynold's appointment as Keeper of Tynedale. Heron systematically used his influence in the dale to ensure that Reynold was a failure, even to the extent of having him kidnapped and then arranging his release, and bringing in thugs from Liddesdale to assault the Carnabies at Stagshaw Fair. The tactic worked: in 1539 Reynold Carnaby was replaced by John Heron as Keeper of Tynedale.

THE RISING OF THE NORTHERN EARLS 1569-1570

The revolt was not unlike that of 1536-37 in that it was a hostile reaction in the north to the policies and acts of central government. It was also similar in that the part played by Northumberland was, at least at first glance, peripheral rather than central. The earls in questions were Charles Neville, sixth earl of Westmorland, and Thomas Percy, seventh earl of Northumberland, the son of Sir Thomas Percy executed in 1537. What prompted them to rebel was a complex of pressures, social, regional and national. Regionally, both were feeling excluded as the result of the new policy directions taken by Elizabeth, who had become queen in 1558. Under her sister, Mary (1553-58), they had been in favour, but now they felt increasingly rejected. The fifth earl of Westmorland's father had been Lord Lieutenant of Durham, but when he died in 1564 the sixth earl was passed over in favour of Sir George Bowes of Streatlam, a man of lesser wealth and lower social standing. Similarly, Mary had restored Thomas Percy to his title and estates and to the wardenship of the East March. Elizabeth allowed him to retain office, but hedged him about with so many restraints that he felt compelled to resign, which almost certainly was the intention. His replacement was a southerner, Lord Grey of Wilton, who, to add insult to injury, was offered Alnwick castle as his residence without reference to the earl. Both men came to believe that Elizabeth had adopted her father's policy of diminishing the power and authority of northern magnates whenever possible.

They were also alienated by Elizabeth's decision to abandon Roman Catholicism in favour of a mild but national form of Protestantism, and here it must be remembered that the Elizabethan Settlement was very recent and by no means certain to survive. The political situation was equally uncertain. The court seethed with rumour and intrigue, particularly directed at the queen's chief adviser, Sir William Cecil (shortly to be Lord Burghley). But the more potent source of trouble was Mary, the ex-queen of Scotland who had been deposed and imprisoned in July 1567 but had escaped to England in May the following year. To those of extreme Catholic views she had more right to the English throne than Elizabeth, while to others she was Elizabeth's obvious successor. Among the many schemes was one for her to marry Thomas Howard, fourth duke of Norfolk, the richest peer in England and by blood very close to the throne.

Closer to home both earls were under pressure from family and followers. Northumberland's wife Anne, the daughter to Henry Somerset, earl of Worcester, was a devout Catholic who strongly influenced her husband's religious outlook. The countess of Westmorland, Jane, daughter of the earl of Surrey the poet who was executed for treason in 1547, was equally conservative in religion, but a much more fiery and determined character than her husband or the countess of Northumberland. Also influential in the Neville circle were the earl's uncle Christopher Neville, and a number of Durham gentry, notably John Swinburne and Robert Tempest. Percy too was surrounded by positive characters, particularly two Yorkshiremen, Thomas Markenfield and Richard Norton. The latter was remarkable in that he was over seventy years old, having been born in 1498; had taken part in the Pilgrimage of Grace; and had eleven sons, nine of whom were to join him in rebellion. All of these people were hot for rebellion since all of them deeply resented the religious and political shifts of the new reign. And their pressure was not easy to resist: leaders they might be, but within the social structure in which they lived the two earls could not lightly ignore the strongly held views and wishes of their clientage.

Rebellion was planned for October, and in preparation the duke of Norfolk left court without permission for his East Anglian estates in September. However, he lost his nerve, and returned to court having urged his northern associates not to go through with the uprising. This threw the northern earls into confusion, particularly as they were aware that they were not trusted by the queen: several times they had defied her summons to come to court, fearing arrest. In the end it was the Crown that triggered the rebellion. In the second week in November, the President of the Council of the North (Thomas Radcliffe, earl of Sussex), who earlier had been convinced of the earl's loyalty, responded to the queen's command and attempted to arrest the earl of Northumberland at Topcliffe. The earl managed to escape, literally by the back door, and hastened to join his fellow earl at Brancepeth. The next day a conference was held which revealed the inadequacy of the rebels. No clear aim or plan of action emerged, and the most sensible suggestions (raising more troops in Northumberland and a dash to seize Mary of Scotland at Tutbury) by the earl of Northumberland were rejected. Instead the rebels indulged their prejudices by marching the four miles to Durham where they destroyed the new service books and celebrated mass in the cathedral, and paraded St. Cuthbert's banner around Palace Green. Having had an enjoyable and satisfying day out, they returned to Brancepeth. In the days that followed they progressed southwards through the North Riding gathering recruits, often, however, only by offers of pay and promises of plunder. Finally, on 22nd November they arrived at Bramham Moor near Wetherby.

At this point they decided to turn back, probably because they had become aware of a royal army gathering in the Midlands, but also because they had failed to rouse other important northerners such as the earls of Derby and Cumberland and the Dacre family. Back in County Durham, they spent several days forcing Sir George Bowes to surrender Barnard Castle. They also seized Hartlepool in the forlorn hope that Spanish troops of the duke of Alva's army in the Netherlands would be sent to their aid. Finally, after a brief skirmish near Chester le Street with loyal forces from Northumberland the earls disbanded their army which in any case was disintegrating as the result of bad weather and lack of food and pay. The two earls then made their way up the Tyne valley and into Scotland, where they met entirely different fates. Westmorland was sheltered by Lord Home who arranged for his passage to the Spanish Netherlands where he was to live out his days as an exile. Northumberland, however, fell in with the notorious Armstrong clan, who handed him over to the Scottish government which eventually sold him to the English government in August 1572. Elizabeth at once had him tried and executed.

Meanwhile, there was a brief secondary revolt in Cumberland organised by Leonard Dacre, who had been trapped in London pursuing a case in the high court during the earlier uprising. His revolt led to the only real battle of the whole rebellion: his force of about three to four hundred men was defeated on 20th February 1570 on the banks of the Gelt Burn west of his castle at Naworth.

From start to finish the rebellion was blunder. It was unplanned and without any strategic aim or tactical plan. The two leaders were probably not wholehearted and most of their followers were hot heads. For the

Neville family it was a complete disaster. The earl of Westmorland never returned and the Neville estate was permanently forfeited. The Percies were luckier. The titles and estates were restored to the earl's brother, but on condition that he lived on their Sussex property at Petworth.

When the details of the uprising are examined, it becomes clear that the large majority of those taking part were from north Yorkshire and south Durham. Although precise numbers are not available it seems likely that at least four thousand men followed the two earls of whom fifty-six per cent were Yorkshiremen and forty per cent from Durham. The Northumberland contingent was only one hundred and forty, a mere four per cent of the total. Moreover, they appear to have come from the south-west corner of the county. A map, showing signs of hasty preparation, has survived, apparently identifying those townships from which the rebels came. It includes ninety-five places in Northumberland, all but twenty-four of which were between the Tyne and Derwent. If this evidence is accurate it suggests that the bulk of Northumbrians who took part were from the Neville properties around Bywell and Styford, and not from the Percy estate. Moreover, of the numerous gentry who rebelled, only thirteen were from Northumberland, and none was of any importance.

Why was the Northumberland contribution so small and restricted, given the leadership of the earl of Northumberland and the dominant position of the Percies in the county? Ideological difference can almost certainly be dismissed. The evidence suggests that there were marginally more Catholics in Durham than Northumberland, but not enough to be significant. What Durham had experienced, which Northumberland had not, was the aggressive Protestantism and estate management of both the bishop and the dean and chapter of the cathedral which had caused resentment and opposition and which may have pushed some Dunelmians into the rebel camp. More significant, however, was the rebels' own failure to march into Northumberland to arouse support, and also the presence in the county of three men prepared to sustain the loyalist position.

The most notable, although not the most active, of these was the earl's brother, Sir Henry Percy, who was Deputy Warden of the East March and Governor of Norham and Tynemouth Castles. His loyalty almost certainly was tactical, and it was definitely given a nudge by the queen who promised 'the continuance of such a house in the person and blood of so faithful a servant as she expects to find him'. Nicely put, and it worked: Sir Henry remained loyal and the Percy tenants stayed at home. He got his reward, of course: after his brother's execution he became the eighth earl, a position he enjoyed for sixteen years until 1584 when he committed suicide under suspicion of being involved in the Throgmorton Plot against the queen's life.

More important was Sir John Forster, the Warden of the Middle March, who had been a stalwart on the Border since the 1540s and was to remain so until the last decade of the century. Throughout a very long career he never wavered as the Crown's man, other than to feather his own nest. The third man was the Warden of the East March, Henry Hunsdon, Lord Carey, who was the queen's cousin, his mother being Anne Boleyn's sister, Mary.

Between them these men commanded a force of over a thousand troops, enough to hold Northumberland, skirmish with the earls in north Durham, and to deal with Dacre's uprising. It is therefore legitimate to argue that the part played by Northumberland was not as peripheral as it seemed. The very failure of Northumbrians to join the revolt in significant numbers, together with the steadfastness of the three loyalists, helped to ensure that the uprising was contained, which was an important contributory factor in its failure. The events also underline how central their Yorkshire properties were to Percy thinking. Again, as in 1536-37, the earl, the head of the house, was in Yorkshire, and Northumberland was left to his younger brother. In contrast, on this occasion, the earl was the rebel and the younger brother loyal. The significant fact, however, is that the family managed to survive.

THE CIVIL WARS, 1637-1651

Between 1637 and 1651 England, Scotland and Ireland were wracked by political disputes and prolonged bouts of warfare. The issues were fundamental: the extent of the king's prerogative power; the role of parliament in the constitution; religious doctrine; and church polity. In the end Charles I's opponents were victorious and ruled the country until 1660 when the monarchy was restored in the person of Charles II. During this period Northumberland, and particularly Newcastle, were heavily involved on two occasions.

The first was the direct consequence of the Scottish revolution which had been precipitated by Charles I's attempt in 1637 to impose his ecclesiastical and doctrinal beliefs on the Scottish church. The reaction in Scotland was violently hostile and resulted in the replacement of the previous constitutional and ecclesiastical arrangements with a structure in which the king was a virtually powerless figurehead: effective secular power was vested in the Estates (parliament); and at the head of the church was an elected General Assembly. Charles twice tried to raise an army to crush this revolt and enforce his will, but he failed ignominiously, in large part because of hostility in England to his style of government. On the second of these occasions in the summer of 1640 a Scottish army, which had been hurriedly but efficiently raised by experienced officers returning from service in Europe, invaded Northumberland. On 28th August a feeble royal force was scattered in a brief engagement at Newburn on Tyne, and on the following day the Scottish army occupied Newcastle, which had been hastily abandoned by the king's commander. At first the Scots were welcomed, partly because there were many of their fellow countrymen working in the coal trade around the town, but also because of resentment caused by the heavy-handed actions of the established church, notably by the vicar of Newcastle, Yeldard Alvey. The honeymoon did not last. The quartering of troops caused annoyance, as did the financial levies which Charles had been forced to agree to pay the expenses of the Scottish army. In the end, the Scots found their position untenable, and consequently they withdrew from Northumberland in the late summer of 1641, apparently without disorder.

With their departure life reverted to its previous normality until the following summer, when the differences between the king and his political opponents dissolved into war. Even before Charles had raised his standard at Nottingham in August, he sent William Cavendish, earl of Newcastle (he had adopted this title because his wife, Catherine, was the daughter of Cuthbert, Lord Ogle) to be the Governor of Newcastle. His arrival had an immediate effect: the town's defences were repaired; forts were created at Tynemouth and Shieldfield; and the government of the town was taken over by the mayor, Sir John Marley, who purged the corporation of his opponents. Newcastle was now firmly in royalist hands, if not totally royalist in sympathy.

The earl was also responsible for raising and commanding the king's Northern Army, in which there was a substantial Northumbrian presence. Nine of its sixty cavalry regiments appear to have been raised and largely if not entirely officered by Northumbrians. Sir Francis Carnaby of Langley's regiment, for example, included Reginald Carnaby of Halton as its Lt. Colonel, Majors Thomas Carnaby of Halton and Tristram Fenwick of Kenton, Captains Richard Carnaby, Ralph Carnaby of Chollerton, Thomas Fenwick of Prestwick, and John Sampson of Twizell, Lieutenant William Newton of Broomley and Cornet Edward Bell of Stannington. Very similar situations obtained in the regiments raised by Sir Francis Anderson of Jesmond, Sir Robert Clavering of Callaly, Sir John Fenwick of Wallington, Sir Edward Grey of Chillingham, George Heron of Chipchase, Sir John Marley of Newcastle, Sir Edward Widdrington of Cartington and Sir William Widdrington of Great Swinburn. In all, a hundred and thirteen Northumbrian cavalry officers can be positively identified. And the same was true in eleven foot regiments: ninety-three officers from the county in the regiments commanded by Charles Brandling of Alnwick, Sir Robert Clavering, Thomas Forster, Edward Grey, Sir Thomas Haggerston of Haggerston, Ralph Hepburn, Sir John Marley, Sir George Muschamp of Barmoor, Sir Thomas Riddell, Gilbert Swinhoe and Lord Widdrington.

It was this army that gained control of northern England for the king in the course of 1643. As so often in the past, the critical event took place in Yorkshire; in this case the earl's victory over the parliamentary forces led by Lord Fairfax and his son, Sir Thomas Fairfax, at Adwalton Moor on 30th June. The north was now under royalist control, except for the important port of Hull. Success in the north was matched by royalist victories in the west country at Lansdowne and Roundway Down which brought Charles I's fortunes to their highest point.

It was therefore in some state of desperation that the parliamentary leaders turned to the Scots, and in September they concluded the treaty known as the Solemn League and Covenant. The practical consequence of this agreement was that in January 1644 a Scottish army comprising 18,000 foot, 3,000 horse, 500 dragoons and an artillery train of 120 guns under the command of Alexander Leslie, earl of Leven, crossed the Tweed at Coldstream and entered Northumberland. Facing them was a totally inadequate force of about 5,000 men, of whom no more than half were properly armed, under Sir Thomas Glemham. Although he was a competent soldier, he had no option but to retreat towards Newcastle, hindering the Scottish advance by destroying bridges. Even in this he was not completely successful: at Felton the bridge over the Coquet remained intact thanks to local women who drove off the soldiers sent to demolish it. Glemham, however, managed to stay ahead of the Scots, whose advance in bad winter weather was ponderous and lacking dash and enterprise, and to reach Newcastle to augment the town forces raised by the mayor, Sir John Marley. They were joined by Cavendish, now marquis of Newcastle, on 2nd February. On hearing of the Scottish invasion he had made the decision to leave the bulk of his army at York, but to bring 5,000 foot and 300 horse to Newcastle. He arrived just in time: the following day the Scottish army appeared before the walls and immediately showed its potential by storming the fort at Shieldfield. To prevent them being of use to the enemy, Marley ordered the town's suburbs to be destroyed.

At this stage Leven had more urgent business than the reduction of Newcastle. Towards the end of February, having beaten off an attack by the small royalist cavalry until which had been posted upriver from Newcastle, he took the bulk of his army across the Tyne by the fords at Bywell, Ovingham and Eltringham. He then crossed the Derwent at Ebchester using a bridge made of trees and advanced towards the undefended town of Sunderland, which he entered on 4th March. To avoid being cut off, the marquis withdrew his small force into central Durham. Newcastle was now virtually surrounded, and to make matters worse the blockade of the mouth of the Tyne ordered by parliament early in 1643 to ruin the coal trade and so undermine the town's economy was becoming increasingly effective.

During the course of March a confused campaign was waged in County Durham. The Scots tightened the noose around Newcastle by capturing South Shields, and two inconclusive battles were fought near Chester le Street on the 20th and Hylton on the 24th. The following month, however, the marquis retreated back to York. His reason for doing so was the defeat of a royalist force at Selby which exposed York to a parliamentary threat. The marquis was once again besieged, but he was relieved by another royalist army under the command of Charles I's German nephew, Prince Rupert. At the same time the strength of the parliamentary forces was increased by the arrival of the Army of the Eastern Association under the earl of Manchester. On 2nd July the two sides clashed on Marston Moor, six miles west of York, where, thanks to the discipline of its cavalry commanded by Oliver Cromwell, the Anglo-Scottish army won a complete victory. Meanwhile in May and June the royalist position in Northumberland was temporarily improved by the activity of the marquis of Montrose. But he withdrew northwards to revive the king's fortunes in Scotland, leaving the way clear for a second Scottish force of 6,000 men under the command of the earl of Callander to reimpose parliamentary control. Newcastle's situation was in fact worse than ever since Callander's troops captured Gateshead, which meant that the town was more closely invested.

The siege of Newcastle began in earnest on 12th August when the earl of Leven with the main Scottish army returned from Yorkshire and established his camp at Elswick. The royalist situation was hopeless, and surrender would have been a logical and sensible course of action. Instead the decision was to fight on, and the man primarily responsible for this was the mayor, Sir John Marley, who was considered by his opponents to be 'atheistical and most desperately malignant'. The siege dragged on for two months. The walls were bombarded and mined, while the defenders returned cannon fire from guns mounted on the tower of St. Andrew's church and flooded any mines they discovered. Twice Leven offered terms but they were turned down on each occasion. Finally, a third offer of surrender on honourable terms was made on 14th October, but with an ultimatum that the town would be stormed if they were not accepted by 8.00 a.m. on 19th. Again Marley and his associates refused to capitulate, and as a result the attack went in at six or seven points where the walls had been breached by cannon fire or mining. The result was a foregone conclusion since Leven committed over 12,000 men against a defending force of no more than 2,000. Nevertheless, the fight lasted two hours and 1,000 Scotsmen and 500 Englishmen died. A few days later the castle and the fort at Tynemouth surrendered to bring the war in Northumberland to an end.

Scottish occupation, however, was to last another sixteen months until February 1647, and for nine of those months Charles I was resident in Newcastle. Following the conclusive defeats of his southern armies he surrendered to the Scottish army in May 1646. In the months that followed attempts were made to reach a constitutional settlement between the king and the parliamentary leaders, but these broke down as neither side was willing to make the necessary compromises. In the end, the Scots became tired of this stalemate and handed over the king to parliament in return for £200,000, half the money owed to them for their services in England.

With peace, however, came reprisals. To the victors those who had supported the king were 'malignants' who had to be punished. The most prominent royalists, especially those who were Roman Catholics, had their estates sequestered. The rest were allowed to compound, that is, to expiate their delinquency by money payments based upon the assessed value of their property. The history of this process is complex in that several schemes were devised and several organisations set up to implement them in the late 1640s and 1650s. Much more research is needed, but at present it is possible to identify over a hundred Northumbrians and Novocastrians who were made to suffer for their active support of the king's cause. Two examples will reveal something of the process and how it affected individual families.

Thomas Rutherford, who had been a lieutenant in Sir Charles Brandling's regiment of foot, was a member of an ancient but not very wealthy Roman Catholic family long established at Rudchester. It is said, although it seems scarcely credible, that his father, Gavin, had thirty children, nineteen of whom were killed in the war. What is certain is that Thomas was part of a well established catholic nexus: his mother was a Swinburne; two of his sisters married into the Grey and Errington families; and no fewer than seventeen of his relatives were listed as delinquents. Consequently, his estate was sequestered in 1650, although under the regulation then in operation, his wife Jane was allowed to retain a fifth for the support of herself and her children. As in most cases, the sequestration was complicated by previous and legally valid pre-war arrangements. In this case, a farm on the estate called Longbank was leased to a Robert Collingwood of Durham, while a man named John Sanderson was entitled to an annuity of £8. In 1653, the estate was bought by a Gilbert Crouch, who in effect was a trustee for the family and acted as such in many similar cases. Consequently, at the Restoration Rutherford recovered his property, but in 1688 he sold his estate to Sir Thomas Riddell, almost certainly because he had failed to recover financially from the events of the 1640s and '50s.

In contrast, James Ogle of Causey Park, a Protestant who had served as a major in Lord Widdrington's regiment of foot and been severely wounded at the storming of Newcastle, managed to survive in body and estate. His property, which included land at Causey Park, Earsdon, Foxholes and Burradon and the tithes of Longhorsley parish produced an annual income of just under £200, which was effectively reduced by £39 as the result of bequests and legacies of his father, Lancelot Ogle. In 1647 James was allowed to compound at a sixth of his estate's value, which was set at £1,944; he managed to discharge his fine of £324 in two annual instalments by October, 1649. Ogle resumed his military career after the Restoration, becoming an officer in the county militia regiment commanded by his former commanding officer, Lord Widdrington.

Unfortunately, he lived only until 1664, leaving a son, William, aged ten, as his heir. Although he had compounded successfully, he was still in debt at the time of his death. In his will he assigned his estate to two trustees, John Clarke of Newcastle and William Armourer of Middleton, for a period of ten years until his son's majority with instructions to pay off his debts.

Why did these and other men fight? Ultimately, the reasons were individual, each man being driven, rationally or emotionally, by particular pressures. One obvious common influence was religion, particularly among those who still adhered to the Roman Catholic church. The number in that category throughout England is difficult to determine, and estimates vary from forty to sixty thousand. What is clear, however, is that their distribution was uneven, and that Lancashire was the county with the greatest number and highest density. How many Northumbrian Catholics there were is also hard to say. Official surveys made around 1600 indicate the presence of about 170, not a particularly large number. However, in so many instances there is a noticeable absence of reference to spouse, children and (where appropriate) household servants, and consequently it is not unreasonable to believe that the real total was several times larger. What does stand out, however, is the uneven incidence of Catholicism. Some parishes (the parish was the unit of record) had none, while in Edlingham twenty-six names (fifteen per cent of the total) were recorded. In fact the parishes adjacent to Edlingham in the north-west parts of the county appear to have been more Catholic than other areas.

Also notable are those described as gentleman or esquire. The families mentioned include Collingwood, Radcliffe, Errington, Swinburne, Mitford, Gallon, Middleton, Rutherford, Fenwick, Lawson, Haggerston, Shafto, Grey and Hebburn, virtually all of whom were highly active in the royalist cause and whose names appear more than once among the officers of the king's northern army.

However, as the case of James Ogle proves, Protestants too took up arms in the king's cause. And, equally, there were men who were staunch in their support for parliament, although at present we know less about them. One very notable example was John Blakiston of Newcastle who was one of the Regicides, that is, one of the signatories of Charles I's death warrant; and in his case too religion appears to have been very influential. Blakiston had become strongly puritanical by the early 1640s, which was ironical considering that his father, Marmaduke Blakiston, was a canon of Durham Cathedral and one of the leading high churchmen of his day.

Blakiston entered the Newcastle commercial world in the 1620s and by 1640 he was sufficiently prominent in the town's affairs to be one of the three candidates in the elections for what became known as the Long Parliament. Initially defeated, he secured a seat when one of the successful candidates died almost immediately. At first he was very much in the shadow of his fellow member, Sir Henry Anderson, who was older and much more experienced and a member of one of Newcastle's most prominent families. But the positions were soon reversed. As the ideological divisions in the Commons became more pronounced and acrimonious, Anderson veered towards the royalist side and was eventually ejected. In contrast, Blakiston became more radical politically and consequently more active so that by 1644 he was serving on no fewer than forty-four Commons committees.

After the storming of Newcastle, however, but with the approval of the House, he devoted much more time to the town's affairs, becoming an alderman and serving as mayor in 1645-46. Clearly, he was the man to whom the leaders of the parliamentary party looked to ensure Newcastle's future loyalty. His last public act (he died in May 1649) was to participate in the trial of Charles I. He clearly did so wholeheartedly for he attended all the sessions, including the one that passed sentence, and his signing of the death warrant argues that he fully approved of the execution and that he was a committed republican.

Epilogue

In the Prologue I stated that the theme of this book was Northumberland as a county where conflict was close to being endemic, principally as a result of its Border location, and that this long phase could be said to have ended when the Scottish army evacuated the county in February 1647.

Life and therefore history, however, are not straightforward. Sixty-eight years after 1647 in the autumn of 1715 Northumberland became involved in the uprisings aimed at restoring the Stewart dynasty to the British throne in the person of James Edward, the Old Pretender to his opponents, James VIII and III to his followers.

Some seventy-seven Northumberland gentlemen went into rebellion, led by two of the county's noblemen, James Radcliffe, 3rd earl of Derwentwater and William, 4th Lord Widdrington, and one of its MPs, Thomas Forster of Adderstone. Almost half of them were Roman Catholics, but all seem to have been driven by a clear conviction that the Jacobite cause was just. The motives of the men who followed them, numbering about 230, are less certain since many were described as their servants.

Happily, there was no fighting in the county. The three hundred or so Northumbrians linked up with rebels from the Scottish borders and together they advanced into Lancashire, hoping to gain the support of the numerous Catholic gentry in that county. Their number was pitifully small, amounting to no more than 1,500 men. Consequently, after a brief resistance at Preston they were forced to surrender to government troops on 14th November.

For ten Northumbrian gentlemen the rebellion was fatal. Two (Edmund and John Ord of Weetwood) were killed in action, and three (William Clavering of Errington, George Gibson of Stonecroft and Edward Swinburne of Capheaton) died in prison. Five, however, were executed after trial: Radcliffe the leader, John Hunter, John Shafto of Thockrington and John (known as Mad Jack) Hall of Otterburn because they were Crown office holders (Hunter and Shafto were army officers and Hall was a justice of the peace), and, rather unluckily, George Collingwood of Eslington. Widdrington was fortunate to be reprieved, while Forster, who almost certainly would have been executed, escaped from Newgate, thanks to the boldness of his sister Dorothy, and fled to France.

As well as losing their lives, Radcliffe, Hall, Forster, Collingwood and Shafto lost their estates, as did Widdrington and six others. The Radcliffe properties went to swell the estate of Greenwich Hospital, while Eslington was sold (for £21,131) in 1719 to Sir Henry Liddell, Bart. of Ravensworth, a friend of William Cotesworth, the government's chief agent in Northumberland. The Liddells were a Newcastle family whose fortune derived from commerce (they were leading members of the Hostmen's Company), and their acquisition of Eslington may perhaps be seen as symbolising the replacement of physical violence by business acumen. If so, it is a suitable end to Northumberland's history as a country of conflict.

Glossary

ACOLYTE: the lowest order of clergy who assisted parish priests. From the Greek *acoluthus* = attendant

ADVOWSON: the right of presentation to an ecclesiastical benefice. The possessor of an advowson was known as the patron

AETHELING: from the Old English *aethel* = noble and *ingas* = belonging to. The term was applied to princes of the royal house

AMERCEMENT: a pecuniary punishment which today would be called a fine

ARRAY: the mustering of men of military age (16 to 60) on the Crown's order, usually on a county basis

ASSIZES: both edicts having the force of law and the courts for dealing with matters arising from them

ATTAINDER: declaring a person guilty of treason by an Act of Parliament and without a judicial trial

BAILEY: the courtyard of a castle

BARBICAN: a double-towered gateway of a castle or town

BARON: a tenant of the Crown with extensive judicial rights within his barony

BARTIZAN: the word simply means battlement, but it is usually applied to a projecting turret at the corner of a tower

BILL: a concave axe on a long haft

BONDMAN: a tenant of a bondland, usually 24 or 30 acres in size, held according to the custom of the manor, not the common law of England. In northern England the word did not imply serfdom

BROADCLOTH: the statute of 1482 defined a broadcloth as having a width of two yards to distinguish it from a 'streit' of one yard

BURGAGE: a plot of land so designated within a borough held by burgage tenure the chief characteristics of which were very low fixed rent and heritability. The owners of burgages were burgesses with full rights as citizens of the borough

BURSAR: a chief finance officer. From the Latin *bursa* = purse

CANON LAW: the word 'canon' derives from a Latin word for a straight measuring rod. Canon Law, the law of the church, was developed between the middle of the 12th century and the early 14th century under

189

the direction of the papacy

CARUCATE: a notional area of land, usually 120 acres, on which taxes or other charges were assessed. The word derives from the Latin *caruca* = plough, and in Scotland the anglicised 'ploughgate' was commonly used

CHALDRON: a measure of coal the size of which is not entirely certain in that it varied from place to place, notably between Newcastle and London, and from time to time. The Newcastle chaldron is reckoned to have been 53 cwt

CHARE: a narrow lane or wynd in a town. The use of the work is confined to the north east of England

COBLE: probably from the Welsh *ceubal* = skiff. The word was applied to small inshore fishing vessels

CONSISTORY: an ecclesiastical court administering canon (i.e. church) law

CORDWAINER: a shoemaker. The word derives from the Spanish city of Cordoba

CORONER: a Crown official elected in the county court and responsible for investigating sudden or accidental deaths

CRUCK: a means of roof support involving two pieces of curved timber resting on opposing walls and meeting above the centre line of a building. In North East England crucks were known as 'siles' and were always made or acquired in pairs

CURTAIN WALL: a wall, not bearing a roof, linking the towers and gates of a castle

DEACON: the third order of clergy (after bishop and priest). From the Latin *diaconus* = servant. Deacons were assistants to parish priests

DEMESNE: a French word derived from the Latin *dominium* = lordship. The demesne was that part of an estate or property retained by its owner in his or her hands and under his or her direct control

DEODAND: from the Latin *Deo dandum* = given to God. The value of the object causing an accidental death which was supposed to be given to charity

DOGGER: a word of Dutch or German origin applied to two-masted boats used in deep-sea fishing

DOWER: a third part of a dead man's estate awarded by law to his widow for her support during the remainder of her life. This right applied only to freehold land, that is, land subject to the rules of common law

DRENGAGE: a pre-Conquest form of tenure involving the performance of services concerned with estate management or hunting. Drengs and drengage tenure survived the Norman Conquest and settlement in many parts of northern England and southern Scotland

EARL: originally a powerful regional viceroy. Later, it was a title of honour below marquis and above viscount

EYRE: a French word deriving from the Latin *iter* = journey. Eyres were wide-ranging inspections of local government undertaken by small groups of royal justices with virtually unlimited powers of investigation and punishment

FIEF/FEE: from the Latin *feudum*, hence the word 'feudal'. It was applied to property, usually land, granted by one person to another in return for service, usually military service

FINE: from the Latin *finis* = end. A sum of money paid in court for permission to terminate a case. The word had no implication of punishment

FULLER: one who fulls cloth. Fulling was the beating of cloth to thicken it using fuller's earth (aluminium silicate) which cleaned it by dissolving the grease

GAOL DELIVERY: the process of trying all suspected criminals currently in a particular gaol or gaols

GLEBE: from the Latin *gleba* = clod of earth. It was the land with which a parish church was endowed; it belonged to the rector during his term of office

HOMAGE AND FEALTY: French words deriving from the Latin words for 'man' and 'faith'. They were applied to the public ceremonies whereby two men (the inferior known as the vassal, the superior as his lord) entered into a precise and formal relationship. The Lord normally granted his vassal a fief or fee, in return for which he required specific services and general loyalty

HOSTMEN: the hostmen were a group of Newcastle burgesses who acquired the monopoly of the coal trade of the Tyne. They emerged during the sixteenth century and were incorporated in 1600, agreeing to pay the Crown 1s. a chaldron for the privilege of monopoly

HUSBANDMAN: the word gradually replaced bondman from the later fourteenth century

HUSCARL: from the Old Norse *hus* = house and *karl* = servant. Huscarls were professional warriors forming the bodyguard of a king or nobleman

KEEL: from the Old English *ceol* = boat. Keels were about 40 feet in length and 16 feet in the beam, and were propelled by a single sail and/or two oars. They were capable of transporting 20 tons of coal downstream to colliers moored near the mouth of the Tyne. Each keel had a crew of three men and a boy. The keelmen emerged as a craft or fraternity during the sixteenth century

KEEP: the central defensive part of a castle. Some keeps were towers. Others were shells, that is, walled enclosures within which buildings were erected

KNIGHT: from the Old English *cniht* = boy. The earlier meaning was a fully-armed cavalry soldier. Later, knighthood was an honourable status which men of certain wealth were required to assume

LAND SALE/SEA SALE: collieries were, or came to be, of two types: small affairs catering for local needs (land sale); and much larger enterprises aimed at the export market (sea sale)

MARK: the sum of 13s 4d, that is two-thirds of a £. It was a currency of account, not a coin

MARRIAGE: the right of a guardian to marry an under-age heiress to whom he wished, or to sell that right

MERCHET: the sum of money paid by customary tenants (i.e. those who held by the custom of the manor) to the lord of the manor for permission for their daughters to marry. In effect, it was a fee for a marriage licence

MOTTE: a mound of earth on which a keep was built. Normally, a motte was created by excavating a deep circular ditch, although wherever possible use was made of a natural hillock

MULTURE: from the Latin *molitura* = grinding. It was a toll paid for having corn ground at a mill. It took the form of a specified fraction of the flour produced

MURAGE: from the Latin *murum* = wall. It was money collected, usually in the form of a toll on goods, for the building and repair of town walls

NEIF: the northern word for serf deriving from the Latin *nativus* = native, that is, one who may not move from his place of birth without permission. Neifs were, in effect, part of the stock of a manor

OXGANG: an eighth part of a carucate. In southern England the equivalent word was bovate from the Latin *bos* = ox

PONTAGE: identical to murage, except that its purpose was the construction and maintenance of a bridge. From the Latin *pons* = bridge

PROCURATIONS: sums of money paid to a church official by those under his jurisdiction in lieu of hospitality during official visits

REEVE: from the Old English *gerefa* (from which grieve also stems) = supervisor. In townships he was a member of the community elected annually by his fellows to be their overseer and spokesman

RELIEF: from the Latin *relevium*. It was the payment made by a feudal tenant for the right to inherit his father's property and obligations. It was paid at the same time as homage and fealty were performed

ROMANESQUE: the style of architecture (often inaccurately described as Norman) whose characteristic was the semi-circular arch. It gave way from the late twelfth century to the Gothic style with its elliptical arch

SCUTAGE: from the Latin *scutum* = shield. The sums of money paid by those who owed military service to the Crown in lieu of that service. The size of the sums was a matter of bitter dispute in the twelfth and thirteenth centuries

SERGEANT: two possible meanings. One was a tenant of the Crown who owed specified but non-military service in return for his land. The other meaning was a full-time farm foreman

SHERIFF: from the Old English words *scir* = shire and *gerefa* = reeve. The sheriff was the Crown's chief agent in each shire or county

SHIRE: the word applied in northern England and southern Scotland to an estate or district within six, twelve or twenty-four settlements grouped together for administrative purposes

SIKE: a northern English word meaning ditch. Sikes were essential for the draining of fields before the introduction of hollow tile drains in the 19th century

SOCAGE: a form of freehold land tenure involving small services and attendance at the landlord's court

TALLAGE: an arbitrary tax imposed by the Crown on its boroughs and demesne lands

THANE/THEIGN: a pre-Conquest land holder of a superior sort with extensive judicial rights and military responsibility

TITHE: from the Old English *teotha* = tenth. The fraction of income which everyone was required to pay to the rector of their parish church

TRONAGE: a tron was a pair of scales and tronage was the toll paid to weigh goods on the official scales of a borough

VISITATION: a canon law term to describe a formal inspection of a church or an ecclesiastical body

WARDSHIP: the right of the Crown or other feudal superior to hold and profit from the estate of an under-age heir of a vassal, or to grant or sell that right to a third party

WETHER: a castrated ram

YARE: a contraption set in a river bed to trap fish swimming upstream

Further Reading

Suggestions for 'Further Reading' must begin with a survey of those books which may be regarded as the foundations of the county's history: William Hutchinson, *A View of Northumberland* (1776); and Eneas Mackenzie, *An Historical, Topographical and Descriptive View of the County of Northumberland and parts of the County of Durham situated North of the River Tyne with Berwick upon Tweed*, first published (in two volumes) in 1811 but enlarged in 1825. Of greater importance, however, is Rev John Hodgson, *A History of Northumberland*, a work he conceived in three parts: Part I, General History; Part II, Topography and Local Antiquities; Part III, Records and Illustrative Documents. Hodgson did not live to write Part I, which was published in 1858 by J. Hodgson Hinde at the behest of the Newcastle upon Tyne Society of Antiquaries. But, between 1827 and 1840, he did write Part II comprising three massive volumes of topographical history, using as his framework the county's ancient parishes and their townships. His main concerns were the churches and their patrons and incumbents; and the land and the families who owned it. The three volumes were:

Part II, Vol. I (1820) – Elsdon, Corsenside, Kirkwhelpington, Kirkharle, Hartburn, Netherwitton, Bolam and Whalton

Part II, Vol. II (1832) – Meldon, Mitford, Longhorsley, Morpeth, Bothal, Ulgham, Woodhorn, Newbiggin, Widdrington, Horton, and Stannington

Part II, Vol. III (1840) – Corbridge, Alston, Kirkhaugh, Knaresdale, Lambley, Whitfield, Haltwhistle, Hayden, Newbrough and Wardon

In the 1850s and 1860s two further important contributions appeared:

Rev. James Raine, *The History and Antiquities of North Durham* (1852) – Norham, Holy Island and Bedlington

George Tate, *The History of the Borough, Castle and Barony of Alnwick* I (1866) and II (1868)

Parallel to these books on the county were two studies devoted to Newcastle upon Tyne:

J. Brand, *The History and Antiquities of the Town and County of Newcastle upon Tyne*, 2 vols (1789)

E. Mackenzie, *A Descriptive and Historical Account of the Town and County of Newcastle including the Borough of Gateshead* (1827)

There matters rested until May 1890 when the eminent historian, Thomas Hodgkin, forcefully pointed out the incompleteness of Northumberland's history. The upshot was the formation of the Northumberland County History Committee to supervise the publication of further volumes covering the hitherto neglected parts of the county. This proved to be a far greater task than the original members of the Committee expected, and it took almost fifty years to complete. Happily, however, by the outbreak of World War II, success was achieved with the publication of the fifteenth and final volume. The complete list is:

Vol. I   Edward Bateson (1893) – Bamburgh and Belford

Vol. II   Edward Bateson (1895) – Embleton, Ellingham, Howick, Long Houghton and Lesbury

Vol. III   Allen B. Hinds (1896) – Hexhamshire I

Vol. IV   J. Crawford Hodgson (1897) – Hexhamshire II, Chollerton, Kirkheaton, Thockrington

Vol. V   J. Crawford Hodgson (1899) – Warkworth, Shilbottle and Brainshaugh

Vol. VI   J. Crawford Hodgson (1902) – Bywell St. Peter, Bywell St. Andrew and Slaley

Vol. VII   J. Crawford Hodgson (1904) – Edlingham, Bolton, Felton, Long Framlington and Brinkburn

Vol. VIII   H. H. E. Craster (1907) – Tynemouth

Vol. IX   H. H. E. Craster (1909) – Earsdon and Horton

Vol. X   H. H. E. Craster (1914) – Corbridge

Vol. XI   Kenneth H. Vickers (1922) – Carham, Branxton, Kirknewton, Wooler and Ford

Vol. XII   Madeline Hope Dodds (1926) – Ovingham, Stamfordham and Ponteland

Vol. XIII   Madeline Hope Dodds (1930) – Heddon on the Wall, Newburn, Longbenton, Wallsend, Gosforth, Cramlington, Benwell, Elswick, Heaton, Byker, Fenham and Jesmond

Vol. XIV   Madeline Hope Dodds (1935) – Alnham, Chatton, Chillingham, Eglingham, Idlerton, Ingram, Whittingham, Lowick and Doddington

Vol. XV   Madeline Hope Dodds (1940) – Simonburn, Rothbury, Alwinton and Holystone

None of these volumes is less than 400 pages in length (and two exceed 600 pages), and all of them include a large amount of evidence drawn from local and national archives.

In addition to his topographical histories, John Hodgson published as Part III three volumes of records : Part III, Vol. I (1820); Part IV Vol. II (1828); Part III, Vol. III (1835). To these the Durham-based Surtees Society has added from time to time volumes devoted entirely or largely to Northumberland matters:

Vol. 46 (1864)   *The Black Book of Hexham*, ed. J. Raine

Vol. 66 (1876)   *Newminster Chartulary*, ed. J. T. Fowler

Vol. 88 (1891)   *Early Northumberland Assize Rolls*, ed. W. Page

Vol. 90 (1893)   *Brinkburn Chartulary*, ed. W. Page

Vol. 105 (1901)   *Records of the Newcastle Hostmen's Company*, ed. F. W. Dendy

Vol. 111 (1905)   *Royalist Compositions in Durham and Northumberland 1643-60*, ed. R. Welford

Vol. 117 (1909)   *Percy Chartulary*, ed. M. T. Martin

Vol. 134 (1921)   *Percy Bailiff's Rolls of the Fifteenth Century*, ed. J. C. Hodgson

Vol. 176 (1961)   *Northumberland Petitions*, ed. C. M. Fraser

Vol. 194 (1991)   *Northern Petitions*, ed. C. M. Fraser

Vol. 202 (1995)   *Newcastle Customs Accounts 1464-1509*, ed. J. F. Wade

Unfortunately, almost all the documents in these volumes are in untranslated Latin. In most cases, however, the editors' introductions are very helpful.

Complementing these large-scale undertakings are the articles published in learned reviews, three of which are of particular significance for Northumberland. The oldest and by far the most important of the three is *Archaeologia Aeliana*, published by the Newcastle upon Tyne Society of Antiquaries, which was founded in 1813. The first four volumes appeared intermittently in 1822, 1832, 1854 and 1855. Since 1857, however, publication has been annual, and the review is now in its fifth series with 152 volumes currently in print. Almost as venerable is the Berwickshire Naturalists Club, founded in 1839, whose annual review contains many articles on Northumberland. Of much more recent origin is *Northern History*, a review of the history of Northern England and the Scottish Borders published annually since 1966 by the Leeds University School of History.

The more specific suggestions for further reading are but a small fraction of the literature relating to Northumberland. One of these, however, must be singled out: Nikolaus Pevsner, *the Buildings of England: Northumberland*, 2nd edition with revisions by John Grundy, Grace McCombie, Peter Ryder and Humphrey Welfare (1992). This is an essential guide to all aspects of building and architecture throughout the county.

CHAPTER ONE

W. M. Aird, 'St. Cuthbert, the Scots and the Normans', in M. Chibnall (ed.), *Anglo-Norman Studies* 16 (1993)

C. H. Blair, 'The Early Castles of Northumberland', *Archaeologia Aeliana* (1944)

A. A. M. Duncan, *Scotland: The Making of the Kingdom* (1974). This provides the most useful introduction to the aims and ambitions of the Scottish kings south of the Tweed.

W. E. Kapelle, *The Norman Conquest of the North* (1979). Absolutely essential to any study of Northern England in the eleventh century.

L. Keen, 'The Umfravilles, The Castle and The Barony of Prudhoe', in R. A. Brown (ed.), *Anglo-Norman Studies* 5 (1982)

W. W. Scott, 'The March Laws Reconsidered', in A. Grant and K. J. Stringer (eds.), *Medieval Scotland : Crown, Lordship and Community* (1993)

M. Strickland, 'Securing the North: Invasion and the Strategy of Defence in Twelfth Century Anglo-Scottish Warfare', in M. Chibnall (ed.), *Anglo-Norman Studies* 12 (1989)

B. Wilkinson, 'Northumbrian Separatism in 1065 and 1066', *Bulletin of the John Rylands Library* (1939)

CHAPTER TWO

C. J. Bates, 'The Border Holds of Northumberland', *Archaeologia Aeliana* (1891). A very detailed study, although superseded in parts by the recent unpublished research of Philip Dixon.

J. M. W. Bean, 'The Percies' Acquisition of Alnwick', *Archaeologia Aeliana* (1954)

J. M. W. Bean, 'Henry IV and the Percies', *History* (1959)

G. McD. Fraser, *The Steel Bonnets* (1971). A popular and readable account of Border conflicts.

D. Hay, 'Booty in Border Warfare', *Transactions of the Dumfries and Galloway Natural History and Archaeological Society* (1954)

C. J. McNamee, 'William Wallace's Invasion of Northern England in 1297', *Northern History* (1990)

P. McNiven, 'The Scottish Policy of the Percies', *Bulletin of the John Rylands Library* (1980)

M. M. Meikle, 'A Godly Rogue: the career of Sir John Forster', *Northern History* (1992)

Sir Arthur Middleton, *Sir Gilbert de Middleton* (1918)

R. Nicholson: *Scotland: The Later Middle Ages* (1974)

R. Nicholson, 'The Siege of Berwick, 1333', *Scottish Historical Review* (1961)

M. C. Prestwich, *The Three Edwards* (1980). Includes a very useful chapter on Anglo-Scottish warfare in the fourteenth century.

R. Robson, *The Rise and Fall of the English Highland Clans* (1989). The most recent study of the Border problem in the sixteenth century.

J. Scammell, 'Robert I and the North of England', *English Historical Review* (1958). A most important article which explains Robert Bruce's strategy towards northern England.

D. W. L. Tough, *The Last Years of a Frontier* (1928). An old but still very useful study of the Border problem in the reign of Elizabeth I.

J. A. Tuck, 'Richard II and the Border Magnates', *Northern History* (1968)

J. A. Tuck, 'Northumbrian Society in the Fourteenth Century', *Northern History* (1971)

J. A. Tuck, 'War and Society in the Medieval North', *Northern History* (1985)

J. A. Tuck, 'The Emergence of a Northern Nobility', *Northern History* (1986). All four articles by Anthony Tuck are essential to an understanding of what happened in Northumberland in the fourteenth century.

S. J. Watts, *From Border to Middle Shire: Northumberland 1585-1625* (1975). An important study of Northumberland at the end of the medieval period.

M. Weiss, 'A Power in the North: the Percies in the Fifteenth Century', *Historical Journal* (1976)

CHAPTER THREE

J. B. Blake, 'Medieval Smuggling in the North East', *Archaeologia Aeliana* (1965)

J. B. Blake, 'The Medieval Coal Trade of North-East England', *Northern History* (1967)

R. A. Butlin, 'Enclosure and Improvement in Northumberland in the Sixteenth Century', *Archaeologia Aeliana* (1967)

R. A. Butlin, 'Rural Change in Northumberland 1600-1800', in A. D. M. Philips and B. J. Turton (eds.), *Environment, Man and Economic change* (1974)

P. Clack and P. J. Gosling, *Archaeology in the North* (1976). This survey includes important studies of Newcastle, Berwick and Morpeth.

M. R. G. Conzen, 'Alnwick, Northumberland', *Transactions of the Institute of British Geographers* (1960). A very important study and in many respects a model for future work on other towns.

J. C. Davies, 'Shipping and Trade in Newcastle 1294-1296', *Archaeologia Aeliana* (1953)

J. C. Davies, 'Wool Customs Accounts for Newcastle in the Reign of Edward I', *Archaeologia Aeliana* (1954)

B. Dietz, 'The North-East Coal Trade 1550-1750', *Northern History* (1986)

M. Ellison *et al*, 'Excavations at Newcastle Quayside: Waterfront Development at the Swirle', *Archaeologia Aeliana* (1993)

C. M. Fraser, 'Medieval Trading Restrictions in the North East', *Archaeologia Aeliana* (1961)

C. M. Fraser, 'The Pattern of Trade in North-East England 1265-1350', *Northern History* (1969)

G. Goodrick *et al*, 'Excavation at Newcastle Quayside: The Evolution of the Sandgate', *Archaeologia Aeliana* (1994)

J. Hatcher, *The History of the British Coal Industry*. The first of four volumes of a comprehensive history of the coal industry in Britain commissioned by British Coal. It includes much useful information on all aspects of mining in Northumberland.

B. Harbottle, 'The Town Wall of Newcastle upon Tyne: Consolidation and Excavation', *Archaeologia Aeliana* (1968)

B. Harbottle *et al*, 'The Medieval Town Defences of Newcastle upon Tyne: Excavation and Survey 1986-87', *Archaeologia Aeliana* (1989). Includes reference to many earlier studies.

M. G. Jarrett *et al*, 'The Deserted Medieval Village of West Whelpington, Northumberland', *Archaeologia Aeliana* (1987 and 1988). These articles supersede several earlier articles also published in *Archaeologia Aeliana*.

J. Nolan *et al*, 'The Town Wall, Newcastle upon Tyne: Excavations at Orchard Street and Croft Street 1987-89', *Archaeologia Aeliana* (1993)

C O'Brien *et al*, *The Origins of Newcastle Quayside* (1988)

C. O'Brien *et al*, 'Excavations at Newcastle Quayside: The Crown Court Site', *Archaeologia Aeliana* (1989)

J. C. Russell, *British Medieval Population* (1948). Although dated in many respects, this is still a very useful guide.

J. F. Wade, 'The Overseas Trade of Newcastle upon Tyne in the Later Middle Ages', *Northern History* (1994)

V. E. Watts, 'Some Northumbrian Fishery Names, *Transactions of the Architectural and Archaeological Society of Durham and Northumberland* (1982, 1986, 1988)

E. A. Wrigley and J. Schofield, *An Introduction to English Historical Demography from 16th to 19th Centuries* (1966). A work of seminal importance to the study of population after 1541.

CHAPTER FOUR

E. Bateson, 'Notes on a Journey from Oxford to Embleton and Back in 1464', *Archaeologia Aeliana* (1894)

G. W. D. Briggs, 'The Church of St. Andrew, Bolam', *Archaeologia Aeliana* (1982)

G. W. D. Briggs, 'The Church of Holy Trinity, Widdrington', *Archaeologia Aeliana* (1989). These two articles demonstrate just how complex the development of parish churches could be.

B. Harbottle, 'Excavations at the Carmelite Friary, Newcastle upon Tyne, 1965 and 1967', *Archaeologia Aeliana* (1968)

D. Hay, 'The Dissolution of the Monasteries in the Diocese of Durham', *Archaeologia Aeliana* (1938)

J. C. Hodgson, 'Temple Thornton Account 1308' and 'Chibburn and the Knights Hospitaller in Northumberland', *Archaeologia Aeliana* (1895)

J. C. Hodgson, 'The *Domus Dei* of Newcastle, Otherwise St. Katherine's Hospital on the Sandhill', *Archaeologia Aeliana* (1917)

W. St. J. Hope, 'The White Friars or Carmelites of Hulne, Northumberland', *Archaeological Journal* (1890)

W. H. Knowles, 'The Monastery of the Black Friars, Newcastle upon Tyne', *Archaeologia Aeliana* (1920)

R. L. Storey, *Thomas Langley and the Bishopric of Durham 1406-1437* (1961). Chapter four gives a good description of the diocesan administrative system in its mature form.

CHAPTER FIVE

C. H. Blair, 'The Wardens and Deputy-Wardens of the Marches of England towards Scotland in Northumberland', *Archaeologia Aeliana* (1950). Blair also produced authoritative lists of Members of Parliament for Northumberland, Newcastle, Morpeth and Berwick in *Archaeologia Aeliana* 1933, 1934, 1935, 1936, 1937, 1945 and 1946.

F. Bradshaw, 'The Lay Subsidy Roll of 1296: Northumberland at the end of the Thirteenth Century', *Archaeologia Aeliana* (1916). Still useful although to a large extent superseded by Fraser.

C. M. Fraser, *The Northumberland Lay Subsidy Roll of 1296* (1968)

C. M. Fraser, 'The Life and Death of John of Denton', *Archaeologia Aeliana* (1959)

J. F. Gibson, *The Newcastle upon Tyne Improvement Acts and Byelaws* (1881). Still the best introduction to Newcastle's municipal development.

R. E. Glasscock, *The Lay Subsidy Roll of 1334* (1975). Includes the 1336 Northumberland assessments.

C. H. Hartshorne, *Feudal and Military Antiquities of Northumberland II* (1858) includes a chapter on the Regality of Tynedale and the text of the 'Iter of Wark', the record of a visit of the Scottish judges to the regality in the reign of Alexander III.

T. Hodgkin, 'Municipal contests in Newcastle 1342-1345', *Archaeologia Aeliana* (1908). Should be read in conjunction with Constance Fraser's article on John of Denton.

John Hodgson, 'A Tynedale Coroner's Inquest 1357', *Archaeologia Aeliana* (1854)

J. C. Hodgson, 'A Border Warden's Court', *Berwickshire Naturalists Club* (1909-11)

C. Johnston, 'The Oldest Version of the Customs of Newcastle', *Archaeologia Aeliana* (1925)

M. F. Moore, *The Lands of the Scottish Kings in England* (1915). Includes much useful information about Tynedale.

R. R. Reid, 'The Office of Warden of the Marches; its Origins and Early History, *English Historical Review* (1917).

R. L. Storey, 'The Wardens of the Marches of England towards Scotland, 1377-1489', *English Historical Review* (1957). Revises and extends Rachel Reid's earlier study.

CHAPTER SIX

J. M. W. Bean, *The Estates of the Percy Family* (1958)

M. L. Bush, 'The Problem of the Far North: a study of the crisis of 1537', *Northern History* (1971).

D. Charlesworth, 'The Battle of Hexham, 1464', *Archaeologia Aeliana* (1952)

D. Charlesworth, 'Northumberland in the early years of Edward IV', *Archaeologia Aeliana* (1953)

J. Gillingham, *The Wars of the Roses* (1981). There are many books on this subject, but this is particularly useful.

J. C. Holt, *The Northerners* (1970). An important study of the baronial opposition to John.

R. Howell, *Newcastle upon Tyne and the Puritan Revolution* (1967)

R. Howell, 'Puritanism and Newcastle before the summoning of the Long Parliament', *Archaeologia Aeliana* (1963)

R. Howell, 'Newcastle's Regicide: the Parliamentary Career of John Blakiston', *Archaeologia Aeliana* (1964)

A. J. Pollard, *North-Eastern England during the Wars of the Roses* (1990). A somewhat misleading title in that the book is largely concerned with Yorkshire.

R. R. Reid, 'The Rebellion of the Northern Earls, 1569', *Transactions of the Royal Historical Society* (1906)

P. F. Ryder, 'The Two Towers of Hexham', *Archaeologia Aeliana* (1994)

C. S. Terry, 'The Scottish Campaign in Northumberland and Durham between January and June 1644' and 'The Siege of Newcastle upon Tyne by the Scots', *Archaeologia Aeliana* (1899). Detailed and important articles on a subject which now needs more research.

Index

Eslington 21, 187
Etal 59, 62
Eure, Sir William 146

Falaise, Treaty of 31
Fallodon 18
Fallowfield 134
Farne 126
Farnham 138
Fawdon 138
Felkington 20
Felton 88, 108, 118, 128, 141, 182
Fenham (Holy Island) 41, 58, 77, 119
Fenton 22-3, 108, 111, 118, 127
Fenwick Family: George 131
    Sir John of Wallington 181
    Thomas of Prestwick 181
    Tristram 131
    Tristram of Kenton 181
Fieschi, Cardinal Luca 43
Fishing 102-3
Ford 22, 55, 59, 62, 108, 117
Forster, Sir John 66, 131, 163, 179
Fotheringay (Suffolk) 115
Fountains Abbey (Yorkshire) 124
Fourstones 153
Fowberry 143
France, kings of: Charles VII 171
    Louis XI 171
    Louis XII 59
    Philippe II 32, 166-7
Frescobaldi of Florence, Italian
    merchant house 98
Friars 131-2

Gascony 36, 45, 94
Gateshead (Durham) 96-7, 100, 143,
    183
Gatherick 80
Gaveston, Piers 40
Geoffrey, count of Anjou 26
Glanton 21, 138
Glemham, Sir Thomas 182
Gosforth, North and South 18, 20, 144
Gospatrick, earl of Northumberland
    10, 19
Goswick 21
Great Whittington 20, 51
Gregory VII, Pope 111
Grey Family: Sir Ralph 172-4
    Sir Thomas I 137
    Sir Thomas II 149

Gunnerton 113

Hackford 86
Hailes, Sir Patrick 50
Halton 20, 51, 175, 181
Haltwhistle 108, 118, 155
Hamburn Hall 87
Harbottle 54-5, 158
Harclay, Andrew 43
Harold, earl of Wessex, king of
    England 8-9
Hartburn 108, 118
Hartford 153
Hartlepool (Durham) 178
Hartley 16, 83, 101-2
Haughton 55
Hauxley 78, 153
Hawkhill 78
Haydon Bridge 88
Healey 147
Heaton near Newcastle 16
Heaton near Norham 20, 59
Heddon on the Wall 32, 35
Hedgeley 138
Heighley 80
Henry I, king of England 19-21, 25,
    118, 122, 124, 126, 132, 153, 159
Henry II, king of England 15, 21, 26,
    30, 155, 158-9, 164-5
Henry III, king of England 32, 35
Henry IV, king of England 55, 167
Henry VI, king of England 167, 171-2
Henry VII, king of England 58-9, 162,
    168
Henry VIII, king of England 62, 64,
    162-3
Heron Family: John 59
    Sir John of Chipchase 176
    Sir William of Hadston 141
    Sir William of Ford 59
Hesleyside 157
Hethpool 22-3
Heworth (Durham) 99
Hexham 20, 75, 80, 82-3, 86, 88, 102,
    105, 108, 112, 114-8, 121-2, 124,
    127-9, 154-5, 172
Hindley 147
Holburn 23
Holy Island 14, 20, 41, 48, 51, 56, 58,
    77, 83, 108, 112, 117-9, 122, 126,
    137, 151-2